OJIBWE STORIES FROM THE UPPER BERENS RIVER

**New Visions in Native American
and Indigenous Studies**

SERIES EDITORS

Margaret D. Jacobs
Robert Miller

Ojibwe Stories from the Upper Berens River

A. Irving Hallowell and Adam
Bigmouth in Conversation

EDITED AND WITH AN INTRODUCTION

BY JENNIFER S. H. BROWN

CO-PUBLISHED BY THE UNIVERSITY OF NEBRASKA PRESS

AND THE AMERICAN PHILOSOPHICAL SOCIETY

Library of Congress Cataloging-in-Publication Data
Names: Bigmouth, Adam, author. | Hallowell, A. Irving (Alfred
Irving), 1892–1974, author. | Brown, Jennifer S. H., 1940– editor.
Title: Ojibwe stories from the Upper Berens River: A. Irving
Hallowell and Adam Bigmouth in conversation / edited
and with an introduction by Jennifer S. H. Brown.
Other titles: A. Irving Hallowell and Adam
Bigmouth in conversation
Description: Lincoln: University of Nebraska Press; co-
published with the American Philosophical Society, [2018]
| Series: New visions in Native American and Indigenous
studies | Includes bibliographical references and index. |
Identifiers: LCCN 2017017420 (print)
LCCN 2017036538 (ebook)
ISBN 9781496202253 (cloth: alk. paper)
ISBN 9781496204462 (epub)
ISBN 9781496204479 (mobi)
ISBN 9781496204486 (pdf)
Subjects: lcsh: Ojibwa Indians—Folklore. | Ojibwa Indians—
History. | Ojibwa Indians—Manitoba—Berens River
Valley—Biography. | Bigmouth, Adam—Family. | Berens
River (First Nation)—History. | Ojibwa mythology.
Classification: LCC E99.C6 (ebook) | LCC E99.c6
B54 2018 (print) | DDC 977.004/97333—dc23
LC record available at https://lccn.loc.gov/2017017420

Set in Charis by Mikala R Kolander.
Designed by N. Putens.

CONTENTS

ILLUSTRATIONS

Following page 88

8. Joseph Green (Ginoozhewinini)
   with his wife and children

9. Alex Keeper (Giiwiich)

10. The dwelling of John
    Keeper Sr. at Little Grand Rapids

11. Sweat lodge under construction

12. Sweat lodge completed and covered

13. Conjuring lodge (shaking tent) under construction

14. Conjuring lodge completed and covered

15. Duck Lake (Barton Lake),
    Waabano pavilion of Ashaageshi (Asagesi)

ACKNOWLEDGMENTS

This book owes its first debt to A. Irving Hallowell and Adam Bigmouth and to their collaborator, Chief William Berens. For many hours and days in the summers of 1938 and 1940, they worked to record and translate the dozens of stories that Adam told about his life, his family, his ancestors and their relatives, and the other-than-human personages with whom they all interacted. Next in importance is the American Philosophical Society, recipient of the Hallowell Papers upon the anthropologist's passing in 1974. I was privileged to work with the papers during a few intensive visits from 1986 to the mid-1990s and to photocopy materials that I have read and mined with great joy and satisfaction ever since. I recall especially the knowledgeable and patient assistance that I received from Martin Levitt and Beth Carroll-Horrocks during those visits.

In 1990 and 1996 I ordered photocopies of the folders holding Hallowell's handwritten transcripts of Adam's stories, written down at Little Grand Rapids, Manitoba, in the summers of 1938 and 1940. I knew they would be interesting, but for the next two decades I was absorbed with teaching and other duties, and with working on other Hallowell materials—publishing his long lost manuscript monograph on the Berens River Ojibwe (1992), gathering the transcripts of William Berens's stories and dreams into a book (Berens, as told to A. Irving Hallowell, 2009), bringing Hallowell's scattered Ojibwe articles into one comprehensive volume (Hallowell 2010), and other undertakings. Adam's files sat largely unread until after my retirement, and until I was able to complete some other long-standing projects. When I finally began to read Hallowell's manuscript pages, I realized how important the material was and began transcribing and organizing it. In this I was encouraged by the warm interest and support of Timothy B. Powell, director of the APS Center for Native American and Indigenous Research (CNAIR) and Brian Carpenter, senior archivist, CNAIR. Keen to see Adam Bigmouth's stories published, they also located a few texts I did not have—stories that resided in Hallowell's folders entitled "Myths and Tales," a rich compendium of Berens River Ojibwe stories, largely unpublished. Brian helped me to assemble the Hallowell photographs that appear in the book and arranged their transmission to the University of Nebraska Press. Charles B. Greifenstein, associate librarian and curator of manuscripts, facilitated the process of granting APS permission to publish the material.

This project has also relied greatly on the research that Mennonite schoolteacher Gary Butikofer carried on while teaching Ojibwe children at Poplar Hill, Ontario, from 1970 to 1990. Butikofer learned the language well and was deeply interested in Berens River family and community histories. He kept copious notes of his interviews, did research in the Hudson's Bay Company Archives, and consulted treaty pay lists and numerous other sources. He also visited Hallowell's widow, Maude Frame, who allowed him the use of Hallowell's papers and lent him Berens River photographs so that he could ask Ojibwe people's help in identifying who was in them. In the early 1990s Maureen Matthews, the CBC radio journalist with whom I was collaborating on Berens River research, and I visited Gary at his home in Richland Center, Wisconsin, and he kindly allowed us to photocopy his hundreds of pages of handwritten notes and use them for research. In 2008–2009, funds from my Canada Research Chair, under a grant from the Social Science and Humanities Research Council of Canada, made possible the transcribing of these invaluable materials in the Centre for Rupert's Land Studies at the University of Winnipeg, under the supervision of my research associate Susan Elaine Gray and assistant Jennifer Ching.

As Gary Butikofer found, Adam and his Ojibwe relatives are a challenge for research because they were often known by different names, both Ojibwe and English. Where questions arose, I turned to Gary, who very carefully read an earlier version of this work, and to Winnipeg researcher Anne Lindsay, who checked the treaty pay lists and Manitoba census data to verify name correspondences and familial relations. My warmest thanks also to Maureen Matthews for the rich collaboration and support that she brought to our several trips to Red Lake, Pikangikum, Poplar Hill, Little Grand Rapids, Pauingassi, and Berens River in the early 1990s and for her exhaustive research on Hallowell's Berens River photographs and her work with the descendants of the people appearing in his pictures. Her colleague, Ojibwe linguist Roger Roulette, began working with us in the early 1990s when we brought him Maureen's recorded Ojibwe interviews from our early trips to the Berens River communities that Hallowell visited in the 1930s. Ever since then, he has been a wise and insightful consultant on Ojibwe language, concepts, and modes of thought. He has carefully gone over the Ojibwe names and words in the text, providing authoritative advice and guidance on both orthography and meanings. His work and knowledge made possible the glossary of Ojibwe personal names that appears at the end of the introduction.

My warm thanks also go to Matthew Bokovoy, senior acquisitions editor at the University of Nebraska Press, and to the two reviewers of the manuscript for their enthusiastic support of the project. At the press Heather Stauffer, associate acquisitions editor, oversaw the preparation of the text and illustrations for publication and was always ready with answers to questions and problems. Thanks go also to the project editor, Joeth Zucco, copy editor, Sally Antrobus, and the indexer, Sergey Lobachev, who worked on the book.

Finally, I wish to express my appreciation to a large circle of colleagues and friends, too many to name, whose interest in Hallowell and his contributions has grown in recent years (they know who they are). My warmest thanks also to the people of the Berens River, past and present, whose names and lives came into focus as we followed Hallowell's trail. They have graciously shared their stories and perspectives over the decades—with Hallowell, with others in the decades since, and with the wider world as they drew up their application for recognition of their communities and region as a UNESCO World Heritage Site. At this writing, official approval of their "land that gives life"—Pimachiowin Aki—as a unique cultural landscape remains in the air (see http://www .pimachiowinaki.org). But their voices are being heard as old stories and memories find new life, and as their following generations chart their own course in a changing world.

INTRODUCTION

In the summers of 1938 and 1940 an elderly Ojibwe man spent a good many hours with an American anthropologist, A. Irving Hallowell, at Little Grand Rapids, a small community on the upper Berens River in eastern Manitoba. Hallowell and other outsiders knew this old man as Adam or Samuel Bigmouth (fig. 1), and he appears as Adam in Hallowell's papers. Among his own people he was known as Gisayenaan or "Our Elder Brother" (Butikofer 2009, pt. II.3, 296). Adam's father was Ochiibaamaan-siins (Otcibamasis or Northern Barred Owl in Hallowell's usage), a highly regarded traditional doctor, and Adam himself was known for his curing skills. This book introduces Adam from another angle—setting forth the storytelling and remembering that he carried on with Hallowell during those two summers, once he found an attentive listener who cared about what he had to say.

The Conversations

Adam told Hallowell dozens of stories about his and his people's lives, experiences, and perspectives. He had met this white man before. Hallowell had spent time at Little Grand Rapids almost every summer since 1932 when he made his first field trip up the river. With him on all his trips was William Berens (fig. 2), chief of the Berens River reserve at the mouth of the river, who in 1930 had steered Hallowell to the upriver communities as the best possible sites for his fieldwork (Berens 2009). Berens supplied both translation and guidance. His support was critical in another way. As a member of the Moose clan, he had Moose kinsmen all along the river, and clan relatives were expected to offer hospitality to one another. These connections provided Hallowell with introductions both to people of the Moose clan and to their relatives through marriage—such as Adam Bigmouth. Adam was of the Sturgeon clan; his wife, Aanii, was a member of the leading Moose family in the area, which was headed by her brother, Naamiwan or Fair Wind (fig. 7), the most famous of the medicine men whom Hallowell met and wrote about (Hallowell 2010, ch. 22). While Adam was talking, William Berens translated and sometimes added his own comments and further information.

During their conversations Hallowell made rapid notes on over a hundred handwritten pages, now preserved in his papers at the American Philosophical Society in Philadelphia (Hallowell 1938, 1940). Adam talked about his youth, his intermittent work for the Hudson's Bay Company, and other personal experiences. In Ojibwe terms, the stories in this collection are all of the *dibaajimowin* type—news or narratives, rather than *aadizookaanag*, myths and legends of ancestral or other-than-human beings. Unlike some other storytellers, Adam implicitly respected Ojibwe sanctions against telling aadizookaanag in summer out of season (Berens 2009, 113). In doing so, he also chose to focus on what evidently most interested him—stories about people.

Adam recounted some successes in curing people but spoke most admiringly of his father, Northern Barred Owl, as "a very powerful medicine man . . . reported to have *killed* mythical cannibals." One story recounted how Owl followed a young patient to the land of the dead and brought her back (see "Spirits of the Dead," Hallowell 2010, 412); and in *The Role of Conjuring* Hallowell told of how Owl conjured to recover lost objects and returned them to their owners (1942, 68–69).

Owl's son did not have quite the same standing. Hallowell found that "although Adam was a conjuror and medicine man too, he did not enjoy the reputation of his father" (1951, 185). Adam had much interest, however, in why people got sick and explained how they were cured, often when a doctor determined the nature of past misdeeds that had caused illness. When patients were cued to remember these deeds and admitted them to others, their health commonly returned.

Some of Adam's stories involved his Sturgeon relatives; others told of unnamed people from "long ago." Relations between men and women and violations of kinship protocols were common subjects, often rather fraught. A good number of stories talked of interactions between humans and their bawaaganag (pawaganak in Hallowell's texts)—spirit guardians who came in dreams to bring blessings and powers, usually benign but sometimes dangerous. Of special note is a series of twenty stories about windigo cannibals (human and other-than-human), people's various means of dealing with their threats and attacks, and windigo cures— perhaps the largest collection of windigo stories gathered at first hand from a single Algonquian speaker. Together, the stories and memories shine spotlights on a wide spectrum of experiences ranging from mundane to mysterious, frightening, disturbing, and sometimes life-changing.

How was it that Adam spoke so freely with Hallowell and William Berens about so many challenging topics? One reason may be that in his last years, he had given up the active practices of curing and conjuring (operating the shaking tent for divination and to secure information from the future or afar) and was willing to turn to reminiscence and storytelling. When he was approached to do a shaking tent performance for Hallowell in July 1932, Adam declined, saying that his powers had grown weak and that his last attempt, the previous year, had failed; the pawaganak would not come (Hallowell 1942, 29n47). Hallowell's original account of their meeting, found among his research notes on conjuring, appears here as a prologue to Adam's stories, as it tells of their first encounter and offers glimpses of the old man's character.

Adam did later say that he was still "using his pawaganak for the wabano" (see "Dream Experiences," pt. 3, this volume, and Hallowell's description of that ceremony as conducted at Little Grand Rapids and Pauingassi in Berens 2009, 190–91). But the Waabano was personally less demanding than operating the shaking tent and curing the sick. By 1938 and in declining health, Adam may have been content to share stories and memories. His comfort level with his listeners must also have been considerable. (Note that materials quoting from Hallowell's texts retain his spellings; "Waabano" and "baawaganak" reflect current preferred Ojbwe orthography.)

Stories from Life: Adam Bigmouth and William Berens Compared

Hallowell in his last two summers of fieldwork, 1938 and 1940, spent considerable time recording life story materials from both Adam and William Berens, but the dynamics and results of these projects were very different. Adam's stories came in a series of open-ended conversations full of anecdotes and subject changes, ranging in a stream-of-consciousness fashion not only across the seven or eight decades of his own life but also into the lives of his father and other relatives and to persons of the past, named and unnamed. His "dramatis personae" (see glossary of Ojibwe personal names at the end of this introduction) extended across several generations of the clan universe in which he lived, which stretched geographically from Lac Seul, a large lake to the southeast of Red Lake, Ontario, to the mouth of the Berens River (see map of the world of Adam Bigmouth, following the glossary). Hallowell did not appear to direct the flow of talk, though he doubtless encouraged Berens, as interpreter, to pursue a few topics of particular interest—notably windigo cases. Berens himself probably helped steer discussions toward topics of interest to him as well.

Given the range of Adam's subject matter, his omissions of a number of topics are interesting. His name, Adam, suggests that he was baptized, and indeed in his later life, missionaries and schoolteachers appeared with increasing frequency at Little Grand Rapids (see, e.g., Schuetze 2001). But Adam never spoke of attending a church or school. He never mentioned any missionary's name or activities. Only one of his stories reflected Christian influence—"A Dream Revelation," in part 3, in which he recounted a dream experience cast very much in an Ojibwe mode. Indian agents also never appeared in his stories, and only once did he refer in passing to a visit of treaty commissioners paying annuities. The only outsiders appearing with any regularity in his conversations were fur traders based at Little Grand Rapids, where Hudson's Bay Company clerks mentioned him bringing furs to trade at various times (for example, the journal of W. M. Chapman, 1912–15). His only stories of warfare centered on battles with windigos and on the duels of mind, magic, and sorcery that arose between local Berens River medicine men—notably between his father, Owl, and Bazigwiigaabaw (Pazigwigabau in Hallowell's texts), both Sturgeons (pt. 5).

The collaboration that led Hallowell to create a memoir of William Berens's life proceeded quite differently. Working in 1940, probably at Berens River, Hallowell and Berens were able to converse directly in English, and Hallowell framed the old chief's life in an autobiographical mode, largely following a chronological sequence. The difficulty was that Hallowell had to leave Berens River before they could finish and was not able to return again. The memoir (Berens 2009) concludes abruptly in about 1904, when Berens was less than forty, after Hallowell had filled about sixty handwritten pages; it ends thirteen years before Berens even became chief of Berens River in 1917. In it, Berens emerges as a personage quite different from Adam. He traveled widely up and down Lake Winnipeg and occasionally beyond. Besides members of his own family, he mentioned to Hallowell about sixty other people he had known or worked for by 1904—traders, missionaries, Indian agents, and commercial fishermen, in diverse and challenging roles. At the mouth of the river, the three decades from the 1870s to early 1900s were times of great changes—from the signing of Treaty 5 in 1875 to the coming of new modes of transport, governmental structures, policing, building of permanent missions and schools, new housing, and so on. Berens's memoir documents these broader historical shifts as well as his own life. As he adapted to these changes, Hallowell saw him and the other "lakeside" Ojibwe as becoming increasingly acculturated, moving away from the old ways and taking on the new (see various chapters in Hallowell 2010 for his notion of an acculturational gradient ranging from the upper Berens River to the lakeside people, and most extreme, the people of Lac du Flambeau, Wisconsin, whom he studied in the late 1940s). Yet as Susan Elaine Gray and I argued in our introduction to the old chief's memoir (Berens 2009, 29, 32), his adaptations did not make him less Ojibwe. His exposure to Hallowell and all the other outside influences seemed, in fact, to reinforce his identity and make him more consciously aware of its importance, especially in his last years as he tried to explain to the visiting anthropologist everything that he knew of the mindsets and ways of his people.

Adam Bigmouth lived in the same time frame as Berens, being perhaps ten years older. He too traveled quite widely but inland, up and down the Berens River watershed and always in Ojibwe country. His was an insider's perspective, immersed in the complex networks of ancestors, relatives, and spiritual beings that colored every story he told; for Hallowell, he was at the "unacculturated" end of the spectrum. His life experiences overlapped with Berens's, yet differed enough that the two Ojibwe elders must have been interested in talking with each other as Hallowell listened. Taken together, they and their relatives opened doors to the range of Ojibwe culture and knowledge that Hallowell was trying to grasp. They presented him with unique learning opportunities, and we are fortunate that he took those opportunities, creating a documentary legacy for anthropology and for the Ojibwe people themselves in following decades.

Adam's Family

Adam Bigmouth and his family lived their lives in a patrilineal clan system that defined their identity and structured their kin relations. He and his male relatives were Sturgeons. Following clan exogamy, they married women of other clans—Moose, Kingfisher, Pelican, and Duck. Hallowell found that as of the 1930s, the most numerous clans were Sturgeon and Moose, followed by Pelican and Kingfisher; their members "constituted 82 percent of the Ojibwa population of the river at that time" (1992, 24). When he mapped the genealogical connections of the people he met around Little Grand Rapids, reaching back into the 1700s, he found that many of them had ancestors and relatives who had come from the southeast and mainly from Lac Seul—a pattern that reflected larger-scale movements of Ojibwe people from Lake Superior westward to Manitoba (1992, 21 and map 2). Adam's father, Owl, still traveled to Lac Seul in the mid-1800s to participate in Midewiwin ceremonies, as recounted in two stories in part 5. The glossary of Ojibwe personal names at the end of this introduction provides a closer view of the kinship relations in which Adam's life was embedded, and the afterword illustrates the ways in which ceremonial life in older times was linked to particular clan and family leaders who had multiple wives and many children.

To understand Adam's background and to make sense of the people mentioned in his stories, it is necessary to sort out a multiplicity of personal names and their meanings. The task is complicated by the fact that each individual was known by different names in different settings. Adam's father, Owl, appeared in Treaty 5 pay lists from 1876 to 1880 as Ah-yas-sa or Ayassa (Small One). Then in 1881 he was listed as "Ayassa or Adam Bigmouth." The Manitoba census for that year listed his religion as "Wesleyan Methodist," so his new name was likely baptismal, but Methodist records from that period are spotty, and in any case he died before a regular mission was established at Little Grand Rapids.

In 1882, when Owl received his annuity at Berens River, he was named as "Bigmouth, Adam . . . Previously paid as Ayassa—By Order." Among Ojibwe people, however, he retained his owl name, Ochiibaamaansiins— the name of a striking owl species, *Strix varia*, with big brown eyes. Gary Butikofer, while teaching at Poplar Hill farther up the river in the 1970s, learned that he was also remembered by two nicknames: Nikazhagayi (He has Canada goose skin) and Ogaawidoon (Pickerel lips; Butikofer 2009, pt. II.3, 296, 292). The latter name may be the origin of the family surname Bigmouth. English speakers often confuse pickerel with pike, their larger relatives, or subsume them under the general term walleye. Both fishes have long, large mouths. Nicknames were common in Ojibwe (and Cree) usage, and were used in a joking or teasing manner. They also served to avoid the utterance of a person's private, powerful name, which each would have received as a child in a traditional naming ceremony; those names were not for casual, informal use. Ochiibaamaansiins was probably Adam's father's ceremonial name, which his son shared with Hallowell and William Berens in friendship. Adam's story "First Rabbit, First Mink" (pt. 1) mentioned that his father's namer lived at Pauingassi, a settlement ten miles north of Little Grand Rapids. This man would have been a grandfather figure who through a dream gave the child a special name and blessing. (For more on Ojibwe naming ceremonies, see Peers and Brown 2000, 537; and Brown 2008, 82–84.)

In 1885 the treaty pay list recorded that Adam Bigmouth (senior),

Owl, had died. His son told Hallowell that his death was caused by a powerful rival conjurer ("Death Due to Sorcery," pt. 5). Annuities were then paid to Owl's widow, "Fanny Bigmouth," who was also known as Ingenie (Injenii in Ojibwe orthography). The Manitoba census listed the family as of 1881: Adam Bigmouth, aged seventy (i.e., born in 1811); his wife, "Ingenie" Bigmouth, aged forty; and his sons, Adam, aged twenty-eight (born in 1853), and Jacob, aged fourteen; the ages should be seen as estimates. (A sister, Makwemod, was married and not present.)

There is more to Injenii's story. She was the younger of Owl's two wives. His older wife was Pasho, a Pelican; she died before 1877. Pasho was a widow and Injenii was her daughter by her first husband, who was of the Kingfisher clan. By sometime in the 1850s, Injenii—Owl's stepdaughter—became Owl's second wife. The records of Pasho's and Injenii's children show that the wives were concurrent. This variation on polygyny was the only such instance that Hallowell found and was not an approved practice; as he later wrote, "marriage between classes of relatives belonging to different kinship generations" was, in Ojibwe thinking, a violation of the incest taboo (Hallowell 1992, 52). But Pasho's daughter was of a different clan, so she at least met the standard of clan exogamy. Ojibwe men who took more than one wife commonly married sisters; Hallowell found six such cases among eight polygynous marriages that he documented (1992, 57.)

Owl and Pasho had two sons, Madoons (Maahtus, d. 1891–92), and Gegek (Kehkehk) (Butikofer 2009, pt. II.3, 293), whom our Adam mentioned as his eldest brother when recounting his boyhood memories. Hallowell's spellings of their names are in parentheses. Sometimes Adam referred to Pasho (unnamed) as his grandmother (see "First Rabbit, First Mink," pt. 1), as indeed she was his mother's mother and quite a bit older. Given the age of his father, Owl, his paternal grandmother (unknown) was almost certainly deceased by the 1850s.

Owl and Injenii had two sons and a daughter. Adam, the eldest, was born in 1853, according to the 1881 census, which may, however, overstate his age. His younger brother was Baachiish (Butikofer: Pachiish), also known as (John) Baptiste, and mentioned as Batis in Adam's stories. A death record at Little Grand Rapids listed John Baptiste as dying on June

27, 1943, aged sixty, which would place his birth at 1883; but Butikofer reported his getting married in about 1888–89 (2009, pt. II.3, 293). Death records commonly err about ages, and early censuses often got names confused; it seems likely that "Jacob," son of Owl and "Ingenie" and aged fourteen in the 1881 census, was John Baptiste, misnamed. Hallowell also recorded a clue indicating that he was older than the census stated (1942, 29n47). When Adam's conjuring effort failed in 1931 as already described, his brother, "another old man (P) [Pachiish], went into the tent but with no success either." The name John Baptiste suggests a possible baptism by one of the Oblate missionaries who visited Little Grand Rapids over the years and later resided there (cf. Leach 1973, ch. 4), but a record has not been found.

Adam's sister, Makwemod (Butikofer: Maahkwemot, d. August 1908), was known in outsiders' records as Jane Bigmouth. Her first husband was Kohkohko'ons or Kokokoos (Little or Young Horned Owl, d. 1882–83); he was a Pelican, much older, and was born at Lac Seul. Adam's story "Love Medicine and Counter Medicine" (pt. 4) tells of how this brother-in-law cured him of a love-medicine attack. Makwemod had no children by that union but had several later. In the mid-1890s her husband was Gichi-ogimaa (Hallowell: Ktciogama, d. 1927), a half-brother of Adam's wife Aanii (Butikofer 2009, pt. II.3, 156, 302, 303).

Injenii (Fanny Bigmouth) died by July 1894, according to the treaty pay list of that year. Her son, "Samuel," the name by which Adam (junior) was listed in the pay lists of the 1890s, received his and her annuities at that time. Adam, in telling of the death of his father in 1884–85 (pt. 5), spoke of how he remained unmarried to look after his mother: "I thought of my mother after my father died—so did not take a wife." After Injenii's death, he wondered, "what should I do?—no place to go. I had to make a home for myself. Finally Naamiwan spoke to me about taking his sister [Aanii]. 'I'll help you,' he said." This relationship cemented Adam's ties to a large family of the Moose clan, based at Pauingassi, which had been founded by Zhenawaakoshkang (Gichi-omoonzoonii or Great Moose, d. 1881–82), a famous medicine man from Lac Seul who established the family's repute. He had six wives, more than any other man in the region; his twenty children and their descendants contributed to the dominance of the Moose clan in the area (Hallowell 1992, 24). His fourth wife, Mangitigwaan, was the mother of Naamiwan and Aanii (Butikofer 2009, pt. II.3, 156–57).

Aanii had multiple connections from her parents on down by the time she married Adam in about 1897. Several of her relatives' names recur in Adam's stories (and Hallowell's notes), illustrating the ramifying kin ties and associations that linked the people of the upper Berens River. Before marrying Adam, Aanii had two previous husbands. The first, in the mid-1880s, was Ahak (Thomas Ross), a Pelican; he was once a patient of Owl and was cured by him (see "Making People Better," pt. 4). Ahak and Aanii had a daughter, Gwiikwishii or Maggie Ross (d. 1967). In 1904–5, Maggie marrried Wiigwaasaatig (Birchstick, John Suggashie), a Sturgeon (Butikofer 2009, pt. II.3, 156, 139, 297), who became chief at Pikangikum and whom Hallowell met in 1932 and probably on other occasions (2010, 373). Birchstick's father, Zagashkii (Sagaski), was featured in Adam's story "Those Two Wives of Tetebaiyabin" (pt. 4). A leader in the Midewiwin, Zagashkii was also vividly remembered for taking his sister (not Birchstick's mother) as the first of his two wives ("Sagaski, the Man Who Married His Sister," pt. 6; Hallowell 2010, 603).

Aanii and Ross had "separated by mutual consent" by the time of the 1887 treaty pay list. In 1892 Aanii married William Keeper (Mezinaawaagwii or Chaahkwiis), a Sturgeon whose first wife, Migizi, had died in 1882–83 (Butikofer 2009, pt. II.3, 342). William was the eldest son of Bazigwiigaabaw (Pazagwigabau in Hallowell's spelling), a powerful conjurer who had been the nemesis of Adam's father, Owl ("Death Due to Sorcery," pt. 5). William, born in Lac Seul about 1852, was "lame, used crutches," and died in 1894–95 (Butikofer 2009, pt. I.1, 14). He and Aanii had a daughter, Winiichipo or Oniichipo, who appeared in treaty pay lists as Maggie Bigmouth. Uniquely among Little Grand Rapids children of her time, she was sent to Brandon Industrial School from 1908 to 1913, registered as Maggie Keeper (her school records are at Library and Archives Canada, RG 10). Interestingly, Butikofer found from treaty lists that only two Little Grand Rapids children were sent to a boarding school in the years from 1901 to 1930: "Maggie Bigmouth and a daughter of Joseph Duck who was an orphan at that time." Maggie later worked as a maid in Brandon, Manitoba, never married, and died in 1926 (Butikofer 2009, pt. II.3, 297–301, 341).

The fact that as of 1896–97 Aanii was recently widowed with a small child may have encouraged her brother Naamiwan to suggest a match with Adam. Aanii and Adam had a daughter who died very young in 1898–99, and a son, Peyak (Payak) or John Bigmouth (1902/3–68: Butikofer 2009, pt. II.3, 297). Their union endured until Aanii's death on 1August 13, 1941; Adam died on July 3, 1942 (Manitoba death index, thanks to Anne Lindsay). Adam occasionally mentioned Aanii in his stories: in "A Dream Revelation" (pt. 3) he spoke of an incident involving "my old wife"; and in "Trouble If You 'Marry the Same Totem'" (pt. 6) she helped subdue a troubled man. Peyak and his only son, Walter (known locally as Warie), were drowned at Poplar Hill on May 7, 1968, evidently leaving no direct descendants (Butikofer, pt. II.3, 297, and pers. comm., January 2016). Few personal recollections of this small family are available. Charlie George Owen (Omishoosh, d. 2001), however, shared his memory of Adam Bigmouth with Maureen Matthews at Pauingassi when she showed him Hallowell's photograph of Adam. Gisayenaan, "Our Elder Brother," was "a highly respected friend of his, and an extremely nice person" (Matthews to JSHB, e-mail, September 1, 2015).

Transcribing and Editing the Texts

When Hallowell wrote down Adam Bigmouth's stories during the summers of 1938 and 1940, he had no mechanical recording devices; his only tools were pens, pencils, and paper, supplemented by his camera. As he kept no daily journal, precise dates and times are lacking, but the visits must have involved numerous sessions of work, given the volume of material recorded. Hallowell's transcriptions of Adam Bigmouth's stories are almost always legible but present numerous challenges. Some sets of pages are numbered, but their pagination is inconsistent and not very helpful for reference purposes. The loose-leaf pages reside in the A. Irving Hallowell Papers at the American Philosophical Society in Philadelphia, in Series V (Research Notes), in two folders entitled "Adam Big Mouth and Windigo—Field Notes, 1938," and "Little Grand Rapids—Field Notes, 1940." A few of Adam's stories are also to be found in a series of folders entitled "Saulteaux Indians—Myths and Tales." Most of those are typescripts, often in duplicate; some are edited handwritten texts that Hallowell evidently wrote out for his typist; and a few pages appear to date from his fieldwork. He did not work over the typescripts very much; they show few signs of proofreading. Among them are four of Adam's stories not in the original Little Grand Rapids texts; they appear, however, to have been part of that collection originally.

As we might expect from a series of conversations, the stories are of anecdotal length, rarely longer than two or three pages. Their subject matter shifted and varied greatly as the conversations flowed. Sometimes a group of stories followed a common theme for a while, concerning windigo cannibalism, for example, but the collection exhibits no overall linear narrative sequence. Accordingly, I read through all the texts and word-processed most of them, identified their main topics, and then assembled those stories with shared themes under headings that best represented their contents. The transcripts follow Hallowell's originals as closely as possible but have been lightly edited for readability; as he was writing with great speed, he commonly omitted connecting words, pronouns, etc., and used abbreviations for kinship terms and much else. Fortunately his usages were consistent, and the texts could be transcribed with a high degree of confidence.

A few texts have been omitted for various reasons. Some were not complete or intelligible, probably because of the pace of conversation and the speed at which they were written down. Some were repeat versions of stories told earlier; in those instances, the most complete version was selected, or two accounts were blended if they offered complementary details that amplified the whole. In some instances a theme was so well represented in a number of stories that further examples were not needed. A few isolated episodes of bestiality, fellatio, and necrophilia were not transcribed; Hallowell discussed some of these transgressions briefly in "Sin, Sex, and Sickness in Saulteaux Belief" (2010 [1939]).

The great majority of Adam Bigmouth's stories have never been published. When Hallowell did prepare some of them for publication, he usually summarized or shortened them; he also rendered them into a more polished English than the translations he got from William Berens, whose wording was more colloquial and doubtless closer to Adam's Ojibwe speech. As Hallowell's meetings with Adam occurred only in his last two summer visits, he drew on those materials rather less than on the data he had gathered and worked over in previous years. In this book, those of Adam's stories that Hallowell quoted from or alluded to in print are referenced in the notes or discussions that follow their texts. Most of their published versions may be found in *Contributions to Ojibwe Studies*, which gathers under one cover most of Hallowell's essays on the Ojibwe (2010). Most of the stories were untitled in their manuscript form; the titles appearing here are editorial additions. The story titles that Hallowell did provide are rendered here in quotation marks. Hallowell's asides are shown in parentheses, and his commentaries are signed with his initials, AIH. Following some stories I have inserted contextual information or at times more extended commentaries to explain, amplify, and offer comparative discussions of their content and to supply further references. Where only brief annotations were needed, they are provided in square brackets following the texts.

Ojibwe personal names and words in the texts pose challenges, as Hallowell's transcriptions are idiosyncratic and at times hard to read. For a list of names and terms that Hallowell used in his published articles, see "Glossary of Ojibwe Words and Names Used by Hallowell" (2010, 569–606). That glossary includes both Hallowell's versions, which correspond closely to the spellings he used in transcribing Adam Bigmouth's stories, and the expert transcriptions provided by Roger Roulette and Rand Valentine, with definitions and explanations. In the texts published here, I have allowed Hallowell's alpha symbol to stand as *a*, and his epsilon as *e*.

To help identify the persons mentioned by Adam, a glossary of Ojibwe personal names appearing in the text follows this introduction. The names, transcribed by fluent Ojibwe speaker and linguist Roger Roulette, include Hallowell's and sometimes Gary Butikofer's variants, their meanings where known, and some basic information on people's relationships. This book draws extensively on Butikofer's research notes from the upper Berens River, recorded from 1970 to 1990. Butikofer transcribed Ojibwe personal names following the system developed by missionary Charles Fiero in the 1950s and listened attentively to the people as he gained fluency in the language. Roulette has kindly reviewed and updated Butikofer's orthography, and with Butikofer's consent, I have supplied Roulette's versions of the names, and their translations, parenthetically in the story texts themselves when they mention Ojibwe persons for the first time, and in the context sections that follow many of the stories. The quoted texts retain spellings of all personal names as Hallowell gave them—with two exceptions. For Hallowell's Cenawagwaskang (Adam's father-in-law), I have adopted Roulette's spelling, Zhenawaakoshkang, throughout as offering a better guide to pronunciation. For his son, the Pauingassi medicine man, I have adopted Naamiwan (Fair Wind), as that name has become established in print (e.g., Matthews and Roulette 2003; Matthews 2016).

Most Ojibwe words that Hallowell commonly used in his writings are left as he spelled them in the texts. They are not italicized, as they appear frequently and italics would clutter the pages; the Ojibwe origin of the words is clear enough. They are glossed on first appearance with transcriptions following the Nichols and Nyholm dictionary (1995), or from Roger Roulette for words not found in that source. Examples include:

atisokanak (aadizookaanag), other-than-human persons
atik (adik), caribou, translated as deer in Berens River usage
cicigwan (zhiishiigwan), rattle
djibaiaking (jiibayakiing), spirit or ghost land
kigusamo (gii'igoshimo), fasts for a vision or dream fast
mandauwizi (maandaawizi), one endowed with extraordinary
     power
matutzwan (madoodiswaan), sweat lodge
migis (miigis), shell associated with the Midewiwin, also used in
     sorcery
nibakiwin (nibikiiwin), owner of the skill of sucking disease or
     harmful agent from the body
ninam (niinim), cross cousin, sweetheart
pagitcigan (bagijigan), sacrificing, offering
pawaganak (bawaaganag), dream visitors, our grandfathers
pekize (bekizi), clean, pure

pimadaziwin (bimaadiziwin), life in the fullest sense
Wabano (Waabano), ceremony seen by Hallowell
wanaman, red ochre, love medicine
windigo (wiindigoo), cannibalistic being who may appear in
   human or monstrous form

GLOSSARY OF OJIBWE PERSONAL
NAMES APPEARING IN THE TEXT

Ojibwe personal names have been spelled in numerous different ways.
A. Irving Hallowell transcribed names as well as he could during his
conversations with Adam Bigmouth in 1938 and 1940, but he was not
fluent in the language and followed a generic anthropological transcription manual (outlined in Hallowell 2010, 570). In turn, Gary Butikofer,
Mennonite schoolteacher at Poplar Hill, Ontario, from 1970 to 1990,
recorded extensive family histories in the area and transcribed the names
he heard using the Charles Fiero orthography, which later served as
a base for the system used in John D. Nichols and Earl Nyholm's *A
Concise Dictionary of Minnesota Ojibwe* (1995). Linguist Roger Roulette
has reviewed the names mentioned in Adam's texts and in Butikofer's
records of the same persons. His updated transcriptions provide the
basis for this glossary, drawing on his deep knowledge of the language
and people of the region. Hallowell's versions (unmarked) follow most
of Roulette's transcriptions as they document the names found in the
original texts. In some instances, Butikofer's are supplied if Hallowell's
were not available, to supplement the record. The names are translated
where possible. Since all these people were related, whether by shared
clan affiliation or as cross cousins to members of other clans along the
Berens River, most entries list their clans and cross-reference some of
their multiple kin ties.

Aamoo. Amo. "Bee." Berens River.

Aanii. Annie (Butikofer).Wife of Adam Bigmouth, sister of Naamiwan. Moose.

Aankas. Angus. Oldest son of Naamiwan, Pauingassi. Moose.

Ahak. Thomas Ross. Son of Ogawapwan. First husband of Aanii. Pelican.

Andwewe. Antwewe (Butikofer). "To listen for, examine by sound." Second wife of Adam's son, Peyak. Moose.

Ashaageshi. Asagesi. "Crayfish." Son of Bapashki (Pahpahski, "Ruffed grouse"): Butikofer 2009, pt. II.2, 77, 86). Had Waabano pavilion at Duck (Barton) Lake (fig. 15; Hallowell 2010, 46). Loon.

Ayaansa. Ayassa, treaty paylist name for Ochiibaamaansiins (Northern Barred Owl). "Small one" (described as "small in stature" in "Pazagwigabau Provokes Owl," pt. 5). Sturgeon.

Baachiish. Pachiish (Butikofer). *Batis, John Baptiste* (fig.5). Younger brother of Adam. Sturgeon.

Bapashki. Pahpaski (Butikofer). "Ruffed grouse." Son of Shote, Osnaburgh; father of Ashaageshi. Loon.

Bazigwiigaabaw. Pazagwigabau. "To stand up from a sitting position." Two wives: We'we and Mahkohkwe, q.v. Sturgeon.

Bezhig. Pesk. "Number one." Brother-in-law of Nabagaabik, parallel cousin of Zhenawaakoshkang.

Biindaandakwan. Pindandakwan. "Stuffing something with brush": Hallowell 2010, 603 (but Roulette finds no mention of "brush"). James Shadow. Son-in-law of Bazigwiigaabaw. Pelican.

Biindakik. Pindakik. "Inside the pail/vessel." Son of Bizhiw; grandson of Zhenawaakoshkang.

Biiwaanag. Piwanuk. "Flint." Family not identified.

Bineshiinzh. Pineshiinsh. "Bird." Samuel Goosehead. Kingfisher clan, from Berens River.

Bikwaakishtigwaan. Pikwakwastigan. "Bluff head, bulbous head." Half-brother of Dedibaayaaban.

Bizhiw. Pishiw. "Lynx." Alt. *Kepekiishikweyaash.* Sandy Owen. Oldest son of Zhenawaakoshkang. Moose.

Booshii. Potci. Bouchie or William Duck, son of John Duck and Taamook (daughter of Bizhiw).

Chaahkwiis. See Mezinaawaagwii (William Keeper).

Dedibaayaaban. Tetebaiyabin. "Daylight all around the sky." Alt. Wazhaashkozid (the smooth one); Andrew Strang. Son of Bazigwiigaabaw. Sturgeon.

Gaa-zhaaboowiyaazid.
Kaashaapowiiyaasit (Butikofer).
"One who is hollow." Older
brother of Ochiibaamaansiins
(Owl). Founded Sturgeon line
(Franklin surname) at Poplar
River.

Gegek. Kehkehk (Butikofer).
"Hawk." Only son of Owl and
Pasho. Sturgeon.

Getagaash. Ketagas. John Keeper.
Son of Kiwitc (Giiwiich, Alex
Keeper). Sturgeon.

Gezhiiyaash. Kezias. John Owen.
Son of Bizhiw and father of
Andwewe. Moose.

Gichi-ogimaa. Ktciogama. "Leader."
Half-brother of Naamiwan and
Aanii. Moose.

Gichi-omoonzoonii. "Great
Moose." Alternate name of
Zhenawaakoshkang. Moose.

Giiwechinwaas. Kiwetcinwas. "Of
the North Wind." Brother-in-law
of Naamiwan. Kingfisher.

Giiwichens. Kiwiichens. Affectionate
term for small boy. John
Keeper Sr. (fig. 4). Son of
Bazigwiigaabaw. Sturgeon.

Giiwiich. Kiwitc. Alex Keeper
(fig. 9), son of Bazigwiigaabaw.
Sturgeon.

Ginoozhewinini. Kinooshewinini
(Butikofer). "Jackfish man."
Joseph Green (fig. 8), son of
John (Midewinini). Pelican.

Gisayenaan. Kihsayenaan
(Butikofer). "Our Elder Brother."
Name for Adam Bigmouth.

Gookooko'ons. Kokokoos. "Little
Horned Owl." First husband of
Makwemod. Pelican.

Gwiikwishii. "Chickadee." Maggie
Ross. Daughter of Ahak and
Aanii. Pelican.

Ikwewiizhenzish. Nickname for
"mother." Daughter of Adam's
brother Baachiish. Sturgeon.

Injenii. Ingenie in official records.
Owl's second wife and Adam's
mother. Kingfisher.

Kehkehk. See Gegek.

Ketagas. See Getagaash.

Kinooshewinini. See
Ginoozhewinini.

Kiiwiich or *Kiwitc.* See Giiwiich.

Madoons. Maahtus. "Diminutive,
awkward, physically clumsy."
Son of Owl and Pasho. Sturgeon.

Maamaan Duck. Eldest son of John
Duck. Duck clan.

Mahkohkwe. "Bear Woman."
Second wife of Bazigwiigaabaw;
her five sons took surname
Keeper. Bear clan.

Makochens. Machkajence. "Little
Bear," affectionate form. John
Duck (fig. 6). Duck clan.

Makwemod. Maahkwemot (Butikofer).
"Bear (spirit) speaking"—not a
growl. Jane Bigmouth. Sister of
Adam. Sturgeon.

Mangidoon. "Big mouth." Adam's
family surname.

Mangitigwaan. Mankihtikwaan
(Butikofer). "Big head." Mother
of Naamiwan and Aanii.

Mezinaawaagwii. "Patterned or
tattooed one," also known
as Tcakwis (Hallowell);
Chaahkwiis (Butikofer). William
Keeper. Son of Bazigwiigaabaw.
Second husband of Aanii.
Sturgeon.

Migizi. Mikisi. "Eagle." First wife
of Mezinaawaagwii (William
Keeper).

Naamiwan. Namawin. "Fair
Wind"; John Owen in
mission records (fig. 7). Son of
Zhenawaakoshkang (Butikofer:
Shenawakoshkank). Moose.

Nabagaabik. Napakaapik.
"Flatstone." Son of Oshkiniiki;
grandson of Nootinwep:
Butikofer 2009, pt. II.3, 248–49.
Also known as Arthur Leveque,
Gichi-mookomaan (big knife).
Sturgeon.

Nikazhagayi. Nickname for Adam
Bigmouth: "He has Canada
goose skin."

Nimanepwaa. Nimanepwa. "Out
of tobacco." Son of Bezhig
(Butikofer: Paishk). Moose.

Noodinweb. Nootinwep (Butikofer).
"Wind sitting." Father of
Bazigwiigaabaw. Sturgeon.

Noojibine. Noochipine (Butikofer).
"Hunting a spruce grouse."
Alexander Bushie, chief, Little
Grand Rapids. Sturgeon.

Ochiibaamaansiins. Otcibamasis.
"Northern Barred Owl." Adam's
father. Sturgeon.

Ogaawidoon. "Pickerel lips."
Nickname of Adam Bigmouth.

Ogawapwan. Two wives, eight
children (Hallowell 2010, 97).
Father of Ahak. Pelican.

Ojijaak. Otcitcak. "Crane." Crane
Strang, son of Dedibaayaaban.
Sturgeon.

Okadjisi. Okachesi (Butikofer).
Brother of Zhenawaakoshkang.
Moose.

Ojiimaazo. Otcimazo (Hallowell).
Ochiimasoo (Butikofer). Older
half-brother of Naamiwan.

Ojik (nickname). *Otcik.* A brother
of Zhenawaakoshkang, had four
daughters, two of whom married
Dedibaayaaban (Tetebaiyabin,
Andrew Strang). Moose.

Omiimii. "Pigeon." Father of
Tcetcebu (Butikofer: Chiichipoo)
whom Owl brought back from
the spirit land. Pelican.

Omichoosh. James Owen. Son of
Bizhiw. Moose.

Omishoosh. Charlie George Owen.
Grandson of Naamiwan,
Pauingassi. Moose.

Otcik (Hallowell). See Ojik.

Owaagigaad. Owagigat. "Bent-legged one." Brother of Biindaandakwan. Pelican.

Pachaagano (derogatory). Timothy Keeper. Married Miskwiimin ("Raspberry"), daughter of Zhenawaakoshkang.

Pachiish. See Baachiish.

Pesk. See Bezhig.

Pahpaski. See Bapashki; Ashaagesi.

Pasho. Owl's first wife, a widow, and mother of Injenii. Pelican.

Peyak. Payak. "One" in Cree. John Bigmouth. Son of Adam and Aanii. Sturgeon.

Pindandakwan. See Biindaandakwan.

Pishiw. See Bizhiw.

Potci. See Booshii.

Sagatciwe. See Zaagajiwe.

Taami. Tomi. Thomas Owen. Half-brother of Naamiwan.

Tetebaiyabin. See Dedibaayaaban.

We'we. "Snow goose." First wife of Bazigwiigaabaw. Sons used surnames Strang and Turtle. Eagle clan.

Wiigwaasaatig. "Birchstick." John Suggashie. Son of Zagashkii. Sturgeon.

Winiichipo or *Oniichipo.* Affectionate nickname. Maggie Bigmouth. Daughter of Aanii and William Keeper.

Zaagajiwe. Sagatciwe. "To come into view over a hill." Midewiwin leader at Lac Seul.

Zagashkii. Sagaski. "To crouch." Sturgeon.

Zhenawaakoshkang. Cenawagwaskang. Shenawakoshkank (Butikofer). "Sound of stepping on a twig." Also known as Gichi-omoonzoonii ("Great Moose"). Moose.

Zhiishiibens. Shiishiipens. "Little Duck." George Duck. Father of Makochens (John Duck).

Ziibi. Siipi. "River." Daughter of Bazigwiigaabaw; wife of Biindaandakwan. Sturgeon.

OJIBWE STORIES FROM THE UPPER BERENS RIVER

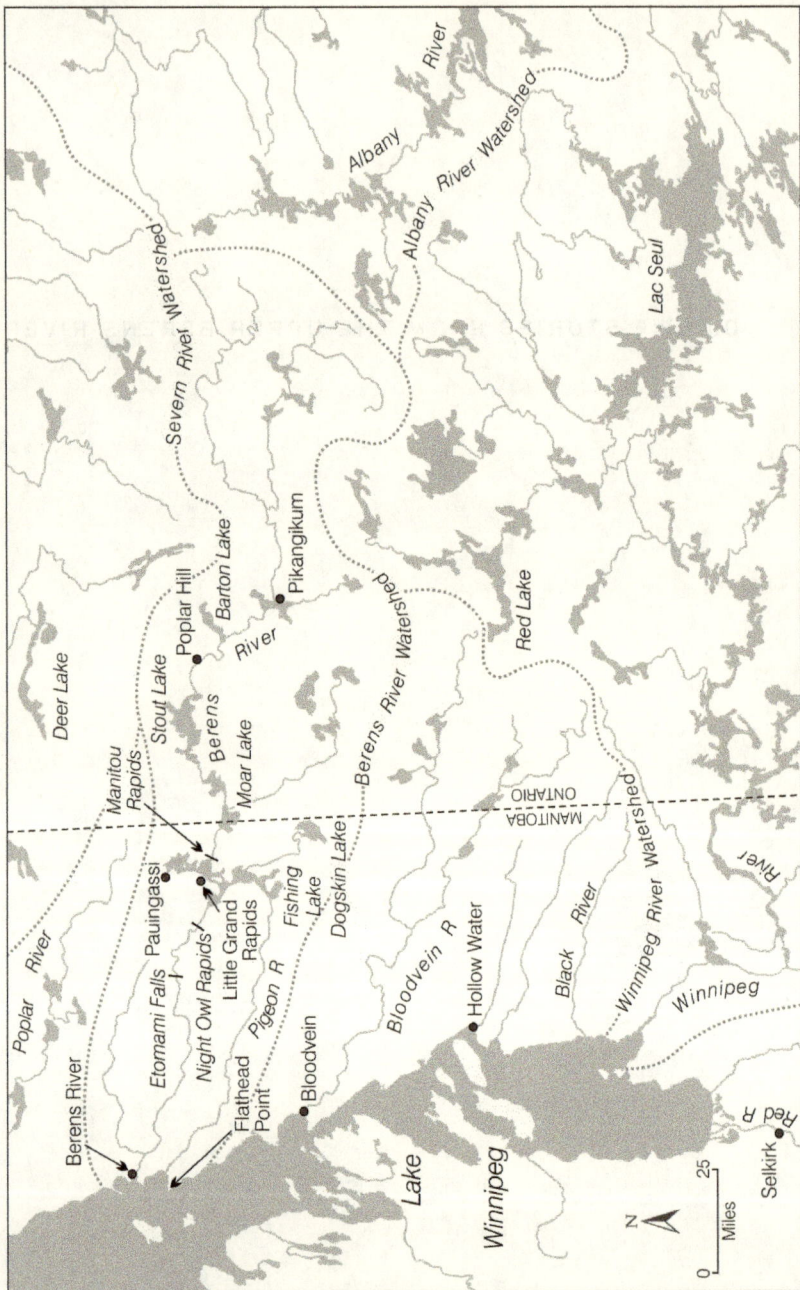

The world of Adam Bigmouth, from his ancestral homeland around Lac Seul to the mouth of the Berens River. Map by Weldon Hiebert. Source: Base map © Her Majesty the Queen in right of Canada, 2016.

Prologue

Adam Declines to Conjure, 1932

The following text, titled "Conjuring" (gosaabanjuge—as a verb), comprises two handwritten pages in Hallowell's field research notes on conjuring. Although undated, it pertains to Hallowell's first trip up the Berens River in 1932 and tells of his first meeting with Adam Bigmouth. He arrived at Little Grand Rapids on July 9, planning to stay only a couple of days before heading to Poplar Hill and Pikangikum. However, on July 10 he decided "to stay over and see a Wabano dance and conjuring—either Adam or John Duck" (field diary 1932). No conjuring performance (gosaabanjigewin) materialized on that occasion, and Hallowell and his party went on up the river to their other destinations. On their return trip they reached Little Grand Rapids at 5:00 p.m. on July 19; this entry is the last one in the 1932 diary. The diary accordingly makes no mention of the event related next, which probably happened the following day.

The conjuring text is most interesting, both as a vignette of how Hallowell conducted himself in the field, and as an introduction to Adam—a reflective person who declined to perform a ceremony at which he might fail and refused gifts that might have tempted him to engage in subterfuge, to "fool the white man."

Adam Big-mouth has been known to shake a tent many times. William Berens at first spoke to another Berens River man who was to ask Adam [to do it]. He was to let us know. In the afternoon we heard that the tent was up from John Keeper. We waited until dusk (and procured tobacco) but received no word. Finally I suggested we go over to Adam's camp. Birchstick [Wiigwaasaatig] said he would go along so W.B., Theo [Panadis], and y.t. [yours truly] paddled over. [We] found from the Berens River man that Adam had given him no answer. So we went in. Found [he had] visitors. After they left, Birchstick took the package I had brought containing a liberal allowance of tobacco and a shirt. He laid this before Adam (who is his step-father) and told him that I had tried to get a conjurer to shake a tent up the river so I could get an answer to some questions, but that no one could do it. Said in addition he knew he [Adam] had shaken the tent. Adam looked at the package, handled the tobacco, and after a while said he could not do it. He had done it well years ago, but the last few times it seemed as if his power was leaving him. Although he was a poor man he could not take the gift and fool the white man. I suggested he wait until the next day to decide but he replied that he knew ahead he could not manage it. Like a fire—bright at first but now he was getting old, not very good. Birchstick suggested that he have a tent put up, and if he could not do it to get someone else. "No"—last year, there was a sick young man, and he thought maybe he could discover the cause of the trouble in the tent. But when he went in it would not shake—pawaganak [bawaaganag] would not come. His brother Baptiste [Baachiish] went in with no better results. Had to admit failure—did not want to risk it again. He has been studying medicine—is going in for that now.

He finally pushed the package from him—which meant a final refusal. (Illustrates a genuine belief in spiritual controllers.)

He said that John Duck [Makochens] conjures, but the last time he did it all the people who were present ran off and left him. He did not even know this but kept on shaking [the tent]. [There's] no belief in his power—Said that he shakes it himself.

W.B.'s father [Jacob Berens] always said that as one gets older the pawaganak leave. Also that to deceive brings a penalty—a man will be driven crazy. A man at Berens River (William Goosehead) developed mental trouble—could not go 200 or 300 yards into the bush by himself—scared that something would happen to him. [He] confessed that he had used his own hands to shake a tent. His mental condition was the penalty.

Persons mentioned

William Berens, John Duck (fig. 6), and "Baptiste" (Adam's brother Baachiish or John Baptiste, fig. 5) are introduced elsewhere in this book, as is Birchstick (Wiigwaasaatig, John Suggashie), who was chief at Pikangikum. Birchstick was connected to Adam through his marriage to Maggie Ross, a daughter of Adam's wife Aanii by her first husband. John Keeper Sr. (Giiwichens, d. 1951), was a son of the Mide leader Pazigwigabau (Bazigwiigaabaw) and his second wife, Mahkohkwe (Butikofer 2009, pt. II.3, 355).

"Theo" is a most interesting personage. Theophile Panadis (1889–1966) was a trilingual Abenaki guide, hunter, and storyteller whom Hallowell had met at Odanak, Quebec, in the 1920s during his fieldwork there. Full of detailed cultural knowledge, he was immensely helpful to Hallowell's research, and his own deep interest in aboriginal life, as well as his practical skills, probably encouraged Hallowell to invite Panadis on his first trip up the Berens River. Unfortunately, Hallowell's 1932 field diary says almost nothing about Panadis, though it lists a few Ojibwe and Abenaki words that they compared and offers a couple of anecdotes. But as Alice Nash discovered in her Abenaki research, Panadis and Hallowell, both newcomers on this river journey, shared remarkable experiences, which Hallowell reported in his academic writings, and which Panadis relived through his storytelling over the next decades (Nash and Obomsawin 2003). In a photograph that Hallowell took of "Our party at first portage above Little Grand Rapids" in July 1932, Panadis stands several inches taller than the four Ojibwe guides and tripmen in the group (fig. 3).

PART 1

Boyhood Memories

Rabbits, Fish, Dogs, and a Caribou-Hunting Tragedy

I remember when I was a boy down at Eagle Lake, my father's hunting ground. I remember he used to start in the morning—make a big circle travelling and would not come back until night, making snares for rabbits. Sometimes my father came back with as much as he could carry. Day after day he used to kill them like that. He used to set a net right there [at the lake] and catch jack fish, tullibee [whitefish], pickerel. In the fall was the best season for otunipi [odanibii, tullibee]—we used to freeze them and smoke them for the winter. Lots of Indians used to visit there in those days. We even froze rabbits and sold them to the [Little] Grand Rapids post—they sent a dog team for them. The Pauingassi men even came to Eagle Lake for loads of fish (in winter).

Old William McKay was in charge of the Berens River post at the time I am telling of [about 1865]. His son (William) was in charge of Little Grand Rapids. In summertime my father used to fish for the Company. Sometimes my father used to be sent to K'tcibanga outpost to guard the building in summer—when the post was closed. Alec Stout was in charge.

When my father was at K'tcibanga one time, he was looking after the company's dogs. Sometimes [someone?] carried a report to Mr. Stout that the dogs were starving. He got mad and came up on a York boat. My oldest brother (Kehkehk [Gegek]) was working on this boat. He wanted to see what this white man was going to do to his father—did not wish any harm to come to the old man. Alec Stout had a reputation of fighting even with Indians. Of course it was only a false report; he found everything OK when he got there. And the same [summer?] every York Boat arrived at K'tcibanga—there was an Indian camp beyond the post—the Pikangikum Indians were there (. . . Pindandakwan, Pazagwigabau [Biindaankakwan, Bazigwiigaabaw]).

That same summer—when Pindandakwan and the others were hunting atik [adik, caribou; deer in local English usage]—that was the time I was very sad and scared. What made me scared was that the party of atik hunters were all weeping when they returned; I did not know why. I heard them talking—this Pindandakwan shot his own brother by accident. They were working together—he could not see—saw leaves moving—he thought it was a deer. They brought the body with them— quite a distance too. (Owagigat [Owaagigaad] was the one who was shot—tall.) I had been with my father to lift nets and just returned to camp when the party arrived. We thought at first that someone was drowned. I was nine years old, able to kill a rabbit. It was just when the deer was in good shape—before pairing—(September); we were hunting for them. I remember some men who used to go down to York Factory in summer—even from Little Grand Rapids. They left before the leaves were out (June), and came back at first snow.

Context

Complex watersheds and name changes complicate the tracking of local place-names. Hallowell in a field note dated July 9, 1932, stated that Eagle Lake was called Moar Lake by newcomers, an identification confirmed by Victor Lytwyn (1986, 112, 199). It lies a short distance up the Berens River from what the Hudson's Bay Company (HBC) traders called Big Fall—later Little Grand Rapids. The next lake above it was Stout Lake, named after the HBC man Alexander Stout. who served there for some time and who threatened trouble over the dogs. Hallowell wrote its Ojibwe name as K'tcibanga, which is a contraction of Kihchiopawankank (Roulette: Gichi-ombaawangaang, big sandy bank).

William McKay Sr., of Scots-Cree descent, had charge of the HBC post at Berens River until he retired in 1871. His son (William McKay, "A" in HBC records) had charge at Little Grand Rapids (Big Fall) from 1865 to 1871. His daughter, Mary, married William Berens's father, Jacob (Berens 2009, 204n12, 13). Kehkehk was the son of Owl by his first wife, Pasho. In winter, large amounts of fish were stored to feed the hard-working sled dogs (see, e.g., Young and Young 2014, 57–58). In summer, dogs were largely left on their own but needed some support to survive.

This story is the first to mention Pazagwigabau (Hallowell's transcription), a Sturgeon and Midewiwin leader at Poplar Hill, who caused much grief to Adam's father, Owl (pt.5). Pindandakwan, of the Pelican clan, and his wife Siipi (Ziibi), a daughter of Pazagwigabau, turn up in Adam's story "This Old Fellow Was Pretty Bad" (pt. 8). Pindindakwan later led the Midewiwin at Pikangikum (Hallowell 2010, 602–4; Butikofer 2009, pt. I.2, 306–7).

First Rabbit, First Mink, and a New Coat

I was so anxious to visit my [rabbit] snares that sometimes I could not sleep. I would not wait even to get anything to eat. My first rabbit—I was very proud then—my father made a feast. All the bones were taken out—we dried it—my parents kept it. In the month of May when the leaves came out, my father was able to kill a few—made a feast. The leader of the feast was his namer. This feast was held at Pauingassi—that is where his namer lived.

Then we went back to Eagle Lake again (headquarters). The following spring my father gave me a steel trap. I set this trap along the shore—there was a mink that passed my trap two or three times but did not go in. My father had caught a mink already; the carcass was hung up outside. My grandmother [Pasho] took a rabbit head—put it on a stick, and told me to take musk out of the mink and rub it on the rabbit's head stuck near the trap. Next day I went again—there was the mink. I was glad—I could not decide what I would buy—I thought of so many things. That night when the skin was stretched, I could not sleep, thinking what to buy at the post.

Then I used the rabbit head—with musk again. I found another mink the next day too, and the following day another—that's three. My father was going to the post—I went along with him to sell my mink. I bought a coat—a white cloth coat with a double row of brass buttons. I was told I had to give more than three mink (three mink = one [made beaver] skin or 75 cents). I managed to pay for this coat of mine anyway. My father used to buy carrot tobacco—tied with string = 3 beaver ($2.25).

Context

Adam Bigmouth's boyhood memories, vivid in themselves, also shed light on life on the upper Berens River in the early 1860s. His emphasis on his father's snaring of rabbits and netting of fish is revealing. The Berens River watershed was part of a region bounded by lakes Superior and Winnipeg that the old Canadian fur traders called le petit nord, the Little North, as opposed to le grand nord, extending from Lake Winnipeg to the Athabasca country (Lytwyn 1986, iii–v; see map, this volume). By the early 1800s the Little North saw intensive competition between the HBC and the North West Company, and stresses on big game animals increased. Moose became scarce in the uplands. In the adjacent Hudson Bay lowlands, the HBC encouraged year-round hunting for caribou skins, and the formerly vast caribou herds had disappeared by the 1830s (Lytwyn 2002, 183–87). Charles Bishop found through archival research that in the Lac Seul region by 1830, "hare and fish had become the chief source of livelihood during most of the year," and the Ojibwe were obliged to make substantial adaptive adjustments (Bishop 1978, 214–17). Meanwhile, the numbers of furbearing animals declined, and the HBC trade monopoly after 1821 meant that there were fewer posts from which to get supplies. Men's hunting of big game and furs was much reduced, and men increasingly turned to what had largely been women's work—snaring rabbits and setting nets for fish. Adam's stories made very few references to caribou hunting: notably, the shooting episode mentioned above, and a hunt carried on at the time of Adam's father's death, around 1884 (pt. 5, "Death Due to Sorcery"). Adam in the early 1860s made the best of the circumstances, taking joy in trapping his first rabbits (misaabooz), for which he was recognized in a feast at Pauingassi, and then trapping his first mink and appreciating his first trade returns. If indeed the rabbit feast was led, as he said, by the man who had named his father, this man must have been very old indeed. The "rabbits" would have been snowshoe hares (*Lepus americanus*); as with caribou, the local English vernacular did not identify them precisely.

Sighting a Fearsome Stranger—and a Sequel

In springtime we used to camp at Eagle Lake. I was a very small boy at that time. The sap was running in the birch trees and I went with my father to cut those trees and collect the sap. ("A kettle of birch bark was fixed so that it would catch the sap. The sap was boiled and put in tea to sweeten it"—AIH.) I had my bow in my hand and my father was holding a kettle when he said to me, "We had better leave this place." Then I looked and saw something sitting on a rock not so far away. He was a fearful looking sight. I could see his white teeth very plainly but his face was black. I can't tell you how his hair looked. It was hanging all around his face. I was so scared I could hardly move my legs to walk. My father held me tightly by my wrist and dragged me along.

After we got to the camp my father spoke to one of the old men. He said, "There is a queer looking stranger near here. Come along with me and we will go and see him." They went back to the rock but the stranger had gone. But when it got dark this thing came closer.

My father had three big dogs at this time, and that same night, as soon as it got dark, they began to bark. Everyone was scared. It was a pitch black night. Then my father took off his shirt and leggings. All he had on was his breech cloth. Picking up his axe he started off in the direction where that stranger was. ("A gun would not go off against a 'real' windigo"—AIH.) But he could not find him. The stranger ran away. The next night the same thing happened; the stranger came closer and the dogs started to bark. My father went again to meet him, naked, with an axe. The stranger ran away again; my father could not get near him.

Flatstone [Nabagaabik] was camping with us at that time. He put up a conjuring tent (figs. 13, 14) and my father went in. Mikinaak [clairvoyant spirit-being in the tent] saw the stranger. He said he was coming towards our camp and was going to kill us. My father told Mikinaak to keep an eye on the stranger. "I'm going to meet him," he said, and he went off. Mikinaak [watching] said, "He [Adam's father] is going straight; he is pretty near now." ("My understanding is that the conjuror did not actually leave the lodge"—AIH.) Then Mikinaak said, "The windigo is running away." (My father never saw him.) "I think he is gone for good." We did not hear any strange noises at night after that.

Later in the spring my father got ready to go somewhere one morning. He did not tell us where he was going or what he was going to do. He met this stranger at the halfway point on Clear Water Lake. He was coming around the other side. That's where the big fight took place. He put that one out of business.

[In another conversation Adam elaborated on this fight, providing a sequel to the story as follows (see "Cannibals," no. 12 in Hallowell n.d., "Myths and Tales").]

I remember what happened once when we were camping at the narrows of Eagle Lake. One evening my father was very quiet. He did not eat any supper. He lay down and slept. In the morning he got up very early and put on his moccasins. But he ate no breakfast. All he said was, "There is going to be a stranger around here and I am going to meet him." He went to Clear Water Lake. There he met the stranger at the last point before you reach the portage. He fought that one. It was a windigo. When the fight was on the trees fell in all directions. We could hear a terrible noise. Then we knew the fight was over. It was the pawaganak we heard—just as you have heard them in the conjuring tent. They divide up the windigo. Mikinaak gets the liver, because that is what he likes. One gets the head—egokwas [Roulette: may be the name of a specific bawaagan]. Pagak [Paagak] gets his share also. The two little fingers of the windigo fell before my father from the sky. "I don't want them," he said, and threw them away into the air.

Context

One human and one other-than-human personage mentioned here recur in Adam's other stories. Flatstone (Nabagaabik), a Sturgeon also known as Arthur Leveque and Gichi-mookomaan, was probably born at Lac Seul and died in 1916 17 (Butikofer 2009, pt. II.3, 252). He led the Midewiwin for some years at Little Grand Rapids (Hallowell 2010, 397n13; 601). Mikinaak, the great or boss turtle, "is always present in every conjuring tent" (Hallowell 1942, 45) and played a key role in defeating windigos—see stories in part 10.

This windigo story and its sequel appear here rather than in part 10, "Encounters and Contests with Windigos," as this childhood experience shaped Adam's awareness of these beings at an early age. It is interesting that Adam and his father at first saw the apparition as a fearsome "stranger." As Hallowell wrote in an undated research note, "Everyone gets uneasy if he does not know who his neighbors are and does not understand what his neighbor is up to, if there are unidentified strangers about, etc. . . . Unidentified persons are potential sources of danger—strangers (piwite [biiwide]) and there is always the possibility of windigo." One is reminded of Mary Black (Rogers)'s comments on Ojibwe "percept ambiguity" (1977); you cannot be sure about what you think you are seeing until you have more clues, and caution is in order.

Two nights after the sighting, when Mikinaak used the windigo word in Flatstone's shaking tent, it carried great power, even though the only signs of the windigo's presence were auditory and indirect—the dogs barking two nights in a row (compare Adam's story of being stalked by a windigo, pt. 10). Adam's father went after him, but never saw him. In undated research notes on a similar windigo episode told by William Berens, Hallowell wrote, "This kind of roaming *windigo* dies in summer—can't stand heat and mosquitoes. [Most are] only found in winter and spring—used to cold (association with kiwitin [Giiwedin, north]" (2010, 99).

The matter-of-fact way in which Mikinaak spoke about the windigo and his movements is revealing. In Ojibwe terms, such personages were real. Mikinaak's presence and his giving of information were assumed and expected, as was his confirmation of the windigo's proximity. The coda to the main story is vague. Evidently Adam told its climactic sequel to Hallowell at another time, and Hallowell preserved it in typed form in his "Myths and Tales" files. He also wrote about the incident in *The Role of Conjuring in Saulteaux Society* (1942, 64) but without recounting specifics. Here as elsewhere, Adam told of how his father dealt effectively and even heroically with such challenges (see pt. 5 and further windigo episodes in pts. 10 and 11).

First Experience with Rum

That same spring [after the windigo battle] we came to Little Grand Rapids to meet the rest of the people there after the hunting was over. After all the people were gathered together, the Company used to keep number 10 kettles (large as two pails) filled up with rum—we did not see tea then. We camped on the island (between Joe Alec's place and the camps on the farther island).

The old people started to drink—some got a little drunk—began to quarrel. We [boys] were pretty scared. Pesk [Bezhig]—he was going to fight his brother-in-law Flatstone. All we boys ran away—two of Pesk's sons and me and my brother and another two. We took a canoe to the mainland and slept there that night. We talked among ourselves—how this stuff acted on these men and made them so crazy. Pesk's oldest son—the oldest of the bunch—said, "I'll go see." So he came back—stole some of [his] father's rum, brought back a quart with him. We put some water in it ourselves, then we started to drink—the first time anyone had tasted rum. One drink we took—two drinks—tastes good—so I went to my father's tent to see if I could find more. When I got there, all the birch bark was in pieces. My mother [Injenii] was there—I could see the kettle covered. I took some in a sly way and filled the pot I had with me—my mother did not expect me to steal anything from the tent. My mother said, "Stay away, they are still drinking." Women did not drink, only men.

I took the pot back—we put water in—had another drink. It did not affect us yet. Soon we heard someone yelling across the water. There was an old man so drunk his canoe got upset. He was doing the shouting—we thought he would be drowned for sure. I was scared—such a swift current; we did not see how they could help him. Some men went out in two canoes and pulled the old man ashore—he could not even walk. About daylight we went back . . . saw a woman and man hitting each other . . . he could not get what he wanted, I guess. The father of

Asagesi [Ashaageshi] was here at that time; Pineshiinsh [Bineshiinzh] was here too (Goosehead). We boys found how it [the rum] worked—we quit.

Context

"First Experience with Rum" is the only instance in which Adam expressed views on drinking. His other stories (like Hallowell's Berens River research notes in general) scarcely mention alcohol; an exception is "Windigo Man Consumes Family," in which a post manager cures a windigo by plying him with rum (pt. 12). Aside from its use at such summer trade gatherings as this, it appeared almost absent from Adam's universe. In older times during serious fur trade competition, and again from the 1950s on with the rise of air transport, bootlegging, and the opening of mines in the region, alcohol problems were much more conspicuous. Evidently Adam was not at all attracted to strong drink after this experience.

Joseph "Alec" (Alix) was one of a few Lebanese free traders in the area and had a family whom Hallowell met in the 1930s. He traded in opposition to the HBC at both Berens River and Little Grand Rapids. On his entry to Canada, his name was changed from Yusef Seba (granddaughter Doreen Silvera to JSHB, August 4, 1999). Asagesi's father was Pahpahski from Lac Seul (Butikofer 2009, pt. II.2, 77). Asagesi met Hallowell in July 1932 at Duck (Barton) Lake and told him of some of his spiritual experiences (Berens 2009, 236n15). Pineshiinsh was Samuel Goosehead (1856–1916, Kingfisher clan) from Berens River, whose wife was a daughter of Zhenawaakoshkang (Butikofer 2009, ppt. II.1, 63; pt. II.3, 156).

Harvesting Wild Rice

After this big time was over, we started down to Long Lake. We went to the Etomami River to gather wild rice up—stayed three weeks. Where it enters the Berens River [at Etomami Falls, see map], for five miles one can hardly paddle through—[the rice grows] terribly thick down to Shoal Lake. [See Hallowell 2010 on the northern range of *Zizania* (wild rice).]

Even the Berens River people [from the mouth of the river] used to go there. There were seven families from Little Grand Rapids and five from Berens River—over fifty people there at a camping ground on the west side of the river. ("Adam used to paddle while his father harvested"—AIH.) Some would exchange rice for rum—some let go two sacks. But those who were long headed kept it for winter. We used to take two bags back to Eagle Lake—100 pounds apiece (each the size of a flour sack). We used it carefully during the winter—enough to keep us till May. Moses [Owen] of Pauingassi goes to Rice Lake every year.

PART 2

Working for the Hudson's Bay Company

Haying and Hauling for the Company

One time when the York boat crew got back to Little Grand Rapids from Berens River, they brought one bull and one cow for the Company. The Company started to raise cattle. When they came to six head, I was ready to help making hay for those animals. Every summer I cut hay—using a scythe—I used to throw hay into a York boat and take it to where it could be dried—lots of handling.

I also used to drive the bull into the woods, harnessed, to haul wood. One time I was going to hitch him up in the morning. His horns caught me and tore my clothes up the front—I was feeling shaky that time. That time there was a new man in charge—Jack Moore [Moar]. He told me, "You go back and harness the bull; if he acts the same way, I'll kill him today." Jack was watching—I hitched the bull to the sleigh. Afterwards in the woods he was hitched to a stump and acted the same way—came at me. I filled up the sleigh with wood, went on top of the load, took a stick, and gave him hell. The following winter they killed him. Then they sent an ox out—that one was alright.

As soon as the river was clear, I was sent to Berens River with a canoe (birch bark at that time). Everything was in short supply here. One time we ran out of grub for three days. One time I went to Pickerel Creek— Bloodvein side. Pipestone Lake [near Red Lake]—that was the trip. The Lake Seul Indians brought pipe stone up here—in the rough. Two kinds—one was softer than the other, both about same in color. [Probably steatite, commonly called soapstone (see Steinbring 1981, 248).]

HBC Manager in Trouble, a Trip to Lake Winnipeg, and York Boat Work

When I was a young man—working already—able to look after myself, I came up from Berens River after a trip (freight). One morning after breakfast, someone brought a message. Everybody had been asked already [and refused] to take this crazy person down the river (only birch canoes at that time). The post manager, Jack Moar, this was the one that was getting crazy. The man did not eat, drink, or sleep. Just on the walk all the time. I said to the messenger that I would take him to the mouth [of Berens River] even if he kills me. Then we took him down—I went with Joe Everett. First night from here [Little Grand Rapids] we only had reached this side of Manitu Rapids. That night we were sleeping good—sun getting up—had breakfast—sun not up yet. Then he got up—he said he was feeling better.

We camped again just above Old Fort [Rapids]. Just about daybreak I woke up. I could see Jack M's bed clothes but the man was not there. I stepped out. I thought this man had run away or had been drowned. I did not go far when I found him walking around. We started off again—got to Berens River before dinner. That last morning, Jack Moar did not eat or drink. We stayed at Berens River for two days—he did not eat. We gave him cow's milk but he would not take it. Then we borrowed a canoe from the preacher. The first day we only got to Flathead Point [on Lake Winnipeg]. He slept good there again, had something to eat. This was the first time he drank tea in the morning. We paddled off again, made dinner at Flour Point. When we got to Rabbit Point it was sundown—forty-five miles from Berens River. We travelled all night and passed Dog Head [where] we saw some lanterns hanging on a sail boat. We set a tent that night. When we were paddling across a bay [Jack Moar] jumped up in the canoe. If he had upset it we would have drowned. We cooked; by the time we finished it was daylight. In the morning he shouted, "There's a boat!" We got up—jumped into the canoe, and put him in the steamboat to go in [to Selkirk].

We stayed there one day and came back. On this side of Rabbit Point, at Split Rock Creek, it was blowing—the sea so big that we afterwards began to take water; the canoe became half full. I was pretty scared that time. We managed to get to shore which was fairly near when the storm struck us. We stayed that night. Next day there was a little rain—fog—blowing hard. We could not manage to sleep that day—mosquitoes so bad. We started later in the day and came to Catfish Creek—blowing hard yet. We stayed and slept there. In the morning the swell was coming in heavy; we got out again when sea became flat again. It was very calm now after this big wind. That's the first time I saw Lake Winnipeg so smooth. After we reached Berens River, I stayed a week or two waiting for Jack Moar to come out [from Selkirk]. Then he came on the boat. We came up the river again.

After we reached Little Grand Rapids, I took bales of fur downriver by York boat. Coming upriver, we pulled the York boat over White Mud [Portage]. When we were hauling the line this rope caught on a tree—very dangerous when you are pulling a boat up against the current. There are two drops. The man next to me—I told him to be careful. He put the line across his body. I told [him] to put the strap on his shoulder: "If anything happens, this line will throw you out." The man says, "I can hold it OK." But when the men at the head of the line were pulling, cutting across the bay, the strap slipped off. I saw something out in the water, saw the man hanging from the rope above the water, the rope was so taut. When the rope got slack, he began to drop into water and spin around—could not stop there. The man braced himself against a rock and got on his feet.

("Adam worked on York boats for fifteen+ years. Three trips per summer: seven nights up the river, three going down. When there are eight men—four tons—10,000 [pounds?] for each man, [paid] $16 a trip coming up; $5 down"—AIH.)

It seems men and women are not so strong now—Why? A young man before he is full grown is after the women, so he loses his own strength and weakens his life as well. I know from my own experience—I'm old now [1940]. I kept away from women—I was a strong young man. I was a strong young man. I used to do heavy work too, no one was a better worker on York boats than me. That's the reason those young fellows are not healthy—bothering the women too soon. I used to shoulder 300 pounds—a barrel of pork over Night Owl Portage. One man carried a sack crossways—he [could] hardly bear it. I tried to see how much I could take—put it through—nobody else could do it that time. Twenty men were drawing this [York] boat over. I was told to give a hand; the boat started to move as soon as I put my hand on it. The people never think, now when I'm walking around, that I was anything at all. I never hurt myself. I never broke a box—[there are] people here who know this. Even a flour sack, after I put a strap on it, I threw it on my back. Another sack on top—did not have to have anyone to load me. That's what I call real hard work. After I got through, I did not throw myself in the canoe on my back. Then after I finished a trip, I went out and set nets—did not lie around on my back—never tired. That's the kind of work I've been doing.

Context

Some people and items need identification in these two stories. Trader John Moar was labeled as "A" (senior) in HBC records to distinguish him from other Orkneymen of that name. After serving elsewhere he worked at Little Grand Rapids as interpreter and postmaster from 1874 to 1885 and again in later years as clerk (HBCA Biographical Sheets 2017). The bull incident probably dates to 1874–75. Joseph Everett was an Ojibwe who had been adopted by the Metis leader Cuthbert Grant. His granddaughter Nancy Everett married William Berens in 1899 (Berens 2009, 19, 210n39). The preacher at Berens River was the Methodist Egerton R. Young, supposing this incident happened in the summer of 1875 or 1876, as seems likely. The Youngs had a cow at Berens River (Young and Young 2014, 87).

The place-names Adam mentioned appear on the inset map in Berens (2009, 36). Telling this story over fifty years later, Adam reversed the locations of Rabbit and Flour points; coming from Flathead Point, they would have come to Rabbit Point first. This was the only trip on Lake Winnipeg that Adam mentioned; Berens may have helped him remember place-names. The steamboat was probably the HBC steamer SS *Colvile*, the first to serve Lake Winnipeg, starting in 1875 (Berens 2009, 206n20).

It would have carried Moar to Selkirk, so that he could seek medical help there or in Winnipeg. Travel up the Berens River to Little Grand Rapids involved some steep grades; Joe Leveque told Gary Butikofer that there were fifty-three portages between Little Grand Rapids and Berens River. When Leveque was freighting for the HBC it took five days to go downriver, and thirteen coming up (Butikofer 2009, pt. II.7, 520). Sizes of loads, manpower, and water conditions varied, of course.

A Company Man Gets Sick

One time I was fishing in the fall with a white man [Willie Jibo]—he spoke to me, said he was not feeling good (company man). He did not eat. Even at night he did not sleep. I said the next day, "We better pull up the nets." We put the fish in the house and dried the nets. It was late; we had to stay there that night—no supper. Next morning we went out in the canoe (birch). When we came to Eagle Lake he told me, "I'm getting better. Let us set the nets again." "No, we better go back [to the post]." "No," he said, "I'm better." I said, "Well—if you want to put down the nets, OK." So we put them down. Joe Green [Ginoozhewinini, but see later note] was there fishing for the Company with his brother. I went to those two boys and said, "My partner is not well." So Joe Green said, "You better take him back."

Next day we started back to Little Grand Rapids. At Pauingassi [Fishing] Lake he lost his senses. After sundown we reached the long portage at the Grand Rapids. He lost his senses again, and started to run away when we had almost reached the post. He came to his senses and was taken to the men's house and left there. I went back the next morning—his sheets and bedding were torn, a chair all smashed. He told me, "If you are ready to go, let me know." Of course I could not take him. That evening I got ready to leave but did not tell him. After he had been locked up, I came to see him. I asked him what he was doing; I said, "Keep still." He said he could not. He'd had no meal yet since he arrived. Then I went and got something to eat. [He] tried to run out—a man got hold of him and threw him to one side. Another grabbed him. This man was spitting blood now. After supper I went back. I found a way to keep him quiet. I sat down for a long time. I asked him if he had eaten. He said he wanted nothing, but that "I might have a good meal if we went together." I started off in the morning, without letting him know. The man got worse. He got away at night and followed me; other fellows went after him and took him back to the post. My father [Owl] had medicine and fixed him up, but it took a long time. We packed up the nets and came back—he was OK then.

Context

Adam identified Willie Jibo in his second version of this story, "The Dangers of Love Medicine" (pt. 5), which relates the reason for his sickness—misuse of love medicine. Jibo, according to Hallowell's notes on non-totemic families in the area, was the son of William Gibeault, described as a Cree from Fort Churchill on Hudson Bay. William was adopted by William McKay, William Berens's maternal grandfather. The Berens River Ojibwe saw the McKay family (and probably HBC employees generally) as white, identifying them with their paternal ancestors; they did not speak of "Metis" or "halfbreeds." Gibeault's surname suggests voyageur paternal ancestry. Butikofer noted that Joseph Green (Ginoozhewinini, fig. 8), son of John (Midewinini), was actually born in 1884–85, after this episode—which predated Owl's death in 1884–85. The young fisherman was probably his father, John, who died in 1893–94 (Butikofer 2009, pt. II.3, 213–14, d. 1893–94).

Guard Duty at Berens River

Down at Berens River there were some scouts came out of the south. Mr. [James] Flett [HBC clerk] gave us rations for night guarding—guns—and orders to speak to them as high as four times. "If they don't answer," [he said], "pull the trigger." There was a separate house to sleep in the daytime, and rations. I did not like that job; did not wish to shoot anyone. I got paid $4 per night. I just felt I might be shot at any time—going around at night any time, a flash of fire.

PART 3

Dream Experiences

A Dream Revelation

When I was a boy, when I was sleeping—all of a sudden I got scared. I was dreaming of the whole world (this country). I dreamed of all kinds of people—white and Indians. Then I saw in my dream this island (the earth) all aflame. Even the water coming down from heaven turned into sparks of fire burning. I heard some people yelling (shouting), saw them crying. I was thinking what a fearful night it was. No one had a chance to live. I heard some man saying: "Somebody is going to come. If this one comes the fire will stop. The one who is going to come, that is God's son." Then I saw something down in the east. It looks like a small bit of cloud. That's where this stranger is—on this cloud. I can even hear something on this earth and something in the water. Like someone preaching. As soon as he reached here the fire went down—even in the water. I was on top of a small hill—that is the point from where I was watching things. And I heard this one say—the reason of the fire is that too much of the earth has been spoiled—the things that are not right on the earth will be burned. That is why the fire came.

From that time I had this wonderful dream, I never said any bad words. Even when I found anything that was left or lost, I never kept it. I always tried to find the owner. I remember once at Treaty time [in summer when annuities were paid] I saw a little bag. I picked it up—did not know what was in it. I asked people who it belonged to. It belonged to one of the white men. It was full of money—this white man he gave me $5 for finding this little sack. I think he was a doctor.

I remember one time I was going to the Little Grand post over there. I saw money lying on the trail where someone had dropped it. I tried to find out who it belonged to. It belonged to Taché McKay. That same winter on a trip, I found a fox in a trap on a lake. I took back the fox, but [re]set the trap. It was a red one. I tried to find out who it belonged to. It seems to me the fox belonged to a Company man. He gave me half of the value. I found a mink once that belonged to an Indian—Peter Ogimaa from here. That one, I did not expect pay.

One time again I trapped a fox—followed his trail—so I came to the place where he was caught [in a trap with a broken chain]. . . . Caught him with a line—chased him. I caught up and knocked him [on] the head. I had a hard time to keep up with this fox—especially on the ice. I came to Little Grand Rapids Post. Tried to find who had lost the trap with the fox in it (broke chain), a silver fox. Joe B. lost it. He gave me half its value. Foxes got a good price then—$100. ("William Berens had [been] paid as much as 300—half cash at Poplar River"—AIH.)

Last year [winter 1937–38], I set a net near Grassy Narrows, along with my old wife [Aanii]. After opening the holes [in the ice], I thought I saw something at a nearby point. After I lifted the net, we went ashore and made a fire. I went to the point and saw a cross fox jumping up. When I came up, I saw there was only one strand of snaring wire holding him. I found a string in my pocket. I tied the string to the end of a stick and snared him with a piece of string. It was a good fox—I did not know whose snare had caught him. I asked the wife of Batis [Baachiish, his brother]—whose snare is it? Payak [Peyak, his son] had some snares over there too. They told me to go and sell the fox because the snare had been thrown away long ago. I did not like to do this. I asked Joseph Green and others. I went to the chief [Alex Bushie], who said it was his snare. I gave him the fox—it was worth $20—He gave me $1. (Laughed.) That's the way I have been treating my fellow men.

Context

This powerful boyhood dream came to Adam unbidden, without his fasting or seeking a vision. The imagery of fire descending from heaven and the waters being set aflame to burn "the things that are not right on this earth"—evokes the prophecy in the Book of Revelation, 20:9–10, 15: "fire came down from heaven and consumed them, and the devil who had deceived them was thrown into the lake of fire and brimstone . . . if anyone's name was not found written in the book of life, he was thrown into the lake of fire." Yet as a boy on the upper Berens River in the 1860s, Adam could scarcely have had contact with missions or clergy, even though his census listing as Methodist implied a baptism by the 1880s. Possibly he picked up a version of the prophecy from other Ojibwe people who had heard biblical stories from priests or ministers or from fur traders, who sometimes recounted Bible stories and passed on elements of Christian cosmology (Podruchny 2006, ch. 3). And certainly mythic elements regularly turned up in dreams (see, for example, Berens 2009, 106–7).

The old Ojibwe mythic story of Aasi, a powerful young man, offers a parallel that may have reinforced the motif of fire destroying evil. In this story Aasi's mother was treated terribly by his father, who took another wife, and by others. After a long journey Aasi returned and exacted retribution by shooting a black arrow into the heavens, causing the earth to burst into flame. After the bad people were destroyed, he shot a red arrow into the sky, and when it hit the earth, the fire went out (Berens 2009, 146–47). Adam's statement that after the dream he "never said any bad words" might suggest to English speakers that he decided to refrain from cursing. But it more likely signified a resolve to refrain from insults and saying bad things about people—a wise practice in Ojibwe country, as verbal insults and aspersions could bring dire consequences if some powerful person, or one with unexpected powers, took offence.

The people whom Adam mentioned give clues to his associations at the time. Taché McKay (1883–1968), son of Indian agent Angus McKay, was living at Berens River in the early 1900s (Red River Ancestry 2017). Skilled in several languages, he often traveled with and interpreted for Indian agents, treaty officials, and doctors. Joe B. was probably Joseph Bushie (Choome [Joome]), 1909-ca. 1946). His father was the Little Grand Rapids chief, Alex Bushie (Noochipine; Butikofer 2009, pt. II.3, 280-81, 285)—the man who gave Adam a dollar for the cross fox.

Fasting in Winter

In winter I went to dream—dug a hole in a snowbank, fixed it up with brush. Then I went and looked for a crust of snow and made a door with the crust of snow. I put my snowshoes outside and went in. I did not even have a blanket—just folded myself up—the coldest day of the year. I was in that den four nights [an earlier brief account says six nights and that he had a blanket]. I did not have any fire, no water to drink, no food to be eaten—quite a long way from my father's camp. I thought of this before I done it—what I would be [facing].

After four nights had passed away I got out of this den. One of my snowshoes had been covered with the snowdrift—wind blowing along the lakeshore. The sun was high when I left the den. Something affected my knees—I could not walk very good. There was a north wind and I crossed a big muskeg. I was facing the wind, and all of a sudden I smelled something—it stank—a long distance away. When I was walking I could smell it getting stronger. As I walked I could see a trail on the snow from a distance. When I came to it I saw that people had been passing the same morning—a fresh trail, and I crossed the trail. After I crossed it I did not smell anything anymore. What I smelt—a human trail—I smelled before I came to it, like an animal does. Not a strange thing—those animals smell a [human] trail before they come to it.

It was getting dark already before I could reach camp. When I got near to it I could hear drumming. John Duck's father [Zhiishiibens] was there. Kiwetcinwas [Giiwechinwaas, "Of the North Wind] was there too (visiting), Spot [Ishpoot], Naamiwan—several families. The reason they were beating the drum was to see if I was living. It was not my father who did this—of course my father knew [that I was alive]—but my mother [didn't know]. As soon as I got in, a basin was handed me to wash, comb my hair. Food was brought—but I could not eat. I went to bed without a bite. After I got home I could hardly stand staying in the tent. Could not take food—except a little to start with. In the morning I took food. I did not feel very good on my stomach after I ate. My father said, "Don't drink too much—just a little water." I did not even put much bed clothes on that first night. Did not take off my shoes. I did not like the smell of the bed clothes. Finally I got a real meal. This [was] where I got my blessing by doing this. I wonder if there is any young man who could do that now—could not stand it. ("Adam would not tell anything of his dreams while fasting. Although he has given up conjuring, he is using his pawaganak for the Wabano. He says his father was a great conjuror"—AIH.)

I went along with my [younger] brother, Batis, one other time. We got hungry—could not stand it that time. ("My father [Owl] wanted us to do that; he sent us," said Batis [who joined this conversation]. "You can't lie at full stretch on your back—but curled up.") Batis said that our father taught us that a person had to do this to live long—to an old age. "There was one other time again when I was off alone" ([said] Adam). "The reason we did it over again," said Batis, "was to be sure of a blessing—not only once—two or three times, to be sure. Pretty near ten nights that time. You can't drink or take food when you are doing that. If you drink before you are through and you swallow a worm, it will be sure to kill you."

Batis said, "I used to have a funny dream. I got hungry—I would dream that someone was giving me meat. After I got through and knew everything—you see this open space [here]—I killed enough animals to fill it in my past life." (Adam: "He means he saw the carcasses of animals all over—that he was destined to kill during his life.")

The main thing for a young man to do is to keep away from women until the age of sixteen–eighteen. I have a young grandson; he is going to be a good hunter too—my son [Peyak, John Bigmouth] has been also. ("[Adam] has put both [two] boys through fasting, adopted grandchildren—Potci's sons; when their mother died, he promised"—AIH.) "It's useful to you," Potci said, "when you get older."

Context

The persons mentioned in this story were all interconnected. The father of John Duck (Makochens) was George Duck (Shiishiipens, Zhiishiibens). George Duck, Giiwechinwaas, and Ishpoot had all married daughters of Zhenawaakoshkang, which made them and Naamiwan all brothers-in-law (Butikofer 2009, pt. II.3, 98, 99 and pers. comm.). Potci was Pochii (Roulette: Booshii), or William Duck, b. 1898–99, a son of John Duck. The two boys who went out to fast were sons of Potci and his first wife, Ihkeweshenshish (Roulette: Ikwewiizhenzish), d. 1924–25, a daughter of Adam's brother Batis or Baachiish, which helps explain the interest that Adam took in them (Butikofer 2009, pt. II.3, 105, 308–9).

A boy who went out to fast had to be clean; and in the bush, away from his family's encampment, he was in a clean place. Hallowell, in a page of notes labeled "Religious purity," cited the Ojibwe term, pekize (bekizi), "pure, clean," to describe this condition. "Animals in the woods, fish and birds, are clean." But animals living with humans are not. Dogs, "always monkeying around shit and piss in camp," were unclean. Hallowell was told that "human beings themselves are not clean," and women less so than men on account of their menstrual flows. But "a boy who has not touched a woman yet, or had women on his mind, even, is pure." Adam in speaking of his youthful HBC work told Hallowell of how he had stayed strong by keeping away from women (see "A Company Man Gets Sick," pt. 2).

Before leaving for his fast, a youth would change his sleeping quarters to "the 'cleanest' place in the wigwam, i.e., towards the rear, in the area reserved for the men"; until then, he had slept near the entrance with his mother and siblings (Hallowell 2010, 452). The shift was "a symbol of his segregation from the women, especially his sisters. At this time it would be fatal to his chances for securing strong guardian spirits if a girl or woman, and worse, a menstruating woman, stepped over his legs or any article of his clothing" (Hallowell n.d., "Sexual Behavior," MSS, series I, file 1, 11).

Boys typically fasted in springtime, in a "nest" that they and their male relatives constructed with poles laid across the branches of a tree

(Hallowell 2010, 452). Adam's fasting in winter, in a den that he himself made in a snowbank, was unusual. On the day that he returned from his fast, he encountered a very bad smell as he approached human trails and habitations. His time in the bush, in a clean state, had made him sensitive, like a wild animal, to human odors and pollution. A boy returning from a fast, Hallowell wrote in a research note, "must not be seen by a woman first. He comes back to camp early in the morning [though Adam returned late in the day]. . . . He waits till the camp is stirring and then whistles. His father knows his whistle and goes to where he is [hiding] and brings him into the camp. Then relatives and neighbors are invited and a feast is held to celebrate his return" (loose-leaf research note, n.d.).

Adam vividly described how, at first, regular food, bed coverings, etc., made him most uncomfortable. Relatives gathered to bear witness to his new status, but as Hallowell learned from others, they would all have respected the proscription, laid down by the pawaganak or dream visitors, forbidding the faster from revealing the dreams and blessings he had received during his isolation and the obligations and requirements that had been imposed upon him (Hallowell 2010, 457). The importance of the occasion could scarcely be overstated. As Hallowell wrote, "The help of powerful persons of the other-than-human category is a necessity. Women may obtain such help but men cannot get along without it." Contact with the masters of the game animals was critical for survival, and a man needed help against both human and nonhuman beings (notably windigos) hostile to him. The special skills and powers that a man needed for curing and conjuring equally depended on the gifts and blessings of spiritual beings. In sum, as one grandfather said to his grandson, "You will have a long and good life if you dream well" (Hallowell 2010, 451–52).

In conversation at Little Grand Rapids, however, Hallowell also heard that boys were not being sent out to fast any more (loose-leaf research note, n.d.). Among the last to go were the two sons of Potci (Booshii), whose deceased wife's father was Adam's brother Batis, as earlier noted. The boys were sent out on Adam's initiative as he had promised, probably in the late 1920s. An easy supposition would be that some missionary was pushing against the practice, but Hallowell was told that the problem was that boys now engaged in "too much mingling of the sexes"—with sisters and other girls, before puberty, so it was "no use to send them." In fact, the local United Church minister of the time, Luther Schuetze, was sympathetic to the power of dreams. When the Royal Canadian Mounted Police arrested his friend Maamaan Duck, on a charge of drunkenness (later disproved), Schuetze begged the Berens River magistrate not to take Duck away, because if he did, many at Little Grand would go hungry. Maamaan, he recalled, "was perhaps the most successful hunter I ever knew, and the most open-hearted at giving." Whenever food was short, "Maman [Schuetze's spelling], as he told me, would dream, and the Good Spirit would tell him where the moose were." Within a day or so he would return "with a canoe load of meat to which everyone was welcome" (Schuetze 2001, 162). Schuetze may not have grasped the role of Maamaan's pawaganak, but he appreciated the power of dreams. Maamaan (1895/96–1980) was the eldest son of John Duck and the older brother of Booshii (Butikofer 2009, pt. II.3, 105).

PART 4

Curing, Helping, Love Medicine, and an Old Man's Jealousy

Making People Better

One time I went to Pauingassi. Joe Green's child had a swelled neck and [swelling] over his ear. His father said the medicine of the doctor he had was doing no good. He gave me a gun. I visited him in the morning and said, "Wait." I went and looked for medicine, dried it a little, smashed it up. After I smashed it good, I put it into a cloth, dipped it in hot water, and squeezed the juice out of the cloth into his mouth. After I did this, in two days, the child did a little talking, then was throwing up—nothing but matter—burst inside his throat. The medicine did this. I did not give any other medicine until the matter was all out; then I gave him some warm water to wash out his mouth. When all was clean, I gave him another kind to drink. In six days he was OK. He is a young man now and working. This was medicine I got from my father.

I remember one time a fellow (T. Ross [Thomas Ross or Ahak, Aanii's first husband]) split his foot with an axe when he was making a campfire. Those fellows [with him] came over here [to Little Grand Rapids, for help]—this fellow almost bled to death. Nobody managed to bring him here. I went to the man where he was. I camped half way—the second day I got there. He could not move; sometimes when we were going downhill, he yelled—afraid he would be hit (winter). My father used his own medicine to fix him. After he got better, he got crazy—just clean out of senses. I used to watch him—I stood in one place—I took him in. One time he jumped out of the house. I was in the store that time. Some of the men yelled out, "He's off!" They could not catch him. I could see him way out on the lake running, where the ice was honeycombed, sharp. Then he ran into the water, reached a flat island close to here, and went across. Part of the men went one way and the other the other. They found strong ice and went out across the lake. They did not catch him until he reached the other side. He had one bare foot—wounded by running on the ice. They brought him home. He was very strong—they bound him with belts to bring him home. When he started to run, he almost pulled all of us along. Finally we brought him here. I asked my father to try and cure this man. He gave him medicine. It only took him two days.

A year ago last fall I went to Poplar Hill—that is the first time I saw my daughter-in-law [Andwewe, Peyak's second wife (Butikofer 2009, pt. II.3, 236, 297)]. When I reached there I heard she was not well. The reason I'm telling you this—just to show that sometimes a person's work is [?]. When I got there, I went into the tent and saw my daughter-in-law lying there sick. She only moved her head, not her body; she could not even move her arms. Somebody might find it strange—this person not sick for nothing. It was raining the next day—the whole day. Even in our tent we were almost flooded out. "What can we do with this sick person?" Kezias says. "I wonder whether we can manage to get her across to the house." We tried to move her. We put the canoe right at the door of the tent and lifted her on a blanket gently into the canoe. The canoe was carried down to the water. We paddled across and took her into the house. [Kezias or Gezhiiyaash (John Owen), Moose clan, was Andwewe's father. He was a son of Bizhiw (Lynx) and grandson of Zhenawaakoshkang (Butikofer 2009, pt. II.7; pt. I.2, 245–46).]

I began to think now—how it would be. I took some rolled oats as rations from here. We cooked them and gave her porridge. When this ran out I bought another sack (six pounds). In ten days' time she started to move her arms. Then I put a little lard in her porridge. After I bought some more rolled oats, I put bacon in the porridge—to boil. Finally she managed to get up. I was feeding her good with soft food. By the time traps were set, she was gaining more strength—I was buying more for her. Finally she had enough strength to wash herself and comb her hair.

She was weak in the spring but could stand up (spring before last). One morning she took a stick (first time) and walked out. Later she did washing and other work. Finally she had a kid and lost it, but carried it on her back.

Payments for Curing—"I saved their lives"

1. Shirt, coat.
2. Pants, shirt & belt.
3. Kettle (big—5 gallon), # 3 trap (3), belt.
4. Pants, big pan, belt—f. up the river
   3 #3 traps—of course tobacco.
5. Shirt & pants.
6. Two pieces of dress good, 2 shirts & tobacco.

"If I can't help them I had to give back the stuff."

Living Well, Being Hospitable

One winter I used to be alone—my wife and three children. I never starved. I never went far either to get the fish and I was well. I used to be a good fisherman and hunt for rabbits—fairly good in fur. Sometimes I used to kill deer [caribou] and moose—don't have to go far to kill a moose. I used to stay here above the rapids [Little Grand]. People used to come in my place and get something to eat. When the Deer Lakers used to pass, they camped when they came through and I gave them something to eat. I had a big tent there. Stayed for a whole winter, did not move much. That's the way my father taught me, to use everything right in the grub line. If you get starved, my father says it will be your fault, not somebody else's; you must not kill anything and not make use of it. I brought up my kids in the same way. ("Firm belief that things will go right on the one hand, but anxiety nevertheless"—AIH.)

An old man here, John Duck's father [George Duck, Zhiishiibens, d. 1902–3], was one of the best hunters at Little Grand Rapids. But he sometimes had bad luck. This was because he made mistakes; he was not careful enough. Never throw grub away. If you have more than you need—give the extra away—that is a good thing too. If I know how to use a gun and set traps and follow the rules and have no accident, I won't starve *unless* someone puts something on me—that is how I know it [that someone is after me].

Context

In time span, these texts range from around 1880, before the death of Adam's father in about 1882, to the late 1930s, when Adam met his son Peyak's wife and made her better. Adam's story of curing the son of Joseph Green (Ginoozhewinini, fig. 8) may date from the 1890s, as Joseph was born at Little Grand Rapids in 1884–85 (Butikofer 2009, pt. II.3, 214).

The ailments that Adam coped with required secular, practical measures; his medical practice was low-key in contrast to some of the remarkable cures that he credited to his father (pt. 5). Hallowell recorded that "Adam claimed he had only used conjuring to bring people Life. His father told him always to love people, not to do them harm, and this is the precept he has always followed. That is why he is alive today. He has done nothing wrong." In transcribing this statement, Hallowell capitalized "Life" as a sign that Adam was using the Ojibwe word, pimadaziwin [bimaadiziwin], sometimes translated as "life in the fullest sense"—"life in the sense of longevity, health and freedom from misfortune" (2010, 301, 322, 559). In the three preceding pieces, as when he told of "A Dream Revelation" (pt. 3), Adam expressed the values by which he lived—views that he echoed in other stories in this collection, especially when he spoke of his father, Owl. Another Ojibwe doctor, Hole-in-the-Sky, with whom Ruth Landes worked in the 1930s, spoke of his father and his values in terms similar to Adam's; "My father said I could learn [bad medicine] if I wished but that I should never *use* it, for then it would never bother me. He meant, if I never sent evil medicine out, it would never become active, and return to trouble the house. . . . No one should know bad medicine, it should be off the earth" (Landes 1968, 60). The first two stories in this section also indicate Adam's reliance on his father's medicines and healing abilities.

In "Living Well, Being Hospitable" Adam described his ethos of sharing and good conduct toward others and with regard to food and animals. His story of hospitality toward visitors from Deer Lake to the northeast of Pauingassi (see map) mentions his having three children at the time, but Gary Butikofer found only two: Peyak (b. 1902–3) and an infant daughter deceased by 1900 (2009, II.3, 297). Records may be incomplete, or perhaps he was fostering other children. In any case, his welcome to the visitors was notable though not disinterested. At Deer Lake the Sucker clan was dominant; there were a few Pelicans and Sturgeons but no Moose or Kingfishers. When Hallowell diagramed the movements and relationships of the clans he knew from Berens River to Pikangikum and Lac Seul (Hallowell 1992, 23, map 2), he placed Deer Lake in a separate box, showing no links to the others. His research notes on Zhenawaa-koshkang (Great Moose), the Pauingassi leader who had six wives, tell a story that explains the distance. Sometime in the early to mid-1800s Zhenawaakoshkang's brother Okadjisi (1.6 on Hallowell's genealogical chart) married a woman of the Sucker clan at Deer [Caribou] Lake:

He did not get along very well with her. One day when they were breaking camp and she had almost finished removing the birch bark rolls covering their dwelling, 1.6 lost his temper and stabbed her in the thigh with a knife. One of the woman's brothers remonstrated with him but 1.6 resented the interference and reached for his gun. Before he could shoot, one of his *kita* [brothers-in-law] shot him. It was winter and 1.6's body was taken and stuffed into a water hole. . . . They did not bother to bury him. This incident was advanced to explain the absence of marriages between individuals of the Deer Lake Band and any of the Berens River people despite the fact that the former constantly traversed the river to its mouth during the summer months when freighting supplies for the Hudson's Bay Company post at Deer Lake.

Fifty years later, in 1989, Gary Butikofer heard a sequel to this story from Adin Kakegumic (Gaakekamig) of Deer Lake. Adin said that a Pau-ingassi man named Inchaapishiish was shot while drinking at Big Sandy Lake. The bullets did not kill him, but the shooters "stuffed him through a hole in the ice" and "he stayed dead." Adin thought that "Naamiwan [Fair Wind] may have been the brother of Inchaapishiish who tried to avenge his brother's death" (Butikofer 2009, pt. II.3. 162–63), but if the story holds up, he would have been a brother of Zhenawaakoshkang and Okadjisi (Okachesi in Butikofer's transcription).

The Suckers' main clan connections were with Island Lake and Sandy Lake to the north; they and Deer Lake all lie in the Severn River drainage (see map). Their most notable family surname was Fiddler, and their stories never mention Moose and scarcely mention other Berens River people (Fiddler and Stevens 1985). Hostile relations continued into the next generation (Brown with Matthews 1994, 66). Adam with his Moose connections certainly knew about the tensions between the Moose and Sucker people. His hospitality to the Deer Lakers was both kindly and precautionary. As Hallowell wrote, speaking more generally, Ojibwe outlooks toward people other than close kin were "colored by the possibility of malevolence," given "the latent mistrust engendered by a belief in sorcery" (2010, 512, 513).

Love Medicine and Counter Medicine

I was down at Pikangikum to help my brother-in-law [Kohkohko'ons] plant potatoes. Seed potatoes brought from Lac Seul. ("These were the first potatoes at Lake Pikangikum. We did not eat the first crop—divided and planted again. Nihtekemeshikum[?] told us about this in 1932. That is how we got our potatoes"—AIH.)

Someone came to me and said, "Take off your clothes; they are going to be washed." I did not think anything of it, so I did. The clothes were washed and brought back; I put the clean clothes on. Shortly after I put them on I began to think about a girl. I loved her all of a sudden. The whole day I had my mind on nothing else. Finally I could hold myself no longer. I told my sister [Makwemod]. She told me to take off those clothes. So she examined the clothes. My shirt—a piece was cut off the tail; my shoestrings cut an inch.

My sister must have told my brother-in-law [Kohkohko'ons]. He said, "You better take a walk with me down in the bush." He asked me what was wrong. I told him about it. "This girl is doing something with you." He opened a small bundle he had with him. He cut the crown of my head with flint till it bled, and on each side of my head (temples) and put medicine there, and gave me medicine to drink. He rubbed medicine all over my heart. He said, "Tonight, see how you will feel. If this medicine does you any good you will know it tonight. Go to sleep." I dreamed about this girl, but I hit her as hard as a person would hit a frog or a snake. My brother-in-law asked me the next morning and I told him about this, how I hit the girl as hard as a frog or snake. "The medicine is doing you good," he said. Two or three days after[wards] we left Pikangikum. I never thought about the girl any more.

Context

The first husband of Adam's sister Makwemod (Jane Bigmouth) was Kohkohko'ons (Little Horned Owl); he was born at Lac Seul and died in 1882–83 (Butikofer 2009, pt. II.3, 156, 293, 302–3). Given his death date, this event probably happened in the 1870s. The story parallels William Berens's experience with a girl's love medicine at Pikangikum in 1888 (Berens 2009, 94–96). Its use entailed risks. Sometime in the same period Owl saved a patient who had lost his senses from misusing love medicine; see part 5, "The Dangers of Love Medicine." Hallowell wrote in 1936 that "the belief in love magic is strongly entrenched, even among the contemporary Saulteaux" (2010, 218).

"Those Two Wives of Tetebaiyabin":
Jealousy, Bear-Walking, and Power

Those two wives of Tetebaiyabin [Dedibaayaaban] were my *ninimak* [niinimag, cross cousins]. Sometimes they used to come and sit by me — one on each side — to tease me. Their old man did not like this and I guess he thought I must be after them. I was living at Pauingassi then and I got sick. Someone tried to help me out with medicine but it did me no good. I thought something was wrong because the dogs barked every night. Other people in the camp told me they had seen a bear around. This is what made the dogs bark. Every time the bear breathed you could see something like a flame (or fire) coming out of his mouth.

John Duck came up from [Little] Grand Rapids and gave me medicine. I was living with Ktciogama [Gichi-ogimaa], and Omichoosh from Poplar Hill was there. He gave me medicine too, but it did no good. I was so sick I could not even sit up. Naamiwan [my brother-in-law] doctored me. He was pretty good, but he did not cure me. I got weaker. I could not walk. I could do nothing without help. I asked my wife [Aanii] to move our camp to Manitou Rapids. So we went there and my brother-in-law (Ktciogama) followed me.

[John Duck was identified earlier. Gichi-ogimaa was a son of Zhen-awaakoshkang and a half-brother of Aanii; Adam's sister, Makwemod, married him after the death of Kohkohko'ons (Butikofer 2009, pt. II.3, 104–5, 156). Omichoosh (James Owen) was a son of Bizhiw (Lynx or Sandy Owen), who in turn was the oldest son of Zhenawaakoshkang and Emihkwaan (Butikofer 2009, pt. II.3, 104–5, 156; Brown with Matthews 1994, 70).]

One night when I was asleep I was suddenly awakened. My strength came to me and I managed to get onto my feet and walk outside. Right in front of me I saw something. It was a bear lying right outside the tent. I saw the flame when he breathed. I said to my wife very quietly, "Hand me the axe." She could not find it. The bear started to go. I tried to follow it but I could not walk fast enough. I spoke to the bear. I said, "I know who you are and I want you to quit. I'm good-natured but if you come here again I won't spare you." He never came back again and after that I gradually got better. I got more strength back every day.

When the fall came I put up some fish for the winter and I did not have any more trouble that winter. When the summer came I went to Duck [Barton] Lake. Tetebaiyabin was there and Sagaski [Zagashkii] was there too. The Midewiwin was being held, and there were lots of people there [see fig. 15, Duck Lake pole structure]. I gave one man a gun. ("That is, to one of the leaders, probably Sagaski, from what follows. Tetebaiyabin was head man of the Midewiwin"—AIH.)

In a certain part of the ceremony, Sagaski spoke up and said, "I dreamed about my brother ("In the extended sense"—AIH) when he was sick last summer. What is the reason this man [Adam] has been sick? That's his fault"—(pointing Tetebaiyabin right out). "That's why my brother has been sick." Tetebaiyabin did not say a word. "If this brother of mine did not know where it came from I guess he would have been gone," Sagaski went on, and Tetebaiyabin had to take it. Sagaski knew he had done it and he always used to say whatever came into his head. He had lots of power himself and was very good at curing people. I did not like Tetebaiyabin from that time on. Before I left, I said to some of the people, "If anybody again tries to do anything that is not good to me they will find I will defend myself, because I will know the person who is trying to harm me. He will know what kind of a man I am." ("I.e., how strong in magic power he was"—AIH.)

The people all left after the Midewiwin. I camped at Poplar Hill the first night. ("This is where Tetebaiyabin usually camped during the summer"—AIH.) Tetebaiyabin gave me a brand new rush mat. He had one of his girls dig some potatoes and he gave me a sack of them to use on the journey to [Little] Grand Rapids. He treated me differently after this.

Another story: How Tetebaiyabin brought death to a young man on account of jealousy. A fellow started to go to Poplar Hill—[he was] there when the Waabano was held. This Tetebaiyabin had lots of girls [daughters]—the young fellows were after them. When this one left Poplar Hill he found himself feeling queer. When he reached Little Grand Rapids he was getting crazy—staying with his sister, and she was watching. When he got crazy he ran around the tent, round and round, as if in the Waabano, grabbing the tent cover, like bark, with his teeth, chewing it, yelling and shouting all the time—"Rats Feet [nickname for Tetebaiyabin] is coming again." This young man died that way; he never got better. Tetebaiyabin did this to him because he was after the girls.

Context

Tetebaiyabin, Sagaski, and Adam were parallel cousins, being of the same clan (Sturgeon) and generation. Tetebaiyabin (Roulette: Dedibaayaaban) was also known as Andrew Strang and Wazhaashkozid (Butikofer: Washashkosit). Son of Pazagwigabau, he was married to two sisters, Kiitawan and Aasamwes, of the Moose clan, and had seventeen children (Butikofer 2009, pt. I.1, 20–23; Hallowell 2010, 97). Cross cousins in Ojibwe kinship usage were potential marriage mates, and as such, they could freely joke with and tease one another (see Hallowell 2010, ch. 5). Parallel cousins (offspring of father's brothers and mother's sisters), if of different sex, were classed terminologically as brothers and sisters, whose interaction was highly restricted.

Adam sensed Tetebaiyabin's hostility to him; and his illness, the dogs barking every night, and repeated sightings of a bear breathing fire confirmed to him that "something was wrong." As Hallowell later wrote, "an evilly disposed medicine man may sometimes disguise himself as a bear," and Adam "became convinced that a certain man [Tetebaiyabin] had bewitched him." The spell was not broken until Adam, finding the bear outside his tent, exerted his own mental powers, shouting at the bear and threatening dire consequences if it ever returned. Hallowell's published accounts tell of the bear-walking part of the story but do not provide the full context: see "Fear and Anxiety" (2010, 233–34), and "Ojibwa Ontology" (2010, 552).

The presence of Adam's wife, Aanii, dates this incident to sometime between his marriage in about 1897 and Tetebaiyabin's death in 1925. "Bear-walking," widely seen in Ojibwe country as signaling sorcery, appears in a few of Adam's other stories: "This Old Fellow Was Pretty Bad" (pt. 8; see also "Bad Medicine"), and "Winter Starving—Sorcery and Bear-Walking" (pt. 9). Numbers of other sources recount similar episodes; see, for example, Richard Dorson, cited in Hallowell 2010, 551, and Selwyn Dewdney (1975, 116–18).

PART 5

Northern Barred Owl, Man of Many Powers

My father was a very good hearted man—kind to everybody. He was not like some of those Indians. Even if there was a sick person he was giving them medicine. He was a doctor. It does not matter what kind of disease it was. He always helped them. Even a person who was crazy ("kiwaskwe [giiwashkwe]—no senses"—AIH), he had medicine for that. Sometimes a person will lose their power to walk—he cured that too.

Owl Rescues and Loses His Father

A long time ago—while my father was living, his father (this grandfather of mine) lived to be very old, blind, and not able to get around well. My father had to help him along when they moved anywhere. One time my father was not there. [When Owl came back] it was four days since they [the others] had left the old man [behind]. My father left with a sled to get this old man. He never had anything to eat for four days. When he had spent two days [out], he was lying down. He felt somebody crawling on him. He took something—a stick—and started feeling around with the stick. He felt something—began hitting at it. He held this stick out over the thing to see if the thing was still alive, then started to feel for it with his hand. He felt something stick his hand then—it was a porcupine that had crawled on top of him. He felt around to where the porcupine had no quills [the stomach]. He had a knife so looked for it and split him down the chest so he could skin him and get the meat to eat. He never lay on anything else but a bear rug.

When his son arrived, he said, "I've come for you." "I'm still alive," said the old man. My father started tying him up to the sled. "I guess I won't live if you don't watch me carefully—the distance you have to take me." My father brought him to the wigwam where they were camped.

Then my father was going away again—expected to be a long time—a month. When he got back, he heard that they had left the old fellow behind again—ten days this time. [They] said they did not know whether he was alive or not. [My father] went to look for him. There was a big lake where the old man had been left. After he started a little ways [he] heard the old fellow making a noise from a distance. He said to himself, he must be a little crazy. When he heard him, the old man was almost in the middle of the lake on the ice. When he saw him the old fellow looked very tall. When he got closer the old man sat down. He was unable to walk any more—packing the bear rug on his back.

"I guess I can't do anything for you now," Owl said. "You always come and look for me when the older [other?] people leave me," said his father. [Owl said] "Let's take the bear rug and I'll drag you on that." "But those bear rugs pull heavy when you drag them," said the old man. He was thin but heavy. My father started off to drag him, sweating something terrible, forcing himself. The old fellow said, "Spare yourself—you'll kill yourself coming looking for me all the time." "I don't think so," [my father replied]. He had a hard time to get to the place where the people camped.

[Now it was] getting close to spring. When the lakes opened up—then he heard again that the people had left the old man behind. He could not find out where. Found traces of him—there were sand beaches where [he found] some marks where he had been crawling around. A long time later they found him. All they found was his bones—all together—found at Ktcibanga [Stout Lake].

Context

Owl's father's name was Pisikawasakakwan; his mother's name is unknown (Bulikofer 2009, pt. II.3, 292). Adam's account of his grandfather's being left alone has a parallel in Louis Bird's story "I Cannot Have Anything from These We-mis-ti-go-se-wak" (Bird 2005, 147–49), telling of a frail, blind old man who was left behind (at his request, as sometimes happened) but who magically survived from the winter into the spring.

Adam told the following stories right after describing his grandfather's death. He did not say the old man's bones were the ones played with by the four fellows, but he clearly made an association with their disrespect and its outcome.

Mistreatment of the Dead Has Consequences

Four fellows recently were playing along the shore. They saw something that looked like a stone and took it; it looked like a big cup. They put it on their heads pretending it was a cap—showed it to their father. Their father said, "You should not be playing with that; it is the top part of a man's head." Those four fellows were sick, and the only way they got better was to tell what they had done.

Again [another incident]—a particular one was out playing—saw a grave—he found a button there. He started opening the grave and started feeling down below. When anybody died before, they used to put all their belongings there. One fellow found buttons—very nice buttons. Finally one of them went inside the grave and started picking up something else perhaps.

All of a sudden this man took sick—the kind that came because he had done something. He went crazy—lost his senses and wandered away. Sometimes his wife would go and look for him. When they found him he would be lying down—sleeping or in a faint. Then again his wife lost him. They had three sons—one just a boy. They went out to look for him. One saw their father from a long way and caught him and took him home. Sometimes he would hear somebody making a noise or yelling—sometimes when walking, he would see someone in front of him. Sometimes when this happened, he would want to go and talk to this man. When he got close, sometimes the man would turn out to be a stump. When the people got to know what was wrong with him, he told what he had done (he used to kick the skull around too). He got better right away. When he was better the people asked him what he had done.

Owl's Ways of Curing

One time he [Owl] got up early and started off in the morning. The reason was that he already found what was the best thing to use to cure a certain disease. He understands this root as if it were talking to him— "your grandfather." He asked him [the root] to cure one of his children at Long Lake. Looked for the best to use—this kid was very sick—but he pulled through.

Sometimes it was not "really" sickness but witchcraft—after he drew this thing out, the person got better at once. If he can't manage it this way, he uses the conjuring tent—his pawaganak [dream visitors] to help him [see figs. 13, 14]. They will know the cause—because if a person does a bad thing, this is where disease starts. Whatever a person did in his past life—and his dreams have something to do with it—some people have bad dreams. When a man is young, he may do something to cause his children trouble; they suffer for this. Even if he doesn't remember, the pawagan will know. Sometimes the pawagan might refuse [to tell]; then a person must die.

Owl Cures Adam and Many Others

I remember one time I made a long trip. I got here [Little Grand Rapids] at sundown—no tea and no tobacco. I just finished my supper and started off at once [to my father's camp at Eagle Lake]. When I arrived at Clear Water Lake, I could feel something wrong with my legs—I had a hard time to reach Eagle Lake. I felt something in the joints of my legs—just managed to get home. I had a hard time to get my shoes off, my leg was swelling—terrible—I could not pull my pants up without splitting the seam. Right away that night my father started curing me. He took a piece of flint, made slashes on my swelled legs all over, and put medicine in warm water. Then he took a feather—dipped and brushed medicine all over my leg. I finally went to sleep. Next morning, there was nothing wrong with my legs; I was well. The reason I got this was because I walked over the trail of a man who had the "bad" medicine—no one was mad at me.

[That is, it was accidental. Trails were said to hold information and power, and medicine carried by one traveler on a trail might affect the next passerby. "The Dangers of Love Medicine" (later in pt. 5) concerns medicine placed on snowshoes. See also "Hunting with Medicine," and "Medicine to Strengthen Dogs" (pt. 14).]

My father only stayed there [Eagle Lake] one day. Somebody came to get him to make another trip to the other side of Pikangikum—Little Clear Water Lake (a day's journey). After that someone sent for him near here (Little Grand Rapids) (first portage east). He got a report that a woman had just had twins; a dog train was sent for the old man. He went. Stayed there two days—in that time she had regained her strength. After that he went back to Eagle Lake. Then a dog train was sent from Dogskin Lake to Eagle Lake—(the present wife of [?]) for him. She had caught cold—had been out fishing, angling. He stayed again two days and the woman recovered.

Around that time, Omiimii's daughter was sick. The next day after my father got there, he could not save her—she died. After she died, he put red yarn around her wrist. After she was laid out, he went and lay alongside of her. My father was lying still, but as soon as he began to move she began to move a little. Then my father raised [himself] up in a sitting position—she raised up simultaneously.

("Explanation—after the girl died, her djibai [jiibay, ghost] went to the hereafter [jiibeyaki, spirit land, south]; the yarn was put on to identify her. The old man lay down to dream. His soul went after her and saw her because she had the mark—he brought her back"—AIH.) [In telling this story Hallowell (2010, 412) rendered the daughter's name as Tcetcebu; Roger Roulette proposes Jiichiibo, a nickname, meaning unknown. Her father, a Pelican, died around 1873, and she died before 1877 (Butikofer 2009, pt. I.2, 259–60).]

Of course there are a lot of people over there [the land of the dead, djibaiaking], and that is why he needed something to spot her—he just got her in time. He claims the other land is much lighter than this. There's a fine good road, but before you get there (odena = city) there is a wigwam, and the one in charge—he tells the spirit to stay and eat something: "I'll tell you what part of this odena the people you want to see are in"—a sort of guide. As soon as you get in, as far as you can see, there are lots and lots of people—everybody that ever lived is there.

Not only once he [my father] did this. Not long ago when this new disease, syphilis, came in he had medicine for that. That was his job—they always sent for him. He could even draw out migis [a magical shell] or anything like that. He was ni'baki'wiwini [nibikiiwinini, one who treats with bones]; he had a bone and a special plate—so people could see it [what he drew out of his patients]. [A small hollowed-out bone was used as a sucking tube to withdraw foreign objects that sorcerers had projected into a patient's body; see Hallowell 2010, 236–37, 586.]

Another young man could not walk. His legs swelled; he was in bad shape. My father used medicine on this fellow. Fixed him up in two days. First he took the drum and sang. After he finished the first song, he stopped: "I can't go on. There's something that brings this sickness. Did you ever use any medicine on your legs to make you [run] fast and not played out? This has now turned against you." "Yes—I used to wear it under my drawers near the knee." "The one who gave you this did not tell you the truth and you did not pay for it. That is why my medicine is a failure. You never paid full for it. Tomorrow you will be getting better." The next day his leg was like an old man's. The swelling disappeared in two days' time and he was able to walk around.

There was a woman at Berens River who went crazy; it was old Boucher's daughter (her husband John Munias). My father was asked to try and cure her. The "sickness" he got out of her—that's what made her crazy. When he got it out she never had a return of it. A needle was in her, with hairs tied around it. It was taken out of her head.

Some people blamed someone else for sickness. Sometimes something drops on your body—some kind of sharp thing—my father used to say such things come. *Uzauwaban* [ozaawaabaan, bile], that's the thing that does it—the name of the disease. Sometimes when a person has a bad stomach, he feels it on his head, like a flame. Feels something in bone.

I remember one time Flatstone was pretty sick alright. My father got something out of his body and told him, "You can't blame any person; this is a sickness that would have killed you." Any disease grows, begins small and gets larger, goes through all your system, even into the eyes which turn yellow. That is why it is called *uzauwaban*. After he cured a person like that, he would give the person a name [of the disease?]. [When he cured] an old man at Bloodvein, [my father] got something out of that man's body.

("W.B. [William Berens] commented that Adam seemed 'mixed up' in the above theory. Of course some *person* is a cause of such diseases [in Ojibwe thinking]. [I] asked Adam whether singing and drumming always accompanied doctoring. Answer: 'No—songs are *not* mashkiki [medicine].' He thought it strange when I mentioned special songs of Plains Indians for particular diseases"—AIH.)

My father used to go place to place. There was one woman across the lake, almost dead. Father was asked to cure her. When he was asked, they brought a blanket and shawl. [He used] two things—was using rattle and nibikiwin [treating with sucking bones]—[something came out]—looked like a gun bullet—she got better.

He was asked again, by a man this time. For three days he could hold nothing on his stomach. [My father] used his cicigwan [zhiishiigwan, rattle]—washed the stomach, and ordered a clean plate—it was dark when they did this. What he drew out, he put on the plate—it looked like green stuff on the rocks. That is why the man could not hold anything. [My father] always did nibikiwin at night, sometimes used to sing.

The Dangers of Love Medicine: Owl Saves a Patient

Wanamin—from the color. [Wanaman, red ochre (Hallowell 2010, 595); earth or clay containing iron oxide.] Medicine wrapped in bark. A man goes to the tent where the woman is, opens it, touches medicine with stick, then goes into the bush and waits—the girl goes right to him. He goes back to the tent and sleeps with her; her parents find him in the morning; he marries the girl.

There are different kinds and strengths—some white, some red, blue, black—like powder. It's dangerous; it may cause children to get sick, or sometimes the man himself—he may go crazy. Old Willie Jibo [from Gibeault]. . . . We were camping down at——. I brought him home—only two of us; we left our fishing and came back, took up nets and dried them. He would not eat. We came home; I was scared, feared he would capsize the canoe. We camped halfway; I did not sleep the whole night. Then Eagle Lake for one night, stayed there, helped by a young fellow. We started in the morning. It was dark above the rapids here [at Little Grand Rapids]. He knew nothing. I started to wrestle with him on the portage; then he came to himself. I took him to the men's house [at the post]. He broke up everything, even wooden beds. Not a big man, but he was shoving the men, kept them busy holding [him]; he was that strong. When he came to his senses, he asked me where we had been fishing and said, "We will go back." "Don't run away from me," I said. I don't recall how many days he did not eat or drink. Then I got ready quietly—we took our rations, did not let him know, started early in morning. He was worse, got away from people who were watching; they could not catch him. A whole day and night they followed his trail . . . saw his trail and found him. He was brought back. They spoke to my father then. Old Jack Moar and Mrs. Jibo gave stuff [to pay for a cure] and my father started to work; saved [Jibo's] life. He got his proper senses again. He was using the medicine to get another girl—he was a married man. *Wrong usage*—not following instructions. [Compare shorter version of this story in part 2, "A Company Man Gets Sick."]

When traveling, if you put this medicine on your snowshoes, even an animal will follow your trail—every animal until he comes to your trap. If you don't do what is right with this medicine, [say] you might drop it where women are passing, then you can't catch anything; everything goes against you.

"You Brought This Sickness on Yourself"

Down at Pikangikum again, there was an unmarried woman. This woman's tent was clean, new brush, etc. She could not move. My father always had someone to help him, but not a special one like skabewis [oshkaabewis, helper or apprentice]. "You brought this sickness on yourself," he said to this woman; the medicine was not doing any good. He asked her, "What did you do?" The woman told him the reason she was sick: "[We] two girls tried to fuck one another." After she told it, she got better—the medicine worked better.

Another girl was sick—could not move her arms—unmarried.

Everybody tried to cure her but no medicine helped her. Finally they came to my father—gave one gun, one trap. This pikogan [bikogaan, domed lodge; see Hallowell 1992, 102, fig. 19] was fixed clean for her; the woman was brought in, in a blanket. He started to work, used cicigwan [rattle]—pretty hard. [He] said this is "not real sickness. Something else. Don't hide anything from me. If you don't hide anything from me you'll get better." This girl told him—this girl when she was a virgin— her chum the same way—(she had a hard time remembering, almost forgot). "Those water animals," [my father said]—"Did you ever do anything with them?" He said this to draw their minds to what may have happened—"I mean, a sucker—I saw something." The girl remembered now. "After we became women this girl and I, [she] used to come on top of me like a man—and she was using a sucker bladder" . . . (almost the shape of a good man and a little larger). After she told this she took some food now. After 2 days—on the 3rd day [she was] able to walk. Now my father had people fix a sweat bath (figs. 11, 12) after this to make him clean. The mother and father would be present in such a case.

[Hallowell recounted these two cases, slightly emended, in "Sin, Sex, and Sickness in Saulteaux Belief" (2010, 317–18). Owl often went into a sweat bath to seek a solution for the ailments he treated and to become clean (figs. 11, 12); Adam made no mention of patients being placed in one. Hallowell was told that women never went in the sweat bath— "this is exclusively a male institution" (undated research page headed "Sexual dichotomy").]

Fellatio between males. ("W.B. [Berens] never heard of cases. Adam heard they did it"—AIH.) In my father's time—a couple of young fellows, they got sick. One had a swelling on his throat, choked. My father tried to cure him. Medicine did no good. He found out what had happened, what these fellows had been doing. The man could hardly breathe. My father knew then what had happened, made him confess. He told what the other young man had been doing to him; "I did not like it." This fellow got better then. It did not happen only once; [I] heard people talk. Some men even used to do that to their wives; then sickness would come; [they would] have to confess.

A wife of Zhenawaakoshkang (one of the older ones) had lots of children. She separated from her husband and looked after herself. She might stay for a couple of nights; then she was off again. She got sick, finally weaker and weaker. When spring came she was so weak she had to be carried in a blanket over portages. She was brought to Pauingassi where her husband was living. Then the camp of the husband moved over here (Little Grand Rapids). They camped right across here—in a cabandawan [zhaaboondawan, long multiple-family dwelling].

This old woman had a lot of young girls. She lay there sick, right across her hips down to the stomach, swelling; taking medicine but it did not help. So the time passed away—she could not pass urine, could not stand up, could not move her legs, paralyzed, her belly swelling. People knew now that ~~she had~~ something wrong had been done.

My father was asked to help. "I don't believe you have been doing right," he said. "Did any of your own children ever do anything to you? "That's true; one of my sons did it" (fucked her). [Owl said], "Too bad you did not confess sooner. If you had said it long ago you would have been better. You should not think of shame. Life is greater than shame. You have been holding this." "I have never been asked to confess," she said.

Owl said, "Your life is going now. But if you see tomorrow morning, I'll try. If I see you here when the sun comes up, I will give you medicine." She was very weak. My wife [Aanii] saw this; she was there. When my wife was sitting there, the sick woman turned from her back to her side—[my wife] heard something roaring inside of her. Aanii thought she would be dead before morning. When Owl got there in the morning, she was dead. (Too late, did not confess soon enough—that was the trouble.) Perhaps C [Zhenawaakoshkang] could not attend to her. [He was still living at the time (d. 1881–82). His daughter, Aanii, not yet married to Adam, supplied a first-hand account, as did Owl, Adam's father. The woman who died was probably Emihkwaan, an older stepmother to Aanii. She had several children and died by 1876 (Butikofer 2009, pt. II.3, 155–56).]

In curing and conjuring, no "medicine" is used. It's just as if a person were covered with something dirty—that is what makes them sick sometimes. When you have some dirt on your hand you wash it off. The pawaganak help to wash dirt off from a person and make him well. They also help to find out what it is that people have done that makes them sick—what "sins" (bad deeds) they may have done to bring sickness upon themselves. Someone may dream, too, what deed it is that another person has done—incest, for example.

We were always at Eagle Lake. A fellow was brought there—sick, married with two children. After he was left with my father, [my father] was given a trap, a blanket, pants, and piece of cloth. The man's neck was swelled down to his chest. My father was sitting thinking—made a sweat bath—thought a lot about it. After he got through, the same night, he took his rattle. He told me to go and raise up the man a little. This man had a rabbit skin blanket. My father used to use the bone [sucking tube]. This time he used a "gun worm." It did not work. There was a big pan set before himself. He took the bone now. I took the blanket off the sick man.

"You brought this sickness on yourself," my father said. "Yes, [the man said]; I remember long ago when I was travelling with another fellow, he used to try and make me suck his prick." Now Owl drew the sickness, put it in the pan; it looked like bouillon, a light soup. "You can expect now that your sickness will be changed," Owl said. He used to sing a song he got from a wolf, and even a dog; that is why no one could hide anything. After he got through, he tried him a second time so the man completely recovered. After he finished, there was no wound or scar. He drew from where the swelling was; previously the man could not eat. The next day the man had boiled fish to eat. In three days he had completely recovered. Of course the skin looked different, a little loose below the chin where it had slacked. [Hallowell's published version, somewhat polished, is in "Sin, Sex, and Sickness," 2010, 317.]

Masturbation brings sickness—bad. A young fellow [did it] when he was travelling. My father gave him medicine—did not work. "Did you ever bother yourself?" He told him to cut it out. "If you quit you will get better. Be healthy like other men. Sometimes at night you do not feel well—that is the cause of that. Not good for you—playing with yourself."

There was a married woman complained of sickness around her abdomen. My father was called in—[went into a] sweat bath. He was expected to look after this woman—that's his job. He gave medicine—[she] could not hold it. "You have a bad sickness," he told her. He told me to tighten up his cicigwan in the fire—Rattled.

This woman shortly after her marriage—"Listen to me," she said to her husband. (My father knew this man did not use his wife right.) "Don't hide it," my father said. "Don't be ashamed—you know this sickness is hard on you and medicine has done you no good. Do you remember anything? You did it in the wrong way."

The woman started to tell. "Even instead of using my cunt he used my mouth when he got off—it used to make me puke—this is the thing he did not do right—my husband did this shortly after we got married." (Some couples when they got married did not know much long ago— liable to do anything.) So the medicine worked fine now—cured her. [Recounted in more polished form in Hallowell (2010 [1939]), 320.]

A newly married couple, long ago—[had a sick child]. A matutzwan [madoodiswaan, sweat lodge, figs. 11, 12] was made first. My father, after he went home, after he sat thinking, [decided] "I think there is something." They sent for him. He took his fire bag (flint, sagatagan [zagataagan, punk, tinder], and pipe) and went to see them. The woman (the mother) and another girl brought brush for my father to sit on—all the old brush was taken out. The child was brought in. That same night when he was singing, [he asked about] something bad. He said to the mother, "Did you ever have a kid before you were married and do away with it? This kid you killed must have suffered long before he died. Your child now is suffering like your [first] child." For a long time she would say nothing—when she knew it was time to tell: "When I made up my mind to marry my present husband, I did not want him to know." "Why did you do it? You should have kept this first child. From now on after you tell this sin, all your children will be alright. It will not follow you anymore." [Hallowell published a somewhat shorter version of this story in "Ojibwa World View and Disease" (1963, 300–1).]

Lots of times my father found persons brought sickness on themselves. My father was a man of no pretences, just like a child. He used to play with young boys despite his great powers.

"Bad Doings": Illness from Causing Animal Suffering

A woman had a sore throat getting worse and worse. A sweat bath was made. My father waited there [he went in] and tried to cure her. He sang—inside the sweat bath—and then said, "I could not! This is not real sickness; it must be bad doings. That is why this life is getting lower." So towards night, they brought him a sacrifice—two traps (beaver), one kettle. My father started to sing but as soon as he started—before he finished, he stopped. "Did you snare a frog?" he said to the woman, "in a pond?" He even moved his arms like this, [showing] suffering—then lifted him [them?] up. Had a queer voice, and his hind legs moving— [cruelty to the frog] was the cause of it. ("William Berens told of hunting frogs with arrows. But he told about it: It's the *secrecy that counts*"—AIH.)

Owl, Finder of People and Lost Objects, Diverting Rainclouds

Sometimes a report would go around that someone had seen a stranger. My father used to see if it was true. On a pitch dark night he would put a looking glass (mirror) before him. He will see a canoe perhaps—how many men in it and other things. ("Used a bigger one than the one in my toilet case"—AIH.) He would tell exactly where they were staying— describe the trees around them, etc. Even if these men were trying to steal fish out of another man's net—he would tell which one they were going to. A pitch dark night—that's the time he used that. He tried to see some persons or something else.

If anyone comes he could see them—used to cover with a blanket. If a person did not believe him, he would bring them to it and they would see for themselves. Between here and Berens River, if you asked him where people stayed tonight, he would be the only one that had it [the knowledge]. He used to tell us the direction people (visitors) were coming from. He knew two or three nights before they arrived. Even if a dog started to bark at night, he knew whether it was a real person or not. Sometimes he knew it was not a good person—when it was dangerous.

One time my father was just coming out of a matutzwan when a man came to him and told him he had lost his gun in the water coming up the river. Otcibamasis [Owl] had the conjuring tent put up, went in and sent one of his pawaganak for the gun—handed it out to the man who had lost it. Even when it's raining—he would fill his pipe and point where the clouds were coming from. They would split and go in opposite directions—no rain at all.

Context

Owl was scrying, or calling up information from a distance through the use of a reflective surface. The practice, using mirrors, crystals, or a pan of water, is widespread in the world. Cree seers empowered by dreams sometimes used "water vision," covering the head and looking into the water to "see what they want to see." Louis Bird said, "It acts like eyes with binoculars; it extends your vision" (2005, 43). In *The Role of Conjuring in Saulteaux Society* Hallowell recounted Owl's retrieval of the lost gun, and another episode in which he retrieved some keys that a woman's baby had dropped overboard from a canoe in the river. If a canoe got overturned in rapids, "Otcibamasis would persuade Mikinaak to fetch all of the goods to the conjuring lodge and he would hand them out" (1942, 68–69).

Owl Invited to the Midewiwin at Lac Seul

("Sagatciwe [Zaagajiwe], Midewiwin leader at Lake Seul, would sometimes send two men for Adam's father—to have him sit in his midewigamig [Midewiwin lodge]. Pazagwigabau was there too. Once he got so mad that he left before things were over. Adam's father got more pagitcigan [bagijigan,offerings] than Pazagwigabau (each man had a share but not equal shares). Sagatciwe treated Owl better." . . . "Pazagwigabau was jealous of Adam's father. People gave Owl lots of things for curing, etc. . . . Owl was much older than Pazagwigabau. Flatstone was younger than Owl—treated [Owl] like a father"—AIH.)

Lots of times, a [sick] person was that far gone he had to be taken on a blanket into the tent. After everything was finished and sacrifices [offerings] were all there, they used to try and see whether the person would get over the sickness. A man would say, "If this person gets better, the old man who has been teaching me is truthful." The man standing who said this was holding the cicigwan [rattle], and all the skabewis [oshkaabewisag, assistants] and this sick person were [on the?] left. The mide took the lead and the sick person was carried in a blanket. This mide, he marched towards the west door, to come circling around [clockwise] with the sick man behind him. He stopped in the west door—said a few words again. Asked for life—hoping it will be true that the sick person will get better. After he got through, he came to the east door and said a few words there again—rattling the cicigwan again. A skabewis [oshkaabewis] went to each side [of the person].

[Then the mide said], "If the sick person can manage to get around this tent it will be true what I said. He will live." As soon as the person got halfway, he was stronger—walking fine. When he reached the west door, the skabewis let go of him. He carried himself with his own strength to the east door. He was told he would have to make one more round. The man by this time could move his legs so fast it seemed to me he was not sick [i.e., Adam was there to see him]. He took his place again. They used the medicine bags now. This is where the shooting comes in. Driving the migis into the joints of his legs and arms—every joint. After this was over, one of those medicine bags was handed him. Of course the ones doing this were in the center of the tent. Now the sick man got up on his feet without help—half trotting around the tent.

Another sick person might be in the tent, having to go through the same thing. If there were four persons, there were lots of pagitcigan—my father got a good share. If six or eight, even as high as ten [sick persons] sometimes. When Owl—my father—got back he had quite a bale of goods; [others were] jealous.

"Midewiwin Miracles"

(Reported by Owl.) There was a man—Kamitcakunawet [?]—who was doing a miracle in the midewigamig. He had four inches of yarn. Then he said to the audience, "If it is true what I said, this yarn will go round the tent." He told S[agatciwe] to take one end of it; the old man held the other end and was told to pull. It got longer all the time like a spool of thread, went around all the way. Sagatciwe kept going; the mide stood still; the two ends met together. Then the people in the tent believed the old man spoke the truth and that the sick person would get well.

Another old fellow at Lac Seul—he stood up in the mide tent. Took his cicigwan and started to rattle and sing. His bag (muskemut [mashkimod]) started to move—a pijiu [bizhiw, lynx] came out and lay on top of the bag, then jumped up on one of the posts. The people started to circle—it kept turning while the people circled. Sagatciwe was holding the rattle in his hand and made a motion as if to hit him—the lynx dropped to the ground—it was only a lynx skin, shipetagon [zhiibetaagon, pelt]. The old man picked it up and put it in his bag (muskemut).

Another man got up and made pretty near the same speech: "If I can get something to move in this bag then we will have a blessing—pimadaziwin." He went around—had his rattle in hand. When he came down to his medicine bag, he rattled his cicigwan over it singing—"wi' wi'—ah ah hai." Something moved inside the medicine bag—pipigiwizes [bibigiiwizens, small bird]—flew out from it. Soon as he came out, he flew up, lit on a post, and watched the people as they circled around in the tent. Sagatciwe did the same thing with his rattle—[and the bird] dropped off from the post. [Now it was] only a skin—no life there now.

Then Sagatciwe said, "If I can make this thing work we will expect Life." He went around the tent first—picked up his medicine bag, carried it around, just about halfway. This bag started to move (something inside); something peeped out of the bag—painted red—a man's prick. Then another painted black; first one then the other peeped out. A medicine woman on the west door, soon as it passed, grabbed it—said [to] the medicine men, "This is what used to make me feel good—this is where all the kids come from." She ran around with it—putting it towards her cunt every now and then in a realistic gesture. This woman was named Eagle. No one laughed—very solemn. Owl saw all these things at Lac Seul.

Context

Sagatciwe [Zaagajiwe] was the chief of the Lac Seul band when Treaty No. 3 was signed in 1873 (Hallowell 2010, 405n94). He needs to be distinguished from Sagatciweas (Peter Stoney), chief of the Island bands on Lake Winnipeg, who was also a Midewiwin leader and the unsuccessful rival of Jacob Berens for the Treaty No. 5 chiefship at Berens River in 1875 (Hallowell 2010, 603).

Sagatciwe evidently had a high regard for Owl's ability to cure the sick people who came to the ceremonies. Owl's great rival, Pazagwigabau, also participated in the Lac Seul Midewiwin, but Adam recalled that he had lesser standing there and was jealous of the respect and quantities of offerings that Owl received. Even so, Pazagwigabau and his son, Tete-baiyabin, had a firm hold on the Midewiwin leadership along the upper Berens River from the mid-1800s until the latter's death in 1925. Hallowell found that these two men "were indisputably the most influential and famous mides up the river." Pazagwigabau's father, Nootinwep (Noodin-web), had also been a Mide headman. In essence, "effective Midewiwin leadership was here confined to a single family line for three generations" (Hallowell 2010, 397; for more on the family, see afterword.)

Bad feelings between that family and Owl ruled out any Mide leadership role for Owl on the river—if indeed he ever wanted it. Similarly, Owl's son Adam was no friend to Tetebaiyabin, although they too were parallel cousins. A few other younger Sturgeon kinsmen became involved in the ceremony, however, and they were on friendlier terms with Owl and Adam. Flatstone, whose Mide teacher was Pazagwigabau, and Sagaski were both associated with Tetebaiyabin in the conduct of Midewiwin ceremonies at Poplar Hill. Flatstone later led a Mide lodge at Little Grand Rapids for a few years, until about 1918. He was assisted by his parallel cousin Bluffhead (Pikwakwastigan [Bikwaakishtigwaan]), who was a half-brother of Tetebaiyabin. The only non-Sturgeon who had a leadership role was Pindandakwan (Biindaandakwan) or James Shadow, Pelican clan, a son-in-law of Pazagwigabau. He assisted his father-in-law at Pikangikum and took over for a while after Pazagwigabau died, but he died in 1909, according to Butikofer (2009, pt. I.1, 2, 306). By the mid-1920s the powerful older Midewiwin leaders had died, and younger ones lacked their standing or commitment. As of 1936 Hallowell knew of only one man, Otci-tcak [Ojijaak] (Crane Strang), a son of Tetebaiyabin, who appeared capable of reviving the ceremony, and he gave no sign of doing so (2010, 397, 398). Its distribution was limited in any case; Hallowell's informants all stated that it was never held at Poplar River, Deer Lake, Sandy Lake, or other Ojibwe communities to the north (Hallowell 2010, 396).

By the time Hallowell arrived in 1932, the people at Little Grand Rapids and Pauingassi were also focused on other ceremonies of their own—the Waabano, and the dream dances with big drums that Hallowell saw at Little Grand, and on Fair Wind's (Naamiwan's) ceremonies at Pauingassi and Poplar Hill. Several of Adam's stories also suggest that people turned away from the Midewiwin because its dominant leaders, especially Pazagwigabau, were much feared and had used their powers to hurt others; see afterword for more details.

Contests with Pazagwigabau

("Owl and Pazagwigabau called each other 'brother.' They were parallel cousins—their fathers were brothers. Yet they were constantly fighting. Owl's son Maahtus [Madoons, Adam's half-brother] was a "humpy"— hunchback. This was supposed to be the result of Pazagwigabau's work. Pazagwigabau's son Tcakwis [Chaahkwiis or William Keeper, Aanii's second husband], who was lame and used crutches but managed to hunt just the same, was made that way by Owl in retaliation" —AIH; Hallowell 1940, Field Notes, single page.)

"Did Anyone Try to Starve Your Father Out?"

Once, Adam remembers. My father managed to kill a few rabbits for only a few nights, [then] caught nothing—made 100 snares, only one or two rabbits out of them. He knew then what was up—he heard something and saw "fire"—like someone carrying a lantern. One day at dusk, he said, "I'm not going to try and kill the person who does this to us. I'm just going to try and drive him away." Of course he could do either one. He made a sweat bath and sang that night. The reason he did this was to drive that person away that was bothering us. Three nights after, things turned out in a different way—he caught lots of rabbits—gradually caught more and more food. The first time he went to his snares he got only three, then more and more, five–six, ten, etc., snares all out—we had lots after that. We had a brother living across the lake—Kehkehk [Gegek]. He heard a noise, someone following his trail. The old man [my father] was trying to chase this man away—he [Owl] thought if he killed the person, his children might be affected someday. Pazagwigabau did this—took him [i.e., his soul] into the conjuring tent too. [Hallowell (1942, 59–61) described "soul abduction," the bringing of a person's soul into the shaking tent for reasons that might be benign or malevolent.]

Pazagwigabau Provokes Owl to a Duel by Sorcery

[Hallowell published this story in his article "Aggression in Saulteaux Society" (2010, ch. 15), describing Pazagwigabau as "the arrogant leader of the Midewiwin . . . reputed to have killed many persons by sorcery." Owl, in contrast, "was a quiet-mannered man, small in stature and said to be kind to everyone. He was not a mide, but he had the reputation of being an excellent doctor and he was a noted conjurer" (2010, 283–84). The story as Hallowell edited it follows; the original handwritten text, very telegraphic, is preserved undated in Hallowell n.d., "Myths and Tales." Some details in the handwritten text were omitted in the printed version; they are added here in parentheses.]

These two men belonged to different local groups and seldom came into personal contact. But [one time] Pazagwigabau had come down the river to the HBC post [Little Grand Rapids] (after the York boats arrived . . . the crew was sitting on the platform in front of the Co. store), and found Owl sitting on the platform of the store with a lot of other Indians. He went up to Owl and said, "You think you are (you made yourself) a great man. But do you know that you are no good? When you want to save lives you always bring that stone (a little one) along. I don't believe it's good (it's no good) for anything." To this Owl replied, "Pazagwigabau, leave me alone. I have never bothered you."

"You are not worth leaving alone," the mide said, and with this he grabbed Owl by the front part of his hair and threw him down. Owl simply got up and said, "Leave me alone." But Pazagwigabau grabbed his hair a second time and when Owl made no resistance, he did it for a third time. [In Ojibwe terms, treating a person's hair in this way would be a terrible offense.]

Then Owl said, "Are you looking for trouble?" That's what I want," said Pazagwigabau, "I want you to get mad. That's why I did this." So Owl replied, "Alright. I know you have been looking for it for a long time. I know you think you are a great mide (man). You are nothing. If I point my finger at you, you will be a dead man. But now I'll tell you something. Don't you do anything to my wife or my child ["ch" in original signifies children]. Do it to me and I'll do the same."

"Ho! Ho! Thanks, thanks," said Pazagwigabau. "Expect me at *kijegizis* [gizhe-giizis, kind moon, February]. (I'll expect you first.) I'll give you a chance to do what you like to me."

Sure enough, during kijegizis Owl was taken sick. He got the shell [migis projected into him] all right, but of course he brought it out. But Owl was not sick long; he easily recovered. Shortly after this, news came down the river that Pazagwigabau was sick. He was unable to walk (went down and down). News spread about that he was getting worse and worse. Every once in a while Owl was heard to say, "Huh! Huh! I guess I nearly killed him. I did not mean to; I was only playing with him." When the ni'kigizis (niki-giizis, goose moon, April) appeared, Pazagwigabau was only barely able to walk about. At the beginning of the summer Pazagwigabau came down the river again with some other members of his band. (In June—when boats were starting down all those Indians met again at LGR.) They camped near Little Grand Rapids where Owl lived. When Owl saw the old mide he walked right up to him and said, "You know who Owl is now! I was only playing with you this time. I did not intend to kill you. But I never want to hear again what you said in this place (another thing like that from you—what you did here). And I don't expect you to do again what you did here. Don't think you are such a great mide! (man)."

(No doubt Pazagwigabau killed people. He called W.B.'s father nin-ingwan ("my son-in-law" [not clear why])—AIH. "Father [Jacob Berens] told W.B. not to go play near his camp. Everybody [was] afraid"—William Berens's comment, added by AIH; this was at Berens River in the 1870s, when William was a boy.)

"Death Due to Sorcery: Adam's Father Killed by Pazagwigabau"

Owl got tired of fighting Pazagwigabau; he gave up. Pazagwigabau killed him—[or else he] would have lived older. We were staying at Eagle Lake at the time—[we] saw this fire. [I] heard a dog barking. I was sleeping in bare feet; moonlight was bright. I went outside, went over to where I heard the dog barking—a kind of collie dog—holding something in his mouth. I told him to let go and he did, and I saw something on the snow—one of those woodpeckers—black ones—I never saw one traveling at night [a bad omen].

Then we left Eagle Lake and camped on the Reserve here [Little Grand Rapids]. I was old enough then to kill atik [caribou]. My brother Batis had not killed a deer yet. After we camped one of my brothers [Madoons, Maahtus], who used to be a humpy, was out angling. He used to take the gun to shoot partridge if he saw any, and took a dog train—along with Batis. "Kill something to eat," he said. Batis shot a buck deer [caribou]; then Flatstone came and his brother Boucher [Poshi, Alex Boucher (Butikofer 2009, pt. II.3. 249)]. They asked me to come along to the post. I did not care to leave my father—he was pretty sick. But he said, "You better go along—maybe you can kill a deer." But I said I did not want to leave him. [He] urged me—"You'll never see me forever anyway," he says. "When my time comes I will die."

So I went with Boucher and Flatstone. When we reached camp, we went for a hunt the next day. Boucher shot two deer and I shot one, a female deer. [Boucher's] wife took the calf and dressed it nicely—dried it, and the deer I killed was all fixed up—smoked, all ready to bring along to camp. I came along with Boucher—had a dog train—about six miles from here. I knew I would not see my father. Across the lake, Boucher said, "Boil a kettle," and we did. But I could not eat. I knew something was wrong in our camp. After we had something to eat, we went on. "Don't think about it too much," says Boucher. When we got to our camp all we found was an empty tent. We left meat there and came over to the post.

I took it hard all right when he died. He never raised his hand on me. I was not married yet. I thought of my mother after my father died—so did not take a wife. After my mother died [Injenii, in 1893-94], what should I do?—no place to go. I had to make a home for myself. Finally Naamiwan spoke to me about taking his sister [Aanii]. "I'll help you," he said; promised to build a canoe. But he never kept his promise. Tomi

[Taami, Thomas Owen, half-brother of Naamiwan] used to make a canoe for me—he used me very well, fulfilled his promise all right.

Context

Adam's stories about his father, Northern Barred Owl, provide the most detailed portrait we have of any nineteenth-century medicine man along the Berens River. Almost six decades after Owl's death in 1884–85, Adam vividly remembered what his father had taught him—his values and rules for good conduct, his methods of curing people, and his medicines. To Adam, looking back, his father was an almost mythic figure who, supported by his powerful dreamed ones or pawaganak, could drive away windigos, defeat rival medicine men, conjure to learn distant information and find lost objects, and most important, determine what was making people sick and how they could be made better.

Ultimately, however, in Adam's view, the Midewiwin leader Pazagwigabau overpowered and killed his father. This presents a historical puzzle. Documentary records indicate that Pazagwigabau died in about 1881, and Owl in about 1884–85, around three years later. The spirits of the dead, however, sometimes lingered and revealed themselves in ghostly form. Hallowell, in writing of such spirits, found that most such manifestations were benign (2010, ch. 22). But Ojibwe thinking allowed for the possibility that "both living and dead human beings may assume the form of animals," and that such manifestations "are inextricably associated with unusual power, for good or evil" (2010, 552, 553). Adam did not say that his father blamed Pazagwigabau for his final illness. But he himself saw an ominous message in the appearance of "fire" and the strange dog barking at night, with a black woodpecker in its mouth. As Hallowell commented, "How shadowy is the line, in Saulteaux thought, between 'humanness' and the essential animate qualities of other orders of being. No wonder, then, that the spirits of the dead are such an integral part of the Saulteaux universe" (2010, 433–34). The spirit of Pazagwigabau was still to be reckoned with.

PART 6

Gender, Power, and Incest

Trouble If You "Marry the Same Totem"

It used to happen sometimes that ndawemaa [persons of the same totem] would marry. Violation led to sickness of children, or a man might even lose his wife—or the woman may die. Some people—they have trouble, do not agree, are fighting and quarreling all the time, then part and go together again. That's the kind of trouble people get that marry the same totem. ("If a man marries a different totem the second time or vice versa, it's OK"—AIH.)

There was a good-natured woman. But the man could not get along with his wife, always fighting her. I saw this man, knew him well. He had children. I saw him once quarreling with his wife—she was cut on the head, bleeding, covered with blood—my wife saw it too. Down at Duck [Barton] Lake—the man was so mad he acted like a drunken man, but he was not drunk. After he did this, we lost this man. I was following the shore. I found him sitting along the lake shore thinking—head down, crying. So I spoke to him. I said, "You're not drunk—your wife is not mad. You better go back; you have some children to look after. I don't think your wife will leave you although she has good reason to go. Seems to me you don't show any love towards your wife." I said it was not the first time I saw this; a lot of times the woman left—sometimes for one year. Lots [were] cured that way. "If you don't want to quit, your wife can report you to the Indian agent." He went back to his wife and quit it for a while.

But again [one time] I was staying in this man's tent when he was sleeping. At night he woke me up—he was quarreling with his wife again—gave me a start. What is happening now? He was using a frying pan to beat his wife. In the morning after eating, his father-in-law, who lived close, could hear the man quarreling with her. So I went over, said nothing; I was just going to listen to what he said. When I got there he was standing in the door. I had sharpened my axe the day before. He was holding it and was going to hit me. (This is a fellow married to his own totemite.) My wife [Aanii] then came. When she saw this, she spoke to him. She said, "You better hit me first." She took the axe from him, saying, "This axe is to chop wood, not to hit people with." The man was trembling—he was that mad. He had four children—three boys, one girl.

Sagaski, the Man Who Married His Sister

([Her] name means "old woman," short for mindimooye.) Their parents died—he raised his sister (Mindjimo—AIH) who was a good bit younger. He was asked for her four times—[he] refused. Then people knew he did not want to give her up. People were talking—"Let him marry his sister then": people will be laughing at them and they will be shamed. He had three boys and one girl out of his sister. They [the sons] died, one after the other. The girl still living [1938], the first.

When his children found out people talked about them, [they] asked their father whether it was true. "Where did our mother come from?" they asked. "Your mother came from the [Hudson] Bay," he told them. "I made a trip to York Factory." Of course his children believed him. Mindjimo was ashamed at first—but got used to it. They used to camp away from the rest. They camped at Duck [Barton] Lake—people never passed there.

Context

In "Trouble If You 'Marry the Same Totem'" Adam recounted from personal experience the story of a marriage gone bad because a man had married a woman of the same clan—that is, a parallel cousin related to him through his father's lineage. Adam noted that violators could suffer sickness or early death. This account, however, mentions no spiritual sanctions but rather tells of secular marital stress and strife as the consequence. This story contains Adam's only quotation from his wife's voice: "This axe is to chop wood, not to hit people with." Hallowell observed in the 1960s that "there are extremely few violations of clan exogamy in my genealogies" (1992, 52).

The story of the man who married his sister is more complex and spans a generation. Sagaski (who called Adam his "brother" in "Those Two Wives of Tetebaiyabin," pt. 4) was a powerful medicine man of the Sturgeon clan. When he came from either Lac Seul (Hallowell) or Cat Lake (Dunning 1959, 112) to Pikangikum by the early 1870s, he was already married to his younger sister. Dunning said that "Sugguski" or "Creeper," as he was called in English, may have left his home community because of local rejection of his incestuous union.

In any case, Sagaski validated his marriage in traditional terms, citing a dream sent by one of his pawaganak, the "Master of the beaver," who "*commanded* him to do as the beaver did" and to follow beaver rather than human mating patterns. His "unusually strong magical powers," reinforced by his many spiritual helpers, spared him from consequences (Hallowell 2010, 224). Hallowell argued that he surely felt guilt about his "incestuous impulses," but "rationalized them in culturally approved terms by appealing to the highest authority in his society—the spirit helpers of mankind." In effect, he was not challenging accepted sexual codes. Rather, Hallowell thought that his case provided to others "an example of what *not* to do." As Adam said, Sakaski kept his family apart. In summer they camped on an island, and he never let young male passersby tent there even for one night (Hallowell 2010, 338–39; 224).

Adam's memories and the research of Gary Butikofer add further details. Sagaski (Zagashkii) died in 1915–16. He and his sister had two sons who died in 1908 and 1901–2 respectively and a daughter who never married; she was living as of 1938. One son married but the other did not. Hallowell's informants indicated that Mindjimoo died early, as a penalty for bad conduct, they said, and that Sagaski later remarried (2010, 339). Butikofer found from treaty lists, however, that she died after Sagaski, in 1916–17. In fact, Sagaski had a second wife concurrently—Chiichiik (Jiichiik), a Pelican; her first child, like that of Mindjimoo, was born sometime before 1876. He and Chiichiik (d. 1920–21) had seven children, of whom four married (Butikofer 2009, pt. I.1, 136–39). Hallowell met one of them—Wiigwaasaatig (Birchstick), who was chief at Pikangikum and supplied Hallowell with a story he liked to quote—about how Birchstick diverted a bear from attacking him by talking to it (2010, 373, 550). Hallowell learned an immense amount on his summer visits in the 1930s; but Butikofer, who taught at Poplar Hill for twenty years, talked at length with the old people, and used documentary records along with Hallowell's notes, was sometimes able to go considerably further.

A Man's Sickness for Hurting His Sister

One man, [Adam] can't recall the name, was sick, getting lower, and went to a doctor to see if he could help. His cock was swelling—he could not put his legs together—could hardly walk. [He was] treated—but medicine did not help him at all—finally time passed—medicine no good. This man *paid enough*—traps, kettle, gun, coat, gave [the doctor] the top price—cloth too. Doctor could not help. The man said, "Make a conjuring tent." The doctor went in; all the pawaganak came in. They talked among themselves and sang. Mikinaak said, "It's pretty hard. The reason this medicine does not work—something came on him because of his own wrongdoing. He has been doing something to his sister, hurting her pretty bad. He is suffering because of that. The conjuror asked [the man], "Is this true what Mikinaak said?" The man said, "No!"—he denied it, did not want to say. "You did something all right—you can't hide anything from pawaganak—you did that to your sister." Finally the man said, "Yes!" This man was just a boy at the time. "I used to laugh at my sister when she cried when I did it—I teased her about it." Mikinaak even told him the time—the spring of the year. After he confessed, he took no more medicine. He got better then. Because the man confessed, the woman did not get sick; it was known then. ("An important psychological point—confession is never secret but facts become public—hence the psychological force of the penalty as a moral lesson"—AIH.)

A Young Man and His Father's Sister

A woman was raising[?] her brother's son in the same tent. This young man was getting to be a fairly good hunter. They were drying meat in camp. The man went to bed. He thinks about his kisigosis [gizigosiins, a diminutive, affectionate form for father's sister] now. He spoke to her: "How's chances?" "Are you crazy," she replied, "to speak like that. You are my brother's son." He said, "Nothing will happen to us." She said, "Yes there will; we might suffer." "No," he said. "Nothing." He got up— only the two of them in the tent. He managed to get what he wanted, then went back to his own bed. He began to worry now—doing it with his father's sister.

In the morning, he said to her, "Nisigosis [inzigos, my father's sister], I better go." "Where to?" she asked. "I'll go somewhere else—I'm ashamed. I do not like what I do." "Where are you going?" "I'm going away," he said. "If I starve to death, all right." "No, no, don't you do it. If you leave who is going to support me? No one. I'll starve to death. It's not the first time this happened. You are not the first one to do this—it has happened before elsewhere." But the young man was worried. She said, "No, you can't leave me. I've brought you up and you must stay here." "I'll go for a while anyway," he said. "You may go for a while—go for a little while. No one knows and I'll never tell anyone. There might come a time to say it but not now."

So the young fellow went off. He came to a high rock and sat down there. He thought about this thing—sorry he did it. He pulled out his cock and looked at it. Found a hair, said, "This is my nisigosis hair," and threw it away. Then he went on—camped that night. Half thinking to go back to her. So he went back the next morning. The night the boy was away, his aunt was crying. Next day at sunrise he arrived. She was so very glad. He spoke to her: "I wonder if it would be right if we lived together now—just as if married." "I don't think so," the old woman said. "It would not look right if we did that. But if you want a woman you better get one for yourself, and if I want a man I better get one." This young man was in trouble because he had tasted something new. He got married in spring—he and his wife lived with kisigosis. The latter got married too after a while. She must have been a sensible woman. Nothing happened—just one slip and it stopped. That may have been why nothing happened. She was not an old woman and had not been married before. The boy was adopted by her to help her.

(William Berens's interpretation: "[There were] fewer people in the old days; almost all relatives [faced] greater temptation than now." "But the assumption is that a man *must* have a woman no matter whom. [There is] no idea of continence so that even asocial behavior is easier to rationalize because of this. Besides, masturbation is considered in the same class of 'sins'"—AIH.) [Hallowell's transcription of this story, quite close to the original, appeared in "The Social Function of Anxiety in a Primitive Society" (2010 [1941], 300–1. His note 25 added that the term for father's sister also means mother-in-law, and that the custom of mother-in-law avoidance made such intimacy doubly problematic.]

Context

The first episode in part 6 reveals not only a man's youthful abuse of his sister but also, by extension, his violation of Ojibwe norms regarding brother-sister interaction. The contextual discussion of Adam's story "Fasting in Winter" (pt. 3) noted the need for boys to avoid contact with women, and especially their sisters, when preparing to fast; sexual relations or even lesser intimacy would guarantee failure of a boy's dream quest (Hallowell 1992, 88). But the convention of brother-sister avoidance extended into all spheres of interaction. As Hallowell wrote, opposite-sex siblings [including parallel cousins] "never participate in common pastimes, games, or other activities together"—in sharp contrast to "the social solidarity that unites siblings of the same sex" [and in contrast to the joking relationship between cross cousins]. Even casual interaction was discountenanced; "siblings of the opposite sex are never seen alone in a canoe together or walking together for even the shortest distance through the bush" (1992, 54–55).

Ojibwe disease theory predicted that the boy's transgression would later make him sick, and confession would be required for a cure. Such confessions were never private; the belief was "that the very secrecy of the transgressions is one of the things that make them particularly bad"

(Hallowell 2010, 298). Confession served to warn others against such acts and reinforce the sanctions against them as well as to alleviate the transgressor's own anxiety—holding out expectation of a cure. Sagaski got away with incest with his sister because of his powers; his relationship, which proved enduring, was also probably consensual. The parents had died, and he was old enough to have already acquired a dream visitor, the "Master of the beaver," who mandated his behavior. He and Mindjimoo evidently did not get sick (the story that she died early did not hold up), and they never had to confess. Their case was unique.

Ojibwe observers thinking about it may have been reminded, however, of a mythic being they all knew about: the small magical man Tcaka-bec (Roulette: Chakaabens), who lived with his older sister—without sexual relations, although he shockingly used her pubic hair as twine to snare the sun (Hallowell 2010, 604; see Bird 2007, 29–36, for a full version of this widely known story). Hallowell noted of the Tcakabec story that "the intimacy that exists between Tcakabec and his sister is . . . completely antithetical to individuals in this relationship in actual life where the very strictest social avoidance obtains between brothers and sisters." As for the "twine," Hallowell added, "I can scarcely imagine a Saulteaux handling a piece of his sister's pubic hair for any purpose. . . . For a Saulteaux strictly avoids even the slightest allusion to sex in the presence of his sister and any allusion to her own sexual parts would be simply shocking" (Hallowell n.d., "Sexual Behavior," 15–16). But powerful personages, human or other-than-human, could bypass conventions.

The story about a young man and his father's sister concerns a vio-lation of a similar set of powerful avoidance restrictions. Interactions between father's sister and brother's son were strictly constrained. Cus-tom required that a man "maintain social distance in relation to all the women his father calls 'sister' and for whom he uses a distinct term. He must avoid women of this class as much as possible and only speak to them directly when absolutely necessary. . . . In the presence of [such] kin . . . any reference to sexual matters, particularly of a bawdy nature, must be avoided" (Hallowell 1992, 54). The story does not explain why this youth was residing in such a compromised situation on reaching sexual maturity; possibly he had been adopted as an orphan. It also appeared that his aunt had come to rely greatly upon his aid; no other adults were at hand. In any case, he was old enough to feel great anxiety about his act—brought to a head by his finding of a pubic hair on his penis. After he returned to his aunt, she managed to resolve the dilemma of how to go on living; they both later found spouses and were spared sickness and confession. As Adam said, "She must have been a sensible woman." Hallowell's further comment added perspective: In Ojibwe thinking, "a man *must* have a woman. . . . [There is] no idea of continence." It was expected that males would take opportunities ("How's chances?"), even when risks were entailed.

Pregnancy Blamed on the North Wind Spirit

Pindakik [Biindakik], one winter, stayed with his mother, only the two of them alone. The woman did not see her husband at all; he was away somewhere. She was always with her son. Sometime after that, in the summer, some people began to notice she was pregnant; a child was born after this. By this time the husband came back (had been away summer and winter). He asked her where she got it. "I got this child from the north wind spirit." The husband must have believed it—he asked her over and over and she told it again and again. If the woman had been a virgin, people would have believed it easier. ("Adam does not believe it. But in old times they might—through dreams, of course"—AIH. Adam's own aside: "Kewetin [Giiwedin, the North Wind] must have been weak; the child did [not] live very long.")

After this happened the man let this wife go. He had 2 wives—was married to sisters. *They could not agree*; that is why they were separated in the first place, and Pindakik looked after her. This old man did not like the older sister [the one who had the child]; he liked the younger one. After a while he began to think that his [older] wife was after someone. The old woman never confessed [about sexual relations with her son], but [was] believed.

Context

Hallowell in a later typescript asserted that the woman invoked the north wind "as a cover for incestuous relations with her son." But, he added, "the behavioral world of the Saulteaux does lend general support to such a possibility, and the occurrence of impregnation by blowing in the myths makes possible impregnation by one of the winds. . . . There is obviously no denial of the *possibility* of magical conception, so that the events in the myths are not utterly distinct from those of daily life. But whereas the mythical events are accepted as incontrovertible, in actual life there may be skepticism or denial, depending on the evaluation of circumstantial types of evidence." Further, in those days, "some people probably did believe her, particularly since she never suffered from any illness due to 'wrong doing'" (Hallowell n.d., "Sexual Behavior," 4–5; see also Hallowell 2010, 460n23). Accordingly, she did not face public confession, although some may have seen the early death of the child as a penalty for her secrecy.

A Father's Violation and Its Consequences

This old man's name was *Piwanuk* [Biiwaanag, Flint]. This man had one daughter. After she grew up to be a woman, after a while he went away along with this daughter—had no one else [no other children]. "You'll carry my [musk]rat traps," he said. In the spring of the year. "Beavers over there. I'm going to set traps." Lots of places now bare ground—snow gone away. So then as he walked, [he said] "I'll have a rest—fill the pipe and have a smoke." He spoke to her—"You'll find out now how your mother felt when I do this to you"—so slipped into her. All of a sudden this woman felt as if she was burning—said, "You're hurting me." But he kept pressing—"That's enough," she repeated. The girl was yelling—then [he] could not hear her voice anymore. "How my girl do you like it now?" She said yes. Began to laugh. They went back home then. The old woman knew nothing of it. After the girl found out how good it was, she gave her father all the chances he wanted.

Then a young man came along and asked for her. Her father let her go. But after she had gone he began to think of her. So this daughter told her husband to put brush around a hole in the ice—going angling. The old man started off, could see the girl quite a piece out on the ice, so rolled himself towards her like something blown away. He got what he wanted again. (His wife was living but did not like her [daughter].)

After he got through, he rolled back again to the water's edge and walked off from there. Now the girl was chopping wood—he went and looked for her again, got what he wanted. Finally his son-in-law found it out. He threw away his wife.

In the spring, the old man was hunting for ducks. Instead of seeing ducks he saw geese and shot two of them. He opened one of the geese— the hen—so he made use of it. The old woman now was cooking these geese—one of them very fat. He spoke to his wife: "Don't you cook the rump part of that goose." "Why?" she asked. "I'll cook this rump." "No, no," he said. "Don't you boil that part." So she did not cook that part.

Another young man came along and asked for the girl—who was now home again. "No," her father said [to her]. "You'll not go this time." Finally the old woman found out what was going on between the old man and his daughter. Did not like this. So she drove the daughter away—sent her somewhere else. A true story.

A Father's Assault

A man long ago, not very old, had returned to camp from a hunt. He had his daughter with him. This season the blueberries were just about right. When the women saw the man coming from the hunt, they said, "Did you see any blueberries today—how far?" "Not very far." "Show us where you saw them; we'll go along with you."

In the morning all got ready and started—the women were keen for these berries. His daughter was along with the party. They found lots of blueberries; the women picked them all day long. "Now my girl," [the father said], "go in that direction—more berries over there." She got quite a ways. The man followed. When she bent down, he got a hard on, I suppose. So after he made up his mind what he was going to do he went to her—of course she knew nothing of what was on his mind. He lifted the girl's dress, threw her down, and shoved it in. The girl started yelling, "Father, father, don't do that." "You keep quiet," he said. Some of the women came running now: "What you doing? (You would deny it if we told this.)" "You are going to make up stories about me," he said. (His mother was supposed to look after the girl.)

[Adam briefly told a sequel to the story. Back at the camp, the man's mother asked him for tobacco, and he gave her some, on condition that he have sex with her. The story ends with no mention of consequences for his transgressions.]

A Young Woman and Her Grandfather

There was one old man who did it to his granddaughter. The girl was sleeping. So this young woman she thought, I wish the morning would come—wanted to try to speak to her grandfather. (This old man was a widower; and this young woman, her father had died.) [She] said, "I'll go see you." After everybody was asleep, this young woman went to see her grandfather. The old man said, "What is it?" "I been thinking of you, made up my mind to come see you." The old man was not young, more than mid-age. The woman took every stitch of clothes off, told grandfather to do the same. So she was stark naked. "If you want to do anything now is your time." So he fucked her. "You are hurting me a little, grandfather. Is that the way the women feel when they do it?" "No," the old man says. "It's pretty hard at first but later on it will be easier on you." This woman said to her grandfather, "I understand now what it means to have a husband." She asked her grandfather all kinds of questions. He told her everything he knew. She asked, "I wonder if a man has 10 connections with a woman, will there be a child?" "No," he said, "it is a long job." "I wonder if a man can make one, if you have long enough." "You might," he says. "If you take another man and marry him your health might give way on you." "What does a woman feel when a child is going to be born?" So the old man told her. "I wonder if I take another man, would he hurt me the same way you have?" "I don't think so. If you give a chance to another man he will know you have been broken in already." So she stayed a long time with her grandfather; did not sleep with him too often as he hurt. She now wanted to find out how it felt from another man. So she got married. Looked after the old man too. When she had her first child she blamed it on the old man. But this was not true. She was just too green. She thought this because he was the first.

The old man must have used magic power to get her in the first place;

no young girl would do that. The old man cautioned her never to tell. ([This was] long ago—not in Adam's time—AIH.)

[Hallowell, writing in 1949, briefly outlined this story in print (2010, 337), describing the girl as an orphan "sent to live with her grandfather." Her "initiative taken, the incest and the nudity make this story a treble shocker." In an unpublished typescript entitled "Sexual Behavior" (n.d., 2), Hallowell recalled that Berens River people asked him "more than once whether it was not necessary for sexual intercourse to occur repeatedly in order for conception to take place. This question has very practical aspects too, since men sometimes have denied fatherhood on the grounds that they only slept with a girl *once*. I feel quite certain that the notion that sexual intercourse must be repeated for conception to occur was a prevailing idea among these people up to a short time ago."]

Old Man Harasses His Daughters-in-Law

Long ago there was an old man with two sons—they went hunting. His two daughters-in-law were left at home. When the night came he crawled across the tent to one of his daughters-in-law—wanted a fresh piece. "No," said the daughter-in-law; "This will never happen—don't want it." He goes to the other one: "You are my father-in-law," she said. "Never mind that," he said to her. "Something might happen on us if we do," she said. "No," he replied. "If you give me a chance you'll live long, and if you don't you'll have a miserable death." (This is Pazagwigabau.) The one he promised to live long did give him what he wanted.

The next night he went to the one that had turned him down. This woman said "No!" "You won't live long then," he said. "No,"—she refused. Finally he tried to spread out her legs, forcing her. She gave him a kick, and he fell over towards the fire. He said, "Thank you, thank you." This woman, she got sick—[on] the same one [leg] with which she kicked the old man. No medicine helped her. Finally she told her husband what had happened—the reason she was sick. The woman died—never got cured. . . . *The other one lived as long as he said.* Of course Pazagwigabau was mandauwizi [maandaawizi, endowed with extraordinary power] and killed the woman. ("Shows how a powerful man could flout custom"—AIH.)

Context

These four stories all involve illicit sexual relations that crossed generations: older father figures acting upon girls or young women in vulnerable situations. Hallowell explained that since generational distinctions are central to the Ojibwe kinship system, "sexual relations or marriage between classes of relatives belonging to different kinship generations violate the incest taboo" (1992, 52). The fathers in the first two stories in this set enacted more than a taboo violation, however; their acts were predatory and hurtful. The daughter of Piwanuk became somewhat of a hostage to her father; even if a consensual element developed, she suffered an imbalance of power and a shortage of options. Then she was "thrown away" by her husband, and later driven away from home by her mother, when they found out what was going on. Meanwhile, the old man added bestiality with a goose to his sins, but this too appeared to bring him no retribution. Adam did not comment on the matter, but the usual Ojibwe explanation would be that he had hidden powers that allowed him to get away with this licentiousness. The second story shares elements with the first, but says nothing of the girl's fate. Again, the man's licentiousness as a father, and later as a son, evidently went unpunished.

The third story features extreme behavior on the part of both a grandfather and his granddaughter. Adam believed the grandfather must have had "magic power"; a girl would not behave this way on her own. Interestingly, Hallowell found that grandfathers, while certainly subject to incest taboos like everyone else, could take verbal liberties with young girls (granddaughters broadly defined) that would not be allowed to others: "In its degree of permissiveness . . . a point is reached where an old man may joke a little with his "granddaughter" even to the extent of making sexual allusions" (1992, 57). In his 1940 field notes Hallowell recorded an example from Adam himself: "One morning W.B. [William Berens] and Adam and I were having our regular session. Three little girls came to the cabin door. Two of them were 12 years and one younger. Old Adam asked what they were doing—[They] said, "looking at wemtigozi" [wemitigoozhi, white man]. He said, 'Why don't you lift up your dresses and show him what you've got?' Both men laughed and the girls ran away. W.B. thought this a great joke and mentioned it afterwards—He said old men in the grandfather relation can say anything to young girls."

It may be imagined that such joking could be misconstrued, at the least. In any case, in the story, neither grandfather nor granddaughter suffered any apparent penalty for their actions, perhaps reflecting the old man's power; and later he came under the care of his granddaughter and her new husband. The question of who fathered her first child was left unanswered. Adam concluded that it was not the grandfather, given beliefs about what it took to make a child.

The fourth story recounts an old man's predatory aggression against his sons' wives, his incestuous assault on one of them, and his death threat, ultimately effective, against the daughter-in-law who repulsed his advances. The perpetrator was Pazagwigabau, whose malign powers and hurtful actions surfaced in a number of Adam's other stories. Pazagwigabau's eldest son, William Keeper, a widower, was the second husband of Adam's wife Aanii, so Aanii was in a position to know about this episode. William's first wife, Mikisi, died in 1883 (Butikofer 2009, pt. II.3, 342–43). The story does not say whether Mikisi was the victim of her father-in-law's curse.

PART 7

The Challenges and Risks of Being Female

"Attempted Killing Because of Refusal of Marriage"

A man was going to get married—[but] this woman did not like him very well. Her old man (her father) moved his camp away from the rest. He was willing [to refuse the man?]. The girl went along [with him]. The man got mad now. When night came, he said, "This girl is mocking me. She knows it already." So he made an image of this girl now ("made of rushes—head, legs, something like a doll"—AIH). "I was going to marry her but she'll get something else now." He put this image in his drum and put the drum covering on; he was going to kill this girl. He started to sing and pound the drum, a water drum. [But] when he pounded, no sound came from it. He could see nothing wrong with it; the covering was OK, no hole or anything. The bottom part had fallen off. He did not know what to think. He fixed it up, started to sing again. It was not long before the bottom part fell off again—the second time.

This young man got mad. He went off and fixed a new image—just exactly how this woman looked. He opened his medicine bag (muske-mot). To be sure this time, he put a migis in every joint—arms and legs and one opposite the heart—another one at the head. This girl began to be sick now. He was going to finish her—all those migis, all went into her body. But she was able to throw them off. He had fixed up a place in a bush where he left the image. He went in the morning to see if the migis were there. But the girl had gathered them from her body and put them in a little tin box. When this young man got there, there was not one migis. (If he had killed the girl [they] would have been there.) So he tried needles now—getting after her stronger, determined to kill her. The next morning the girl did the same thing—she got the needles out of her body. When the man went to look, he did not find the needles; he had been singing all night too. He thought, "What shall I do next?" Really the girl was beating him. He could do no more—she had more power than he.

This was a man named Nimanepwa [Nimanepwaa]—"I have no tobacco," a Lac Seul Indian—a mozani [Moonzoonii, Moose clan]. He never got a wife—the girls did not like him—he was getting old. When he was staying in a camp once in summer, not so long ago—two [ten?— see below] years ago—he was staying with another man, using mosquito nets and a candle. The net caught fire; the tent caught fire too. They were drinking. The one that was with him was pulled out but died. Nimawepwa burnt to death right there. [Nimanepwa was a son of Bezhig (Pesk or Paishk); he died on May 29, 1927 (Butikofer, pers. comm., 2017).]

[Hallowell then asked Adam about "women—using magic power to kill." Adam replied, "Woman *will only protect herself*—will not project magic. The girl in the story could have sent the migis and needles back but she didn't. She had the power all right. The women long ago seemed to be scared all the time. Women had dreams that made them strong but it seemed they did not make use of it (that power)." In the manuscript this passage is immediately followed by another story touching the same theme: "Windigos Killed by Two Women" (pt. 10).]

A Failed Rape

Some young men were having a council—talking about a young girl— not full grown. That is what the council was about. They will try to fix the girl in some way. This female was not sleeping with her mother, but in a separate place. After all were asleep in that camp, these young men went to the place where she was. They lifted the blanket carefully with the girl on it. She did not awaken. They walked very carefully; as soon as she started to move they stopped—(four were carrying it).

So they took her far enough so nobody would wake up when she started to yell. One man had an awful hard on—he started. But before he touched her, he broke off, could do nothing. The second one had a hard on—he touched her, but then his broke off. The third touched her, but the same thing happened. (There were more than four altogether.) Foolish men they were—none of them could do anything. They had to let her go. She went home. Men could not harm her. They started to laugh at each other now. She was alone, "but none of us could manage it." Something must have helped her. They left her alone then. For a long time those fellows did not bother with any woman.

Old women used to say if you touch a girl before she has her first blood, she will have no children. Cf. with boys and pawagan. Young men used to be single a long time.

"Sometimes a Girl Does Not Want to Get Married"

She was asked to marry but refused an old man, Kokokos [Kohkohko'ons]. Young men were after this girl but she refused them [too]. So one young man went to the four oldest men, the oldest he could find in the camp. The old men spoke to this young man: "You go up in the bush and clear out brush—a place where we can sit. Right on bare ground—no brush. And in the center of this place put some sand." So after this young man got through doing what he was told to do, when the night came, the four old men took their places in a circle. There was a little day sky—no other light so anyone could see. So these old men took their [medicine] sacks there in the bush. This young man he put up enough pagitcigan [bagijigan, offerings] to pay these four old men.

One of the old men—he opened [a bag of] wanamin [wanaman, love medicine]. He chewed the end of a little stick. After he picked up the medicine, a little of the medicine (powdery) stuck to it. The young man was handed the stick and told to touch bark where the head would be (no drawing)—went to the tent of the girl: "Come back after you do it." He did it and returned to the bush. One old man started to sing a song now. You can hear the girl come running already to where these old fellows were. The girl started to dance in front of the old man that was singing. After she got through she took off her leggings, threw them to one side. The second old man started to sing now—knows what this girl intends to do. He was going to defend her but did not have the power to bring her senses back. This fellow did not continue; he told the other three, "I don't know this kind of song." He was sorry for the girl when he saw how she was acting. When the others finished singing she had taken off all her clothing. When she came to this old man she passed him. The leader started to sing; the girl danced. After this she was naked by this time. Right in front of this old fellow she spread her legs. He started to fuck her. After he got through she went to another one. The one who defended her did not bother her. The second one did it. After he got through she went to the third. Same thing. The young man spread out a cloth in the center and placed her there. She was laughing. The leader now started curing her. She started coming to her senses now. She did not know, of course, what she had been doing. This other old man who pitied her did not touch her. She started to cry now. [The leader said] "You would not accept any young man."

The young man helped her put on her clothes. He was sorry. The young man took her back to her tent quietly—everyone else was asleep. She was so ashamed—you could hardly see her in daytime. The father of the girl knew nothing about it. The man who tried to defend her said, "Let the son of the leader marry her," and gave her medicine to accomplish this. The father of the girl in the meantime found out. So he gave the defender some pagitcigan to help the girl more; [he] said, "I'll help you." The leader, he had three sons. The defender said, "I'll help you." (The leader had moved.) He fixed a place and took the young girl and her parents. What he was going to use was nicely covered. "I want you to turn your mind to any one of the sons of this leader you want." And this girl, she knew one of his sons was a very good hunter.

Then he put out two sticks—one standing towards where the old man was camped (he did not want the leader to know). He took the sticks in both hands, then opened what he was going to use. "Sit alongside this stick" [he told the girl]. The one standing stick, he blazed on one side, then opened a little parcel and gave the stick to the girl. He took wanaman, and touched the other (standing stick) where it was blazed. He opened his bag, [took out] something wrapped. Then he opened two things—one an image (carved) of a man and the other of a woman. Now he tied the stick with a little string. ("One end of the string [was attached] to upright stick, the other held by girl. The man did not touch string. Like needles on a string, about one inch apart. If they don't move [it] won't happen"—AIH).

"You hang onto this (the female)," [the man said to the girl]. He chewed the medicine and spit on the string; he had tied the male image to the standing stick. There was a little hole in the heart of each image where the heart would be. "Hang on to the end of the string," he said. He brought the male and female images together in the center of the string, then took them apart now. The man started to move, and the other one (female) too. The male moved towards the female; just held, no one moving them; got together. All of a sudden this young fellow thought of this girl. He could not think of anything but her. He got ready and started off. "Where are you going?" said his father. He did not say where. He went right into the girl's tent and sat alongside of her. He married her. Kokokos [the old man she had rejected] told this story. The old leader [not Kokokos] must have been ashamed of himself.

[In her Ojibwe fieldwork in the 1930s, Ruth Landes heard "old and contemporary tales" in which "the victim falls into a hypnotic relationship with the sorcerer, showing abnormal or overwhelming lust. The victim, male or female, trails the medicine-wielder or 'owner' and makes shocking sexual displays and demands in public" (1968, 65).]

Sex and a Girl's Injury

Long ago, there was a girl from Bloodvein and a man from here [Little Grand Rapids]. The girl was after the man. One day in the bush, the girl grabbed the man and hung on, tried to pull [him] into bush. (The man told Adam to go and wait for him somewhere—AIH.) He fucked her—[I] heard her squealing—my partner called me then [to] come over there. I went over—saw the girl had fainted—knew nothing. There was a creek not far—[we] laid her down and put water on her forehead. She came to her senses but could not move. We could not stay with her. The man told me not to say anything. The girl was lost—late in the evening, the man was worried—found her there. Holding her up, [he] brought her down. She dragged her legs, could hardly walk. This fellow was well hung—an awful size. No wonder this girl could not stand it. His son at Berens River the same way. The girl got all right but had to have medicine—probably was torn inside. His son did the same thing to his uncle's girl when she was about 17. Tore her—she could not walk. William Berens's mother examined her. He got three years in penitentiary.

[Hallowell's manuscript "Myths and Tales" errs on this, saying eight years. In "Myths and Tales" this story is paired with that in the two paragraphs that follow here. In the manuscript it is titled "Human Parallels to Long Penis of Wisakedjak [Wiisakejaak, trickster]," suggesting an undercurrent of Ojibwe male humor for both teller and listeners; see Hallowell (2010, 340–41) regarding sexual stories told about this Ojibwe "trickster-culture hero." In Hallowell's original transcript of Adam's stories, the second story occurs a few pages later and is more telegraphic, yet has a few details not found in the edited typescript. The following text follows the original more closely, with connecting words added and sequence improved.]

Okawapwan [Ogawapwan] was a small man with a very tall woman for a wife, and a big prick. The head of it used to stick out along his leg beyond his anzian [aanziyaan, breech cloth]—purposely, even when facing his daughter-in-law. It was as big as a tin can—almost like a horse. Everybody knew of it, even at the mouth of the river. Once there was a big feast at Pauingassi; all were sitting about. When eating, he took the top part of the fish and stirred the kettle with his cock. His wife was mad; the others laughed. She threw the fish out and washed the kettle.

Then he tried to catch a girl who called him "little prick." He jumped up and chased her and got her down on the flooring. But he could not get his cock in. The girl started to cry now—one woman was laughing; the old man was sweating, so he let her go but said, "don't call me that again." An old woman was there and saw the whole performance.

[This final sentence, added in the typescript, suggests that Adam had heard a first-hand account of the episode. Hallowell (2010, 97) listed Ogawapwan, a Pelican, as one of five Berens River polygynists; he had two wives and eight children, one of whom was Ahak (Thomas Ross), first husband of Aanii.]

"I Don't Want to Let Her Go": A Father Resists a Suitor's Demands

There was a married man—asked an old fellow to give him one of his daughters. "No!" This old fellow, he left and camped a long way off from the other bunch. X followed and asked for the girl again. Put something [a gift?] before him. Would not eat. Said to the old man, "I did not come here for nothing; I want to take back what I expect from you." So the old man said, "It is hard for me. I don't want to let her go. You have one wife already." X pulled out his knife, put it before him. "Now is your chance. Will you give me the girl or not?" The old fellow said nothing. X said, "Answer my question." The old fellow said the same thing, "I don't think so." X grabbed his knife. Both jumped to their feet. But the knife was grabbed from X by a third man. X was killed with his own weapon—stabbed all over, his guts out but still fighting. [This was a] brother of Zhenawaakoshkang.

[In the margin of this text, Hallowell wrote that the girl was of the Sucker clan. The contextual discussion following "Living Well, Being Hospitable" (pt. 4) tells of another murder that fueled deep tensions between the Moose and Sucker clans in Zhenawaakoshkang's generation. By Adam's time, they did not intermarry.]

A Wife's Murder

A man was going down this river to the mouth. He had his family with him—started from Little Grand Rapids. Between here and Berens River he said to his boy, "You better go around and shoot some rabbits and partridges." The boy took his gun and went off in the bush. ("Don't know what the old man is thinking about," the boy said.) When the boy got off, the old man started to fight his wife, stabbed her even in the stomach, dragged her body to the river and threw her into the river. The woman tried to hang onto the rocks, [but he] meant to kill her. She went down and drowned. The young boy got back at sundown. "I don't know where your mother got to" [the old man said]. At first the boy did not think much of it, thought she had gone somewhere. In the morning he went off in the canoe to the mouth of the river.

My father [said Adam] was paddling down the river, behind. He saw something, a body floating up already, clothing dropping off. My grand-mother [Pasho] took the body ashore and fixed a place for burial and buried it there; she saw the wounds in the stomach. The young fellow never knew. The man's name was Otcik [Ojik], a wicked man. Nothing happened to Otcik. The boy might have found out later but did not believe his father had done it. No one ever accused Otcik to his face — scared of him — not because of mandauwizi [extraordinary powers]. [His two sons suffered] blood from mouth — one died of T.B. This must have been because of the murder — blood from wounds. Otcik had two wives after the first.

[Hallowell added three asides: first, "sic" regarding what the boy knew, apparently indicating that the account was ambiguous. Second, regarding blood from wounds, Hallowell noted "sympathetic magic — this idea always gives a clue." And third, he said Adam added, "Something is sure to come on you, even on your death bed." Otcik was a brother of Zhenawaakoshkang. Two of his daughters married Dedibaayaaban; see "Those Two Wives of Tetebaiyabin" (pt. 4).]

Context and Commentary

The stories in parts 6 and 7 have much to do with gender relations and women. Hallowell did not publish explicitly on these topics, yet they run like a leitmotif through much of his writing and in his research notes. He regretted that he could not do more on the subject. As he wrote to R.W. Dunning on October 27, 1955, one of his graduate students, Dorothy Spencer, spent part of the summer with him in 1934, and his idea was "that she would tackle the women." But the interpreter they hoped for had moved away, and no replacement could be found (Berens 2009, 112). Hallowell compensated by recording his own observations about women's and men's lives, interactions, and views of one another, along with what the men told him. His unpublished commentaries on the myths and tales he collected along the Berens River also paid attention to issues of gender arising in those stories.

In conversations and in studying the myths and tales, Hallowell was struck by a gendered double standard that placed women at a considerable disadvantage. On a handwritten undated page, Hallowell outlined the six findings that follow, rather bluntly stated under the title, "Aggressive attitude towards women." Under the list he wrote: "All reflect a basic insecurity in men."

> W.B. [William Berens]: "Women get blamed for everything." [In a 1995 conversation, Margaret Simmons, a granddaughter of Berens, heartily agreed with her grandfather's comment.]
> Terms for hunting animals are the same as for hunting women.
> Women must yield submissively and at once to men's sexual impulses—pursued and "taken."
> No man would commit suicide if disappointed in love—plenty more [women available].
> Use of love medicine to force women—no consideration of them as persons.
> Or men will bewitch a woman who won't yield.

The following paragraphs draw in part on a paper that Maureen Matthews and I presented to the American Society for Ethnohistory in November 1995, building on our Berens River researches and extended conversations with Margaret Simmons and Ojibwe linguist Roger Roulette, as well as on Hallowell's papers.

ITEM 1: When William Berens told Hallowell that women got blamed for everything, he had in mind the many ways that women could frustrate or endanger male activities, livelihood, and even health. When Adam and other young males fasted to establish ties with dreamed visitors, they had to avoid their sisters and other females before fasting, or the pawaganak would not come to them. Hallowell found: "From all accounts, the older Indians were very strict about this," such that male sexual activity before fasting was probably kept to a minimum (2010, 332). Speaking more generally, Adam said men who "bothered the women" at a young age would not be strong and healthy (see "HBC Manager in Trouble," pt. 2). Older people told Hallowell that "a man would have more mental power if he kept away from women and did not marry"; he could conserve his power and not waste it.

Similarly, women were not to step over men's legs or possessions; to do so would make the men weak and poor runners.

The core issue for men had to do with women's "uncleanness," related to their menses. Hallowell's notes recorded the term *winewisiwin* [wiiniziwin, uncleanliness] for catamenia, or as Baraga's dictionary translated it, "monthly flowings," which men saw as both threatening and repulsive. (One man described them to Hallowell as "slime between the legs.") The root verb is wiinizi, "being dirty or impure"; in contrast, bekize is the state of "being clean or pure"—or "religious purity," as Hallowell glossed it. The Cree employed the parallel concept pikisiw, "someone is clean," in speaking of the condition that a male needed to be in on a dream quest (Brightman 1993, 79). Fasting in the bush occurred in a clean place, away from women, dogs, and other sources of pollution. Wild animals were also "clean," and their "bosses" (manidoons, diminutive spirits) were offended and kept them away from hunters if a menstruating or pregnant woman came near. Also, such women were not to lift fishnets, tend snares or traps, or have contact with animal remains; their actions and condition could threaten both food security and male hunters' livelihood and powers. More profoundly, they put at risk men's abilities to call spirits into the shaking tent, to heal people through the sweat lodge, and to conduct Midewiwin or Waabano ceremonies. Menstruating women did not take part in ceremonies because they would "put them into disorder," as Roulette put it (Brown and Matthews 1995). Berens River Ojibwe women held no ceremonial roles except occasionally after menopause when, as Hallowell was told, "they are considered to be more like men." The medicine woman in "Midewiwin Miracles" (pt. 5) was postmenopausal. Yet William Berens and Adam Bigmouth both acknowledged that some women had powers to counter sorcery or even to kill windigos (see "Windigos Killed by Two Women," pt. 10), even though they did not seek them deliberately as males did through fasting.

Men could not easily assess or predict the nature or strength of women's powers; the male "insecurity" that Hallowell observed arose both from uncertainty about them and from the men's concerns about contact with menstrual substances and other bodily fluids.

One powerful myth that William Berens recounted was "The Birth of the Winds, Flint, and the Great Hare." In its opening episode, the young male fasting and dreaming for a blessing wakes several times to find his blanket wet; a woman urinates on it each night, ruining his quest until he finds means to escape (Berens 2009, 128). Hallowell commented regarding this and other myths that "on the one hand we have in Saulteaux society a heavy weighting of male dominance, and on the other the conception of women as "unclean" and therefore a potential menace to the proper functioning of men in relation to supernatural entities. Thus there is a great deal of psychological realism reflected in the myths in so far as women are portrayed as the sources of frustration and danger that have to be overcome by men" (Hallowell n.d., "Myths and Tales," file #26, "Sex").

ITEM 2: Ojibwe and Cree men, when speaking of hunting and courtship, used much the same vocabulary and imagery for both. At Pikangikum in the 1950s, R. W. Dunning learned the term, "*Neno-che-an* [onooji'aan]—literally, I hunt or flirt with someone. The same term is used for both flirting with girls and hunting game" (Dunning 1959, 101). William Berens told Hallowell of a dream he had one time when his hunting was going badly. He dreamed of two girls on a trail, one of whom "was setting a table with lots of good things to eat. . . . 'This is all for you,' she said." He woke up, headed straight for a deadfall he didn't usually visit, and found in it a fine female fisher (Berens 2009, 102). Of the Rock Cree in northern Manitoba, Robert Brightman wrote: "From the point of view of male hunters, sex is a metaphor for hunting, and women are metaphors for animals." In Cree dream experiences, "animals elect to interact with men in the form of human women, and sexual or other encounters with these 'women' predestine events of successful foraging" (Brightman 1993, 127–28). Richard Preston found metaphorical parallels between hunting and sexual relationships among the James Bay Cree (2002, 214).

These statements, of course, also imply that both animals and women often elected to be pursued. Hallowell gathered stories showing that "the reputed 'hunting' of girls by boys, if viewed realistically, indicates that the girls did not run 'to get away,' but rather to be pursued—and caught! In the initiation of sexual activity, Ojibwa girls and women often play anything but a passive role" (Hallowell 2010, 332). Male aggressiveness could be a major threat, however, as Adam's stories of sorcery and hurtful attacks demonstrated, and young men's behavior sometimes got out of hand, even without sorcery. Hallowell was told how some women devised a "Cure for a young man who ran after women all the time." The women got together and said, "We'll fix him." One of them waited for him in the bush. "The others said, 'If he gets after you, you hang on to him and don't let go (i.e., before he does anything).' It happened that way—one after another came up so that the women had him. Tore his pants off, then his shirt; one held him by the hair, head down; held on the ground, bare naked. One pissed on his naked belly, etc. Turned him over and rubbed asses against the back of his neck (did not shit). Now the oldest said, 'You'll know enough now. You've bothered the women right along. You know the women now.' The fellow jumped into the water. It was not kept a secret. Everyone laughed at him. He was different altogether after that—so ashamed. None of the women would have anything to do with him after this" (Hallowell, research notes; his published version of the incident, somewhat abridged, appeared in 1949 [2010, 333].)

ITEM 3: Some of Adam Bigmouth's stories show that not all women yielded to men "submissively and at once." But Hallowell noted in connection with Adam's story "A Young Man and His Father's Sister" (pt. 6) that Ojibwe men had no notion of continence. On some handwritten pages titled "Saulteaux sex," Hallowell commented on an Ojibwe assumption "that there is a kind of natural right to sexual gratification," in contrast to Western culture, "where restraint and continence are given a value in themselves." Continence is "in fact thought abnormal—since the contemporary natives can't quite believe the priests are truly celibate," suggesting that Catholic priestly transgressions would not have struck Ojibwe men as surprising.

Further, "Because of the cultural support of male dominance and the sexual accessibility of women, the male ego is peculiarly sensitive to *rejection*" (2010, 335). Rejection could be taken as personal insult, leading to the use of love magic or sorcery. On a parallel note, Hallowell was struck by the lack of companionship (after puberty and before marriage) between the sexes; there was no sharing of games or other recreation. This meant that young men sought out women simply as sexual objects or as wives. Concomitantly, the myths and stories that Hallowell recorded were strikingly free of elements of romantic love and yearning (n.d., "Myths and Tales").

ITEM 4: The statement that no man would kill himself over disappointment in love echoes this theme; even once married, a man could find other women if he wished. Hallowell noted that among the numerous sexual transgressions that could lead to sickness and penalties, one was conspicuously absent; the "sin" of adultery or alienation of affections was never mentioned.

ITEM 5: The use of love medicine on women leads back again to hunting parallels. Crees used hunting medicine in efforts "to exert a seductive influence over a dispositionally reluctant quarry"; and similarly, the Ojibwe classified hunting medicine with love magic as "bad medicine techniques . . . that subvert the autonomy or welfare of others" (Brightman, citing Black 1977; see also Landes 1968, 65). Brightman added: "A clear correspondence exists between the lethal effects of sorcery on human victims and the use of hunting medicine to kill animals" (1993, 191, 192). Of course, women as well as men could use love medicine, as both Adam and William Berens experienced, but women's efforts at seduction were relatively mild and more easily countered than the assaults launched by male sorcerers with their migis shells and other resources.

ITEM 6: "Men will bewitch a woman who won't yield." As Adam recounted, however, in "Attempted Killing Because of Refusal of Marriage" (pt. 7), some women found powers to resist such sorcery.

But then again, episodes of male physical violence also presented dangers. The last three stories in this series tell of a girl who invited a man's sexual aggression and was hurt by it, of a suitor prepared to kill an old man in order to take his daughter, and finally of a man's murder of his wife. All these stories were directly known to Adam: he was present when the girl was injured; the old man's attacker was a brother of his future father-in-law, Zhenawaakoshkang; and the body of the murdered wife was recovered from the Berens River by Adam's family and buried by his grandmother. In light of the last two stories, it is curious that Hallowell, in an article published in 1940, stated: "Within [the Saulteaux] behavioral world, murder has occurred again and again but always as the result of sorcery, not of overt physical aggression" (2010, 275). Possibly when he wrote those words, he had not yet heard Adam's stories of physical murders.

The following photographs were taken by A. Irving Hallowell during his Berens River summer fieldwork in the period between 1932 and 1940. The originals reside in the Hallowell papers at the American Philosophical Society in Philadelphia. All were taken at Little Grand Rapids, Manitoba, on the upper Berens River unless otherwise indicated. For Ojibwe names and their variants, see the glossary following the introduction. APS reference locators appear at the end of each caption.

Fig. 1. Adam Bigmouth (Gisayenaan), summer 1938 or 1940. APS A186.
Graphics:6600.

Fig. 2. Chief William Berens at Berens River, probably 1932. APS F51. Graphics:6761.

Fig. 3. "Our party at first portage above Little Grand Rapids," July 1932. Left to right: J. J. Everett, Gordon Berens, Antoine Bittern, Theophile Panadis, and William Berens. Panadis was an Abenaki from Odanak who accompanied Hallowell and the others on his first trip up the Berens River. Gordon was William Berens's son, and Antoine Bittern was his son-in-law. Note the two square-stern canoes and the "kicker," a small outboard motor, on Gordon's shoulder. APS A45. Graphics:6429.

Fig. 4. John Keeper Sr. (Giiwichens), William Berens, A. I. Hallowell, and Antoine Bittern, probably 1932. Note the Ojibwe men's footware; locals found rubbers most effective on slippery rocks. APS F92. Graphics:6693.

Fig. 5. Baachiish (Batis or John Baptiste), younger brother of Adam Bigmouth. Little Grand Rapids, 1938. APS A128. Graphics:6545.

Fig. 6. John Duck (Makochens) in front of his Waabano pavilion. APS A182.
Graphics:6596.

Fig. 7. Naamiwan (Fair Wind, John Owen), son of Zhenawaakoshkang (Butikofer: Shenawakoshkank), at Pauingassi. His sister, Aanii, was married to Adam Bigmouth. APS A206. Graphics:6615.

Fig. 8. Joseph Green (Ginoozhewinini), son of Midewinini (John Green), with his wife, Kwananii (daughter of John Keeper Sr.) and children. APS A153. Graphics:6571.

Fig. 9. Alex Keeper (Gllwlich). APS A115. Graphics:6532.

Fig. 10. The dwelling of John Keeper Sr., bark and canvas. His daughter Noonaawas (Bella Keeper) is on the right, with two of her nieces (Butikofer). This was the largest traditional dwelling that Hallowell saw at Little Grand Rapids. APS A89. Graphics:2060.

Fig. 11. Sweat lodge under construction, with two men. APS A180.
Graphics:2066.

Fig. 12. Sweat lodge completed and covered with quilt. APS A177. Graphics:6592.

Fig. 13. Conjuring lodge (shaking tent) under construction, with five men. APS A190. Graphics:6603.

Fig. 14. Conjuring lodge completed and covered. APS A192. Graphics:2055.

Fig. 15. Duck Lake (Barton Lake), Waabano pavilion of Ashaageshi (Asagesi; see Hallowell 2010, 46). It may have been used earlier for the Midewiwin; see part 4, "Those Two Wives of Tetebaiyabin." APS A281. Graphics:6685.

PART 8

Bad Medicine and Old Men's Threats

Bad Medicine

A mide will make a little grave and an image of a man out of grass or anything. This represents the man he is going to kill. He buries him [the image] in the grave and mentions the moon in which he will get death sickness. He leaves it there—no one knows where. The man will get sick—everything is settled; no mide or anyone can do anything to save the man. He will die on the scheduled time. Then after the man is dead and buried—the same night—the mide will put on a bear skin and go to the grave ("This is the power of a bear skin kashipetagan [gashkibitaagan, stringed pouch]. But he does not appear as a bear on the way, but like the 'moon' (fools fire?)"—AIH.) He appears as a bear at the grave. He goes there to scoop out the eyes of the corpse and cut off the tip of the tongue which he keeps in a death-box, so he knows exactly how many people he has killed. If a relative of the person who died goes to the grave, i.e., if he thinks something is wrong, he may hide nearby—before sundown—no one knows he went. Then when the mide appears like a bear, he may shoot him, and no one will blame him or call him a murderer because they will know what happened, and the mide will be proved guilty anyway because he had no right near a grave at night.

(Hallowell's notes: "No name of any mide who was thus killed could be recalled, but W.B. [William Berens] often heard his father and

89

grandmother mention actual cases which happened long ago. When a mide was killed in this fashion, his body was cooked and his relatives forced to eat him. His wife might be given the head. The man who killed him would go to one of the leading men—another mide—and arrange the feast to which the relatives would be invited. If they refused to eat they would be killed themselves. The 'medicine' necessary for the above purpose was associated with the fourth degree of the Midewiwin. It could not be withheld but every person was cautioned in its use. This is why everyone was so afraid of those who had gone high up in the Midewiwin. No person could resist this type of medicine—it was sure death.")

[Ruth Landes (1968, 52) wrote that "the Ontario and Minnesota Midewiwin in the 1930s was structured as eight successive grades of curing. . . . The first four or five grades were considered desirable but the last . . . were considered dangerous because they taught sorcery," presenting "dangers of excessive power and ambition." Pazagwigabau had doubtless attained one of the higher grades. Landes heard stories of sorcerers visiting the graves of their victims in the form of bears, to extract their tongues (1968, 64–65).]

("If a mide was paid by someone to do the deed of killing someone, would the mide be considered 'guilty' of murder? The chief [of Little Grand Rapids] said yes, in his opinion, but he thought Pazagwigabau would not hesitate if he was paid"—AIH.)

(Hallowell's further note: "Adam denied anyone knew how to use bad medicine now; he said it was never told [taught?] to him. Flatstone and Bluffhead [parallel cousins, Sturgeon clan] were the last to know about this at Little Grand Rapids. Pazagwigabau was known to have killed several people. His son-in-law found a box with eyes of people he had killed gouged out, also the tip of a tongue. He must have gotten these after the people were buried—went to the cemetery not in human form but in that of a bear. A bear of this kind can manage to go underground too. That is how he must have got them. His son-in-law saw Pazagwigabau looking in the box; he looked at it after his death [in 1881–82]—burned it. Tetebaiyabin [his son] used bad medicine too, He used it on Adam.")

[See "Those Two Wives of Tetebaiyabin," pt. 4.]

This same old fellow—everyone was scared of him. There was a young man who visited at Poplar Hill—brother of Levick [or Levique; see Berens 2009, 112]. This man when he came home, he saw something at the rapids—Winisk rapids, this side of Poplar Hill. Right on that high rock on the side of the river—he saw two animals there—something like lions. It was the old man—mandauwizi [maandaawizi]—mad at the young men *because they did not camp at his place but went right through* ("trivial offence"—AIH). Flatstone here knew what was happening, that Pazagwigabau was going to do something to his son [Levick's brother]. He knew he had greater power—wanted to save his son. He knew what moves to make, so he beat him. (Tetebaiyabin [son of Pazagwigabau] knew as much as his father—a great medicine man.)

"This Old Fellow Was Pretty Bad": A Son's Death and a Father's Retaliation

One time a young man fell into some rapids, and an old man pulled him out. Then the young man became sick—a long, long time, losing strength. The old man did his best to treat him.

His father saw a "fire" ("no special term"—AIH); it looked round like a moon. This is what someone was using [against his son]. Blood came from the young man's mouth (name Bazil—Pindandakwan's son). He was very weak—almost dead. So he told his father, "I want you to do something. Clean that kettle" (a small copper HBC one). He hung it above his head to one of the tent poles. He slept good that night. He told his father, "Handle this kettle very easily—set it right." It was covered. "Lift the cover," he said. It was full of blood. (Where did it come from?) The fellow got a little better. He sat outside the wigwam now. His mother said, "I wish my son would get better." But they were still seeing the fire every night—as if someone were visiting them. The young man got better—then weaker again.

The old fellow that was doing this was living with another man—(X). X was wondering what the old man was doing. Late at night when the fire was out in the tent, X watched how the old fellow put fire to sagatagan [zagataagan, tinder], then covered it up with a blanket—(kneeling, covered himself too). X did not know what it meant.

Pindandakwan was away—when he got back to camp, he heard his wife crying (they had one boy and one girl). He found his son was dead—this woman wept the whole day. Pindandakwan was not crying. He fixed up a place in front of the tent where the body lay at night. "Don't take it too hard," he said to his wife. "I know what happened. But the man that did this may not be far behind our son." ("Body was usually kept inside"—AIH.)

He put birch bark all around the corpse. He fixed up his gun—cleaned it. (The mide men had something to counteract magic power—shot was no good.) After Pindandakwan cleaned his gun, he painted his face and hands black. He put medicine in his gun and watched the corpse so he can [see] what is going to happen. He saw the fire coming—making a circle around it—like walking. Then he heard a voice—"This is finished." He saw a bear trying to lift the bark on the head side—he was going to take the part he wanted. Pindankakwan shot him then. He heard a man's voice—(the old man had covered himself up again).

Meanwhile X was watching in that tent. The old man threw his blanket quickly and fell right over on the fireside. X saw this—he got up, lit a birch bark, made a little fire, and woke up his wife. He said to her, "You hold this birch." He was afraid he would be blamed. He knew the old man was dead—blood running from his mouth; he was not far behind the young man, as Pindandakwan had said. So X, he got ready early in the morning and went over to tell Pindandakwan that the old man was dead—then found out the young man was dead too. X told the next camp too—he knows already that the young man "did not die for nothing." People came to bury them both. X was sure what the old man was doing—and knew that he was killed in turn. This old fellow was pretty bad. X got no blame at all. (Pindandakwan did not shoot with a regular bullet or shot—[used] some kind of migis.)

(William Berens told Hallowell that Mide men sometimes used snow, "then feathers for a wad and charcoal for a bullet—my father told me they used this." "How did the gun go off?"—AIH. "A man dreamed what to use"—Berens. Pindandakwan would not get sick [for this action]—he was simply defending himself. Same in principle as killing a windigo—AIH.)

Context

Pindandakwan (d. 1909) and Siipi (Ziipi, a daughter of Pazagwigabau) had seven children in the 1880s and 1890s. Treaty pay lists record the deaths of two sons, unnamed, in 1895 and 1898 (Butikofer 2009, pt. I.2, 307–8); one may be the victim in the story. Hallowell summarized this story in "The Ojibwa Self and Its Behavioral Environment" (2010, 525–27), noting that in Ojibwe thinking, a powerful person's soul can leave the body and take on the appearance of an animal (525). More generally, "*multiform appearance* is an inherent potential of all animate beings. What is uniform, constant, visually imperceptible and vital is the soul. A sorcerer, being a person of unusual power, is able to leave his human body in one place and appear in another perceptible manifestation elsewhere" (526). "Bear-walking" recurs in "Those Two Wives of Tetebaiyabin" (pt. 4) and "Winter Starving—Sorcery and Bear-Walking" (pt. 9).

Adam did not explain why Pindandakwan's son Bazil came under attack. The attacker was unnamed. Pindandakwan was a powerful Mide practitioner, and Hallowell found a recurrent pattern of sometimes intense rivalry between males with magical powers, the contests between parallel cousins Owl and Pazigwigabau being a strong example. Covert rivalry and sorcery arising from perceived insults and offenses may have led to this old man's killing of Bazil; possibly he could get at the relatively defenseless young man but not at his powerful father. Flatstone's comment in "Bad Medicine" that Pazagwigabau was planning harm against his son offers a parallel; a sorcerer might target a rival's family members, aside from the enemy himself.

An Old Man's Winter Threat

An old man—in the morning—people getting ready for something. "Ch[il-dren], I'm going to tell you something—In four nights I am going to destroy you (winter)." One fellow listened carefully. All scattered to hunt.

This fellow spoke to his wife: "What I am going to use won't come from far either." He got up early. He was not a common Indian. He knows something. The woman knows her husband knows something. He went and killed a moose—very fat. He came home and brought all the fat—the fattest part of the animal and some meat besides—the best part, all cooked. When everything was prepared he spread out a birch bark in the center of the tent and put the cooked meat on it. The man spoke to the old man: "You see this grub—sit down and eat. If you can finish it I'll go off once more."

This old man had a dog (dogs used to be kept inside). The old man filled his pipe. After he got through, he said, "Now, my dog—there is a feast before us. Try to grow." The dog jumped up and shook himself—he grew big—about the size of a year old deer [caribou], and came around the tent. As soon as the dog came opposite to the man who put up the feast, he [the man] grabbed him by the jaw and back of neck and cracked him. He said, "I will do the same to you if you scare my children." The old man put his head down and started to eat. But he could not finish— this man beat him. He depended on the dog.

This is what was meant when [the younger man] said he would do what he wished without going very far. The old man did not live long; he died the first part of the summer.

Context

This is a rather enigmatic story. The old man's powers and threat were connected with winter, and his plan to "destroy" the people probably involved ruining their winter hunts. The man who "knows something" and brings home the fat moose forestalls his plot by setting up a kind of eat-all feast, such that the old man can do nothing unless all the meat set before him is consumed—an impossible task once his host kills his monster dog companion. Eat-all feasts usually involved the participation of all present; here the host abstained. Robert Brightman observed that on occasion, "The feast becomes not a celebration of community but a shamanistic duel between human adversaries . . . the meat is a medium for rivalry between human beings" (1993, 234–35). None of Brightman's Rock Cree examples, however, included this sort of one-sided contest in which only one party must satisfy the eat-all requirement. The old man failed the challenge, his threats came to nothing, and he died when summer came.

"Orphan Boy Proves He Has More Power Than an Old Conjurer"

There was an old man who was pretty bad ([Adam] heard the story). He never went around among the other Indians to camp with them. He camped alone—had a big crossbar in his tent on the door flap. If he was not pleased with the way you closed the door, [he] moved [took action]. When one man "slammed" the door, he made a kosabandjigan [gosaabandjigan, shaking tent] and killed the man that displeased him.

There was an orphan staying with his grandmother. This boy fasted. Those [the other] young fellows were talking about this man, wondered who would be bold enough to go see him to try him. So this young fellow said, "I will go see him." "You better not go—he will kill you." "I would slam the door too," he says. "I don't think he can beat me. Just watch me from a distance. Then you can see I will slam the door—I'll go visit him." He walks right up to the tent and goes into it. When he went in he slammed the door. "Ho, I'll visit my grandfather." The old man burst out laughing. "Sit down, grandson."

The old man was roasting a jackfish. He turned—and started to fuck his wife. The boy started to laugh. This was what he was watching for. When the old man was wiggling his ass the boy put the hot jackfish right on his ass, ran the hot [roasting] stick across. The grandfather turned to one side. "You almost burnt me," he said. The boy sat there laughing and talking. "Now I'm going to leave you, grandfather." "That's right, that's right." The boy went out and gave the door a swing to slam it. The old man laughed: "This is a funny thing that is mocking me." Early in the morning he moved his tent away and put up a conjuring tent.

Then the boy was fixing something where he sat [at home], then he went out with some young fellows. The old woman [his grandmother] did not know what he had done. He had made a small conjuring tent inside the tent. In the evening, he said to his grandmother, "Go and get some of this wet sand." "What are you going to do with it?" The lad said, "I'm going to use it." So she went to the water's edge and got the sand. The old man had killed a lot of men. No one could compare with him.

After sundown, the lad acted funny, as if he was losing his mind. Finally he knew nothing; people could not hold him. He broke loose—away he went. His old grandmother was worrying now: "Too bad this grandson of mine went there [to see] such a wicked old man." He went and came back three times. Then he took the sand and packed the little conjuring tent with wet sand. Now he came to his proper senses, when daylight came early in the morning.

That same night when the old man was shaking his tent, there was not much power. It was getting slower, then stopped altogether. "What's the matter?" said one of his sons. "Are you asleep?" No answer. He lit a birch bark to see what was going on inside the tent—lifted the cover, took the birch bark off. It was just blocked up with sand. The old man was buried in sand, smothered—of course, the tent could not move—he was killed.

Early in the morning the sons came to the camp and said, "Our father is dead." The people said, "It's this orphan that killed him." They gave him lots of presents; they were glad the old bugger had been killed. In that tribe the orphan was the first to be invited to everything after that. He became a great leader. The reason he beat the old man was that the old man had never dreamed of the sand. The boy knew more. ("Illustrates the idea that there is no absolute security; someone new may arise to overthrow established reputation"—AIH.)

Young Man Overcomes an Old Man Who Bewitched Him

There was another old man—wicked, much the same, always looking for trouble. If you didn't watch what you say he might think you were talking about him and get mad. A young lad was staying with his father. The old man for some reason got mad at the lad and moved his camp in the morning. The lad at night got crazy—ran in and out—people could not hold him. He started to bleed from the mouth. At daylight, the old man [his father] said to his son now, "You know that old fellow is very wicked; you should have been careful." The young man could not move. He said to his father, "Go up in the bush—among those flat rocks—there's a boulder. The father started out. He found a boulder on a flat rock—a good size. The lad said, "Did you find it?" "Yes, I found a big one." "Take me over there," the lad said—so he went with his father. The young lad filled his pipe and smoked. He walks around the boulder—it gets smaller. Walks a second time—it gets still smaller. The third and fourth time—it's very, very small now. He picks it up; took it back to the tent, put it near his pillow. The second night, he started to get crazy again—out and in. He said to his father, "I am in my senses now. Spread out something in front of me and put the stone on it." [Then he got] crazy again—grabbed it, and away he went.

In [the old man's] conjuring tent a crack was heard. The tent stood still—no sound. "What is up?" [the people said]. "Are you asleep?" No answer. They lifted the covering. They saw something inside—opened it all up. There was a big boulder, as big as the conjuring tent—filled it right up. They tried to roll the big boulder off, but they could hardly find the old man. All that was left was hair on the boulder, smashed right up. The old man was beaten. The young fellow got better. He turned out to be a great man—everyone looked on him as a big boss—all felt good now.

"We Are Only Playing": An Old Man's Magic Tricks

There was an old man and a young man. The old man showed the young man some of the things he could do.

The old man walked out of the wigwam and said to the young man, "Stand outside here and hold this door. After you stand there awhile go back in again." The young man held the door closed a little while; then he went into the wigwam. When he got inside he found the old man who had gone outside ahead of him sitting inside. The old man said, "Did you see me come in?" The young man did not answer. The old man said, "When you turned and came in, that's when I came by you. Watch closely; I'll do it again." So the old man went out again. The young man followed him. He looked around but could not see him anywhere. He turned around and walked back into the wigwam. There was the old fellow sitting there. He did it four times but the young man could not catch on to how he did it.

The old man handed him a knife. "Go and throw this knife away somewhere." So the young man went out and threw it away. Then he came back in again. "Did you throw that knife away?" "Yes," the fellow replied. "You never threw it away. You have it," the old man said. "No, I threw it away," the young man replied. "No, you have it." "No, I threw it as far as I could." "Take a look at your hip," said the old man. The young man put his hand on his hip and the knife was there. "I told you, you did not throw it away," the old man said. "Try it again." So the young man went outside the wigwam farther than he had before and threw it away. Then he came back. "Did you really throw it away this time?" the old man asked. "Sure." "Are you positive?" "Yes." "Let's see now. Move that foot (pointing) and we will see if you did." The young man moved his foot. There was the knife. He was standing on it. "I told you it was not thrown away," the old man said. "You were trying to hide it." "No," said the young fellow. "I threw it as far as I could."

The old man handed him a flint. "Go and throw this away," he said. After the young man had gone out and come in again, he said, "Did you throw it away?" "Yes, I did." "No, you never did, you have it." "No, I threw it away," said the young man. "You want to keep it for yourself. That is why you have put it where it is," said the old man. "No, I did as you said," replied the young man. "No, you never did." "Yes, I did." "Well, then," said the old man, "look in your tobacco bag." The young man looked. The flint was there. "Try once more," said the old man. "Throw it as far as you can." So the young man went out and threw the flint as far as he could. Then he came in. "Did you throw it away?" asked the old man. "Yes, a long way." "No you didn't. You took it on the sly," the old man said. "No, I never took it." "Let's see," said the old man. "Untie your moccasin. I think you hid it there so I would not know where it was." The young man untied his moccasin, took it off, and the flint was inside. "Ah, you could not throw it away," said the old man. "You better hand it back to me now." So the young man gave the flint back to him.

This old man went on trying this young man in a lot of different ways. He said, "Take my pipe and put it outside." So the young man took his pipe outside. When he came in the old man was smoking his pipe, He looked carefully. It looked exactly like the pipe he had just put outside. "Go outside and get the pipe you put outside," said the old man. The young man went out and found the pipe was gone. The old man did this twice but the young man could not find out how he did it.

Finally the old man said, "That's all I'm going to do." Then the young man took off his coat and gave it to the old man. He also gave him some tobacco so that nothing would happen to himself, his wife, and his children. The old man said, "I don't think I'll take what you are giving me because we are only playing." ("I.e., it was not a real magical contest in power"—AIH). "Perhaps you will freeze if I take the only coat you have." But the young man forced the old man to take the coat. Everybody was scared of this old man.

Context

The theme of older men whose threats and magic powers pose serious dangers to others is common in Ojibwe and Cree stories (for more examples, see Brown 2006b). The fact of their having lived a long time while escaping sickness or other penalties for their misdeeds was a sign of their accumulated powers and their ability to defeat any challengers. As Ruth Landes wrote, "A sorcerer was the Ojibwa ideal strong man, defining and holding at bay the terrible forces of existence, manito and human. His skills were inseparable from his alarming personality . . . jealous, greedy, bullying, and extremely ambitious" (1968, 59).

The stories also highlight a second theme—that of intergenerational competition and conflict. The first two old men are challenged, insulted, and defeated by young males; an orphan who had just fasted successfully, and a "young lad" staying with his father. An orphan could have unsuspected powers, according to Cree storyteller Louis Bird, because he lacked love, and was lonely and "in a state of fear"—needing strong dreams for help (Bird 2005, 125; see also "A Windigo's Head . . . and an Orphan Boy's Cure," pt. 10). Hallowell noted the high risks the two youths took; they could not measure the old men's power. "But in such matters it is not possible to be wise before the event. One has to risk defeat in attempting to achieve the ends desired" (2010, 285). The lads succeeded in bringing violent shamanic death to the old men and received much acclaim. The paths they followed thereafter are unstated; we may wonder if they in turn became strong medicine men with "alarming personalities," continuing the cycle of male shamanic violence in their own generations. In the last story, the old man was "only playing," but his magical trickery forestalled any chance that the young man would challenge him. Finally the youth felt compelled to oblige the old man to accept his gifts, as only by that act did he feel that he and his family could deflect the man from using his powers to harm them.

Another theme is one of social isolation. These old men, being both aggressive and feared by others, lived in relative solitude. They might have wives, but no children were living with them. Visitors were played with or not welcomed, and young people were warned to keep away. When Pazagwigabau came down to Berens River in the 1870s, William Berens, then a boy, was warned by his father to keep away from that camp.

PART 9

Starvation Threatened and Real

Naamiwan and His Brothers Threatened by Hunger

In the first part of the winter [troubles began, one time]. The cause—men talking; there was some misunderstanding—insult. One was a Norway House man—the bad one.

In the first part of the winter everything went well. Then those hunters, when they were tracking, the animals all ran away—they could not see them. They went down to a lake to catch some fish, angling, caught a few but not many. They had not moved camp far when they saw something—a wolf. They used to hang snowshoes near the water's edge—the wolf was after them to eat the babiche [sinew netting]. They even mixed partridge shit with it [the fish] to keep them alive—they were so starving (Naamiwan and Otcimazo [Ojimaazo]). One was married already—Otcimazo.

Then they split camps. Naamiwan went one way—Otcimazo the other. Naamiwan went to look for Tomi and Old Moose [nickname for Bizhiw, Lynx]—went towards Deer Lake. He had lots of food on that side. Naamiwan just about reached there. They cooked the blood soup and animal fat to start with. Just like sick people. Not very long after, they got their strength back.

Otcimazo went the wrong way—he was the one that was the focus of trouble. He was a pretty good man. Now he was at a point—told his family to go ahead—he stayed there hid, to take a look at the wolf that was following. The wolf was bigger than the ordinary kind. He shot the wolf but did not kill him. Next morning when he moved camp again, he sent his children ahead—he quit moving—nothing to eat for several days now. There was a girl and a boy. When they came to the mouth of the river, they saw a band of deer [caribou] there. They told their father. As soon as the old man came along, the deer began to run off at full gallop. He went after them. Just when they reached the shore and tried to climb up a little hill, he saw something black—a deer bleeding from the back of his neck. Pagak [Baagak] was the one that did this (he used him). Now his children had something to eat. I can't say whether he killed the wolf or not. [Pagak was a skeleton being who was sometimes heard in the bush or seen as a flying skeleton. He caused fright, but he could also be a helpful dream visitor (Berens 2009, 100).]

Otcimazo killed two deer again shortly afterward—three again—now he had lots of meat. Went off again—killed five, then quit for a while. After he got his strength back, he was working hard to kill all he could—that's the way the Indians tried to starve one another. People did not know for a while whether he was alive or dead—they lost track of him. Many thought he had starved. Then his eldest brother, the one called Moose, went towards K'tcibanga [Stout Lake] because he had lots of grub for his family. Naamiwan and Tomi went to look for Otcimazo. When they struck his trail and followed it, they knew then that he was alive. When they got to his camp, they found he had loads of meat. But Moose did not know this; he heard Otcimazo was starving, moving on.

My father [Owl] was at Eagle Lake that time—his hunting ground. Moose came all the way over from K'tcibanga to Eagle Lake to see my father and took him to his own camp. He did not expect to see his brother Otcimazo—[he was feeling] just like a sick man. After my father got there, Moose gave him three traps, made a sweat bath, and told my father to go in to try to find out whether Otcimazo was alive or dead. My father beat the drum and sang four nights. Sometimes he quit for a while, then sat thinking and began again. After four nights this Moose made another sweat bath. My father sang inside again. "Now my son," he said, "I know you are thinking a lot about your brother. You will see him yet. I can see him; he is living. You will see him and all his family.

Try to believe what I am telling you." Moose felt easier in his mind. In the spring of the year already—duck hunting, deer; Moose helped my father a lot. My father had left his canoe at Eagle Lake. Moose said, "Don't you hurry to leave—I'll take you over to where your canoes are lying when open water comes." (Everyone liked my father.) Moose gave us pounded meat and fat and the ribs of the deer and the brisket—dried—gave us that for the road.

My father asked the men at Pauingassi when we got there whether they had heard about Otcimazo. "Yes, he is living," they said. So the news spread out. Then Moose came down to Pauingassi to see his brother and my father. The latter said, "I've told you the truth—I know you were scared—worrying a lot." Moose was well pleased. He said, "When are you going to [Little] Grand Rapids?" "Just when the leaves are full grown, I will be going." And the Pauingassi men came down and camped just where I am camping now—a big cabandawan [zhaabandawaan, long lodge]. Zhenawaakoshkang was here already. We came along with Moose (from Eagle Lake, via Pauingassi). Otcimazo came here and stayed for the summer.

It's a bad thing when people try to starve one another. Not an easy death. Lots of people will do things like that for almost nothing—if you even brag a little, or just to try you out—to see what you can stand. [Even] teasing may lead to trouble—may make one a little ashamed, or make a person suffer a little.

Context

The "bad one," in the hunters' minds, was probably Tapastanum, the most powerful medicine man in the Norway House area (Lindsay 2012). The men linked their near starvation to presumed sorcery; the ominous appearance of a large wolf was a sign that the bad one was the cause of their hardships, trying to starve them out.

Naamiwan and Otcimazo were half-brothers, sons of Zhenawaakosh-kang. As Naamiwan was not yet married and his first child was born "before 1877" (Butikofer 2009, pt. II.3, 194), this episode probably dates from before the mid-1870s. Hallowell spelled Otcimazo in this text with an initial *A*, but with *O* in his Moose sib genealogy. Butikofer listed him as the second child of Zhenawaakoshkang and Emikwaan (pt. II.3, 156); he died in 1909. Tomi was Taami or Thomas Owen, another half-brother. Butikofer found that HBC records of the time referred to Zhenawaakoshkang's eldest son, Bizhiw, as "Moose" or "Old Moose."

Winter Starving—Sorcery and Bear-Walking

Long ago the Indians were drinking. One Indian, he threatened another fellow with starvation (a man will say anything when drunk). "Expect me this winter—The poles of your wigwam will all be white frost on top." He told him the moon—mid winter—February when it is half gone. "That is the time you will freeze to death (in your own tent)." This man, he prepared himself—gathered all kinds of food—oil, grease etc. So he had lots of grub. In the beginning of fall, he started to hunt. When January began, he could hardly catch anything—it seemed as if the animals had disappeared. He made one of those wooden tents where he expected to stay for the winter. He could not kill anything now, so he had to start to use the grub he had prepared in summer and fall. Of course in the old days there were no sacks. He kept things in birch bark vessels. He was well stocked. He would be all right as long as his grub lasted. The time was coming closer.

When the time came, he made no fire. Of course he had water. He did not make a fire for several nights. He knew that the man (his enemy) would be coming. As he lay under his blanket, he kept his gun by his side. He heard something outside. It was snowing that night. Even the tent poles were covered with snow. It sounded as if someone was going around his tent. He heard a man's voice outside. It was a bear going around. Right in the door he spoke—with a man's voice because he was made that way. He said, "Ah, quite a while ago this fellow died."

The man took up his gun; the snow on top of the door was fooling [the bear]. The door began to lift and the bear put his nose into the tent. He was coming into the tent to take a certain part of the person—(the witch has a box—keeps a part [of each victim]—an eye, a tip of tongue, etc.). The man shot him between the eyes as he was coming. He heard the voice of the man now. He ran out after the bear. It dropped every now and then. He killed that bear and made a fire in his tent. Everything was all right now. He killed moose, bear, rabbits, fish, anything he wanted. So he saved himself because he knew what to do. The other man died. These two men were not very old either. The other man was sitting in his tent; he just fell back and blood came from his mouth and his nose. He had his family with him.

The man's father-in-law had wanted him to stay with him, but he did not want them [his wife's family] to get into trouble, so he went by himself. His father-in-law sent his sons (brothers-in-law) to look for him. They found him all right—did not expect to find him alive. The news spread all over that the witch had died. It all started because, when they fought while drunk, the witch was licked when he tried to grab a knife to stab the hunter. So then he threatened the man with sorcery. He failed both ways.

Starvation and Magic: Wicked Old Man Destroyed by Midwinter Lightning

There was one old man long ago. (Version 2: "not long ago. All the people were at the mouth [of the Berens River]. In the fall when hunting season begins everybody used to come up this way. One old man was a bad one.") This old man used to stay in one place. . . . This old man [Amo, Bee] stayed at the place; everyone that passed was supposed to give the old man firewater—or else he killed them. So many used to die out of this place. One fellow passed by, going to hunt. The wicked old man said to the stranger, "We will spend the night together and have a good smoke together." Now the two old men had a drink together. The other old man was a good doctor (version 2: "a great doctor, helping people"). The wicked old man (Amo, the wicked one) said, "I heard about you—people talking about you, you are very strong." Amo kept on talking; G.B. [Grey (Cloth) Balls, a small fellow] said nothing, taking it all in. G.B. then had to leave—went to another tent. Amo followed him; he said to G.B., "Did you hear me? People are talking about you like manitu" (version 2: "mandauwizi [maandaawizi], one is endowed with extraordinary power"). He took him by the hair and threw him over. G.B. said, "Time for you to leave me alone; you are only like an old cunt anyway." [He was] mad, could stand no more.

His sons took him away to another tent; they did not want a quarrel. Amo followed. "You watch out for me this winter," Amo said. "I am going to visit you. About mid-moon in January; that is the time. You will see the clouds. I'll be that tall." "Yes," said G.B. "Try to speak the truth. You'll bring your life to me when you visit me." [Citing this incident in a typescript, Hallowell named G.B. as Grey Balls (n.d., "Aggression"); in another handwritten version of the story, he used "grey cloth balls" and gave the Ojibwe name as "cibingwekinweciu" (Roulette: jiibiingweginiahiw, "winking testicle"). Hallowell observed that "old cunt" was "the worst verbal insult in the vocabulary of the Saulteaux" (n.d., "Aggression," 4–5).]

[In January] G.B. could not get any grub—he was that starving, eating whiskeyjack [gray jay]. One morning he said to one of his sons, "You go up to that river—go on the north side, kind of a sandy bank—you go look there." So the young man went there—not far. He found a lump like a snow bank—knew there was a bear's den there. He killed it. In winter a bear is very fat. After using the bear meat, the time is coming close. (Version 2: "They were hungry again—coming close to March".) G.B. told his son where to go again—said, "Go in that direction (pointing with his lips), not very far. (Version 2: "I see three tracks—seems to me I see the end of this trail"). Moose—three of them. He killed them and hauled the meat, had something to eat.

The time is coming now—Amo is coming. G.B. can hear something—can see fire, something like a moon—two days—sticking out way above the trees because Amo said he would reach the clouds—that tall. G.B. was not a large man. So he went [to another camp] with his wife and family four nights. You can feel it now—every step Amo made was like the earth was moving. (Version 2: "The fourth night he moved camp to where he was going to fight. Everybody scared.") In the morning the old man [G.B.] was still there in bed covered up. One of his sons said [to him], "That's what I told you—not to mock that old man—look at what we see now." G.B. was still lying down. It was a fine day.

Finally G.B. threw his blanket off his face and said, "I guess Amo is pretty close to our last camp by this time." He got up, put on his moccasins, took a piece of string, and tied himself up. He spoke to his son, took a little axe, an old fashioned one, after he got out: "As soon as I get started, look up; see if you can see a little cloud over there." The son did so and saw the cloud. Soon the cloud spread out as the old man was walking. Now thunder was heard. Just like midsummer the way you hear the thunder—sometimes four streaks of lightning there (version 2: "[it went] into this monster. Did not take long to finish him"). It was not long before pinesi [binesi, thunderbird] disappeared—(mind you, in January). It turns into a fine day again, can see a little bluish smoke spreading out in the air. G.B. went back to his own tent. "Amo has been killed," he said. This Amo—just as if he had been split by lightning. G.B. told his sons to go and see this windigo. The sons were afraid to go. (Version 2: "The body showed signs all over where it had been split with lightning.") G.B. took his axe from his belt now. After he put the axe away, everything was over.

After the hunting was over, in spring [they went downriver]. G.B. keeping behind, all the other Indians going ahead. When he got to the mouth of Berens River—the Hudson's Bay post when Indians used to camp long ago, he saw something there, a red looking thing—saw a grave—birch bark—that was Amo's grave. Amo's sons were there too. G.B. pretended he did not know. Soon as he got out from his canoe, he called out, "Cook something, Amo. Amo, you are pretty slow this time, not coming down to meet us." (Version 2: "Why didn't Amo come down. He used to come when there were strangers; why didn't he come? The sons said nothing.") Amo's son said, "I been talking lots of times to my father about what he has been doing."

Now then after that, lots of Indians were glad of this—more free-like. A lot of those people gave clothing to G.B.—shirts, etc., because they were thanking him for saving people's lives. He even got some firewater too. My father (Owl) was very young when this happened [ca. 1820s?].

Hunger Defeated: A Fight with a Monster Man and Giant Dog

There was a man long ago who was getting short of food—starving. He was using a hook—angling but could not catch any fish. When he was angling, even his hook and bait was covered with ice under the water. Finally he was getting weak from starvation. So he and his wife went out on the lake—a stormy day; they could scarcely see anything. After they struck out on the lake, they saw someone coming along, walking towards them on the ice. The woman said, "What will we do now? Look at what is coming." (This thing had been sent by somebody of course—someone trying to starve him out.)

The man filled up his pipe, turned it all around. The man approaching on the ice had a big dog along with him (not the kind we have). Almost the size of a year-old colt. The woman said to her husband, "What will we do now?" The man said, "I'm not able to fight the two at one time." The woman said to her husband, "I'll try to fight the dog and you can fight this (monster) man." The woman started to fight the dog while her husband took on the other one. When the fight started, the ice that was thick could be heard cracking every once in a while.

It did not take very long till the woman killed the dog; the man was still fighting. After she killed the dog, she helped her husband to kill the monster. (Of course it was the pawaganak that were doing the real fighting.) The monster was killed too. A woman sometimes is greater than a man in magic power; she may have more pawaganak than her husband. When night came, you could hear a lot of noise—pawaganak feasting on that monster. Mikinaak gets the liver, Pagak the head. Everything a man dreams of participates in the feast.

This fellow had tried hard to kill something but failed. After this, he killed everything—beaver, atik, etc. Sometimes [such an attack] is done just to find out how strong a man is—not because he deserves it.

[A second manuscript version of this story refers to the monster man as a windigo, the killing of which saved the man's life (Hallowell, n.d., "Myths and Tales"). However, the man died soon afterwards; "all his power went with the pawaganak he used."]

Magical Starving of a Thief

A man might set traps for beaver that did not really belong to him, on another man's hunting ground. The thief could not catch this animal or any other, all of a sudden. For a long time he could not kill anything. Even the bed of poplar leaves [around a trap] the beaver will eat, but the trap remains untouched. Because the man that owned this beaver was not pleased, he was using magic power to starve the thief out. First thing [the thief] knew, one of his children got sick—the kid died.

This man was now the one using his power—wanted [the thief] to look out. Sometimes when [the thief] had his traps under water he even caught a whiskeyjack—teasing him like that to let him know, or a mouse might be caught. The whole winter he was punished this way, could not kill any kind of fur. If he caught anything it might be a squirrel or a rabbit, not much good to him. Spring came, hunting over, he killed the fish all right. But when he was hunting after deer he tracked them all right but had no chance to see them, could not get near enough. Sometimes he heard something behind him when he was tracking deer. That's the way one case turned out.

(William Berens: "[Someone might] make a weapon out of a beaver tooth if a man has stolen beaver and project it. If [the thief] does not get it out he will die—a warning.")

[A second story about beaver theft cited sickness and death as penalty, rather than starvation.] "Kitam and his brother found a beaver. The man who owned this beaver had set traps already—a fellow from Lac Seul. Kitam took them out of the water and threw them to one side, and put his own traps in their place. The Lac Seul fellow, of course, expected to get something when he got there. He found his traps [thrown] all over. He got mad. It was the first part of winter when this happened. In the spring both Kitam and his brother fell sick. In [the time of] open water both of them died. They were punished." Gary Butikofer's research identified Kitam and his brother as sons of John Turtle of Pikangikum; they both died around 1928–29 (pers. comm., 2017).

Context

The preceding stories have a common theme: winter situations in which people experienced hunger or suffering because hostile beings, human or sometimes monstrous, came after them, or because of their offences against others. As Adam said, "It's a bad thing when people try to starve one another. Not an easy death." Naamiwan and his brothers survived the threat of a "bad one," but only after Otcimazo suffered great hardship until saved by the intervention of Pagak, who must have been one of his pawaganak. In "Winter Starving" and "Starvation and Magic," sorcerers initiated a round of insults and threatened their victims with hunger and death in midwinter. The latter prepared themselves and took extensive precautions. One man tricked and shot the "bear-walker" when he came to collect body parts from his victim, whom he presumed to be dead. The other had pinesi (thunder) as a helper and was able to destroy his attacker with lightning—in January.

In "Hunger Defeated" a starving man and wife confronted a monstrous man and his huge dog, "sent by somebody of course." In a great fight both the man and woman managed to kill the monsters; "Of course it was the pawaganak that were doing the real fighting." Here, as in his story "Windigos Killed by Two Women" (pt. 10), Adam highlighted women's often unsuspected powers: "A woman sometimes is greater than a man in magic power; she may have more pawaganak than her husband.") At night the pawaganak came to feast on the monster's body, just as they would feed on windigos that they killed (see Adam's stories in part 10). But these stories of starving did not mention windigos except once in one version of this story, even though among the Cree and in other Algonquian stories, windigo monsters are commonly linked with starvation.

The stories of the hunter who took strong magical measures against a man who tried to trap on his beaver grounds, and the brothers who scattered another man's beaver traps, teach that such acts may have grave consequences. The intruder's child died and he almost starved; he may finally have survived, but he suffered severely for trespassing and interference with another man's claims to a particular beaver locale. The brothers' early deaths were seen as the penalty for their destructive behavior. Adam's stories were concrete and personal; some told of ways that individuals coped with difficult situations; others warned against offensive behavior, and all offered implicit advice for survival and achieving pimadaziwin (bimaadiziwin), "life in the fullest sense" (Hallowell 2010, 559–61).

Starvation Killing of an Adopted Boy

There was a man and wife who had children of their own and an adopted boy. They were always good to him, gave him a little more grub than the rest. But the other children were getting thinner all the time, so weak that some of them quit playing. All they could do was collect a few sticks and keep the fire going. The man was too weak to go out and kill anything. The woman seemed to be in better shape than the man who had been on the go from morning to night. They saw nothing but death facing them.

[The man] talked over with his wife the possibility of killing the adopted boy. He was the fattest. The boy started to cry (they started to examine him). The man hit him with an axe from the rear on the head. They took one leg first and cooked it. When they gave the meat to the children, they vomited. But the old people held it and it tasted good. Finally the kids managed to eat, little by little.

There was another camp not very far away. Two nights after this happened, a visitor; he pretty nearly came in time to save the boy's life. The man was sorry for what he did. The visitor gave them some food, some meat, and made periodic visits. The children gained strength, and the man too. When the kids started to eat deer's meat they began to vomit again (perhaps from overeating). This visitor helped them quite a while. When spring began, he left them alone—the hunter was now able to fend for himself. The reason the kids threw up when they got animal meat was because the human meat was not quite "clear" in their stomachs.

The man did not get sick because he told what had happened. He did not try to make a secret of it or go on with it; [he was] also under pressure of starvation. No magic here or anything of that sort.

A Man Rescues His Father-in-Law from Starvation

My father used to tell this story. There was an old man who had a son-in-law. The son-in-law and family moved to their hunting ground [in winter]. He left his father-in-law behind—moved camp pretty near every other night. Finally he thought of his father-in-law—wonders how he is getting along. He spoke to his wife: "I wonder whether your brothers have managed to kill anything?" "Don't know." (This fellow had gotten lots of meat.) "I guess I'll go and find out."

When he approached the camp, he could see no tracks of his

brothers-in-law. When he came to the water hole—it was not opened lately. He could see a little smoke from the wigwam. He found his father-in-law's family all lying down. His father-in-law says, "We are starving to death." They had given up—just picking up branches to keep a fire going; mostly unable to move. The man had a day's rations with him—he gave them a little, and went to his own camp to get frozen blood for them. He went back to them—very late, made a fire, got a big pot of water, and put this blood in it and a little grease. After he cooked, it turned into soup—thick, and he gave them a little to eat. So he left the blood soup with them and went home again, brought a whole sled-load of dried meat. He kept them on blood soup for four days. Soon as they were able to stand up on their feet and had some strength, he gave them meat, chopped fine and boiled, bouillon and all. When they got over this, he gave them all the help he could. After they were able to manage for themselves, he went back to his hunting ground. He had lots of grub and kept giving it to his father-in-law—beaver and all kinds of food. Later on, the brothers-in-law were able to hunt for themselves.

Context

The above two stories are the only ones in this series that talk about what might be called secular starvation—that is, hunger that was not attributed to some malignant or offended being, human or non-human. The desperate act of the adopted boy's family was accepted as understandable by the man who came to their rescue and evidently by others who heard their story. Because the father did not conceal the deed, they suffered no penalty such as sickness or death; also, as Hallowell noted in a brief published account, "they developed no cannibalistic proclivities" themselves (1963, 302). No one defined this episode as involving windigo cannibalism.

The second story also has a rescue element, as a son-in-law goes off to check on the welfare of his wife's father and her brothers and tides them over through their hard times. These episodes, like others involving starvation, took place in winter, a time when hungry, cannibalistic windigos might have been expected to appear, whether as monsters or as transformed human beings. But Adam's stories of hunger did not draw a firm link between windigo manifestations and famine. Further, these victims of famine, unlike victims of windigo cannibals, survived their suffering, whether by means of careful planning, mental and magical powers, the help of their pawaganak, the aid of rescuers, or a combination of these.

PART 10

Encounters and Contests
with Windigos

Zhenawaakoshkang Pursued by Windigos, Saved by Pawaganak

Zhenawaakoshkang was hunting atik [caribou] in summer. He tracked
some kind of a person—a man. He came to a muskeg—shady place.
He saw this person had been digging down next to the ice (a trench;
some parts of muskeg never thaw). The old man wondered what kind
of thing would make this. He went to another muskeg where the track
led. He knew already this is windigo—two of them—one man and
one woman. The old man tried to sneak around to one side; did not
want his presence known. But the windigos knew him already. They
followed him and he ran for his life. Then his pawaganak told him,
"Two are following you." Now when he was running, wondering what
would happen, he thinks of all the pawaganak—which is the best to
help him. The windigos were heading him off to where his canoe was.
He had his family there.

When he reached there, his pawaganak were fighting already. Both
windigos were killed. The old man saw the female. She was lying on
her back. He saw her cunt—scales all over, so dry. The man was lying
the same way. His cock was like a dry hide—so hard. He did not look at
them very long. On the feet side and [by the] head he saw something
lying—some kind of an animal. On the feet side there was a big wolf
sitting, and a wolverine on the head side. At the feet of the female was

a raccoon, and a badger on the head side (the big ones, not the ordinary kind), guarding the corpses so they could not get up (come to life).

When night came, all the pawaganak came and shared them up. The old man, when he was sitting, something dropped in front of him. He heard a voice: "That's yours." He told him he did not want it. His wife said, "You better not keep it; it might fall on [harm] our children. He told the pawaganak he did not want anything. A second time his wife said not to take it (a hand and part of an arm). ("To eat part of a windigo is equivalent to an act of cannibalism, and cannibalism in turn is reputed to bring sickness or misfortune on oneself or one's children"—AIH footnote, "Myths and Tales" manuscript).

Owl Saves His Brother from a Windigo

Once my father saved his brother from a windigo. My father was camping at Long Lake and his brother was camping on Poplar River. My father's brother was so scared that he was going to give himself up. He took one of his children in his arms and bowed his head. My father knew what was happening. He got all his pawaganak together—just like an army—and there was a terrible fight. The earth was shaking when the fight was on. When it started the noise was so terrible that my grandmother [Pasho] was the only one that did not fall asleep (faint) at the awful sound.

My father had dreamed of Wemtigozi [wemitigoozhi]. ("A name given to white men, although not the literal meaning"—AIH.) This pawagan had a weapon something like a sword. It was sharp on two edges and had a handle. When Wemtigozi entered the fight he said to the others, "What are you doing? You should have killed him long ago." He climbed up on the clouds and cut off the head of the windigo, just as clean as if you split a potato. The body of the windigo still went staggering around after he had lost his head. The monster's shouts were so loud that his voice was heard at Deer Lake. ("A distance of some miles from Long Lake where the fight is reputed to have taken place"—AIH.) This woman I got now [Aanii], her father [Zhenawaa-koshkang] was living at Deer Lake. He heard the noise of the fight and got ready to meet the windigo. He started in this direction. But one of his pawaganak said to him, "It is not close, that sound you hear. That one is killed. You have heard his last shout." (Later during the same summer he told my father this.)

After the windigo was killed my father was dizzy and confused from the fight and the terrible noise. He did not know in which direction to go home. My grandmother went out looking for him. He had a rattle in his hand and my grandmother heard this as he went staggering around trying to find his way. She called to him. When he came to our wigwam the door was too small for him. He was that big. (The windigo almost reached the clouds.)

When spring came my father learned that the thing he had fought was made out of a dream. It was sent by a Norway House man against my father and his brother. It might have been Tepastenam [Tapastanum] or his brother. ("A Norway House man famous all over this part of the country for his magical powers. I had met his sons [in 1930] and the narrator knew this"—AIH.)

[This vivid story, which Adam must have heard in his boyhood, is preserved in Hallowell's manuscript "Myths and Tales" (n.d.). Adam's father's brother was Gaa-zhaaboowiyaazid or Kaashaapowiiyaasit, who died before 1875, according to Butikofer (2009, pt. II,1, 56–57; pt. II.3, 293); see afterword for more details. On Tapastanum see Lindsay (2012).]

Owl and Zhenawaakoshkang Drive One Away

Otcibamasis [Owl] was once going to use a gun—he had an axe too. He remembered to hang onto the axe and let the gun go. An axe is the proper thing to use (against a windigo)—no confidence in gun. He went along with Zhenawaakoshkang one time; they came close enough to reach the windigo with the axe. (They found him sitting on a bare rock. Just as my father was about to strike him with an axe the windigo ran away.) He ran away. When he saw this, my father said, "The windigo is running away." Zhenawaakoshkang said, "You will make him mad; he'll kill us all now." Zhenawaakoshkang is the only one Otcibamasis ever took along; others did not have the heart. If some old people could listen now they would not deny it, because they heard it themselves. [A typescript of this story is in Hallowell's "Myths and Tales" (n.d., no. 12d); details from this version are added in parentheses.]

Old Man Escapes from Cannibal by Becoming an Otter

My uncle (Flatstone?—AIH) told me about an old man who was out shooting ducks. He lay down on his back by the waterside to sleep. He had barely closed his eyes when he felt as if someone was breathing on his face. He opened his eyes just a little bit to see what was happening. There was a windigo bending over him like this (demonstrated). The old man thought of an otter he had dreamed of when he was a boy. As quick as a flash he slid between the windigo's legs, down the rock and into the water. He did not come up until he was far away from the shore. He saw the windigo looking into the water for him. It was a narrow escape.

Adam Stalked by a Windigo

Myself at one time in the spring of the year, I was hunting [musk]rats. Only the river was open—not the lake. I took the canoe and went out in the open streak; there was ice in the river close to shore. When it was getting dark and I could shoot no more, I made a fire to cook supper, close to the water's edge. I was pretty scared that time: across the river I could hear someone passing—cracking branches. I went down to the canoe. As soon as I got in, I paddled as hard as I could to get away from this noise. There was a kind of a poplar point as the river got a little bigger. When I got opposite to it, I was paddling quite a piece out. I heard a sound as if something was passing in the air. I saw a big stick thrown out at me, but it did not reach me. I kept on going. I went on to the opposite side of the river. Before I got to that side, he was across the river already—headed me off. I went to the other side. He went back—headed me off again. It was spring and the nights were not long—it was this way the whole night long. I camped right on a high rock.

In the morning I went and set a bear trap. I came back to the river again (the place where he bothered us) late in the evening again. I had to pull the canoe over to a lake. The sun went down before we could strike another open place that night. There was a crack on the ice; I wanted to see how to pull the canoe over. When I went back to camp, I heard him again. I took the canoe out on the lake—big—when I got to the other end it was almost daylight. I heard no more [noise] and made a fire. After this I heard something again. "How am I going to get away from him?" I thought. I was scared. I thought I would go to the other side of the island. I heard something again. I went back to where I left the canoe. As soon as I sat down, he came a little close. I was a little mad now; he had chased me long enough. I said to myself, "the number of my days has been given to me already." I took the axe and I took the gun and went in the direction of the sound. As soon as I got close, he made a break for it. Between the islands there was a place not frozen; he was heading for this. I kept after him. I could hear him on the weak ice. He fell in and yelled. I turned back. I can't say whether he managed to get out or not.

I had killed some ducks and had them in the canoe. I was getting pretty weak. I knew there was a camp close by, so I made for it with my ducks which I intended to share with them. The camp was not there; the people were so scared when they heard the noise that they had moved. I started for Little Grand Rapids then; I left my canoe on the other side. The ice was getting weak but I thought I would try it. I came across to the post, then went back again to the place where I had set the bear trap. When I reached it I could see it had dropped; a bear was in it. I was still a little frightened but there was nothing new. Towards evening, it was calm; I came to the mouth of the lake. I heard someone—could see splashing in the lake. When I was watching, I could see a band of ducks; the moon was shining. I shot the ducks; of course I had the bear too. Then I heard another splash. I shot quite a few ducks before morning. (This was about the second year of Treaty [about 1877].)

I went to the same place later—it was raining that morning. There was a sandy bay in which I thought I would pull in. I saw fresh bear tracks there. I tried to see if he was following the lake shore—put the canoe in now and then. The tracks were still fresh. When I came around a point I saw him—but quite a way off. He was digging. I shot him. I could hear him squeal and saw him turn over and over. I went back to get my canoe. I watched where he struck the bush and told my partner to go there and follow him. I tracked him there—he climbed up a tree, then threw himself down. When I came there, [I saw] a kind of hollow with a covering of branches; that's where he was lying. This was where he had wintered. I shot a second time and killed him. My partner came running. Not quite dead yet; we felt him. I killed a few ducks and we made camp. Back to [Little] Grand Rapids the second day.

Context

Hallowell retold and discussed Adam's windigo story in two different articles. In fall 1938, soon after hearing it, he commented at some length:

> To an outsider the fears of the Berens River Indians . . . appear to be "neurotic," in the sense that they occur in situations where no actual danger threatens. . . . Can we speak, then, of "cultural neuroses" that are characteristic of whole populations? I think not . . . the Berens River Indian is responding to a *real* danger when he flees from a cannibal monster, or murders a human being who is turning into a *windigo*, or when he becomes apprehensive in a certain disease situation . . . the Indians themselves are able to point out plenty of tangible empirical evidence that supports the interpretation of the realities that their culture imposes upon their minds. They are naïve empiricists but not naively irrational. (Hallowell 2010, 240)

Add to that the sensory experiences of anyone who has camped alone at night in frozen northern woods—the cracking of trees, the falling of snowy branches, the breaking and shifting of ice in early spring. In such an environment, persons for whom windigos were real would indeed hear and fear them. Recounting the story in 1951, Hallowell noted that Adam made thirteen references to hearing the windigo; auditory stimuli were very powerful to people who were primed by culture and experience to interpret them in that way (1951, 183). Ojibwe hunters lived in a universe of sound very different from our visually biased or ocularcentric world.

Burning a Shoulder Blade Brings Windigo Attack: Two Cases

1. Away down among the Suckers, they [when practicing scapulimancy] burnt a shoulder blade by mistake (must not be done). On it was a picture

of a person—something like those cards (Rorschach, that I had with me that summer—AIH). The same person whose picture it was came to their camp. They knew it when he was coming near—it was as if the ground was moving. Soon as the windigo came, the fires could not burn—they turned all black, he was so powerful. He was that tall—his head was amongst the clouds. Three Suckers—they went to meet him. They had their pawaganak to do the fighting for them. They barely killed him. One man got sick and died afterwards, a second sickened—just as if the windigo owned them. The other one was not very healthy afterwards (Adam Fiddler).

Same thing might happen—my father [said]—if kids burnt a bone by mistake. My father would then take a rabbit shoulder blade. He would burn it and the windigo would never reach us. My father never got stuck; he always knew what to do. ("The moral of this story was that the narrator's father [Owl] was more powerful than these men. He always knew just what to do and never suffered any ill effects"—AIH footnote, "Myths and Tales" manuscript.)

2. One time there was a young kid, about the size of Joe Alix. He threw a rabbit shoulder blade [in the fire] by mistake, did not know better (it had some kind of a picture burnt out of a human being). This boy's brother was the first to know that something was coming on them in that camp. The people had to move. They tied the boy up to tent poles and left him in the camp. If this monster-windigo reached the camp he would eat the boy and spare the others. The brother was away at the time. He returned and found his brother tied up there. The windigo— every step he made, the earth shook.

When the brother came to the camp where this brother was tied up, he made a kind of a speech. He saw the windigo coming already, higher than the trees. This monster was as high as the clouds, so this fellow started to fight it now. He killed the monster. All different kinds of memengweci [memegwesi, little people] helped him, and Pagak too— came upon him and pressed his body to the ground—memengweci his legs, and of course Mikinaak. This windigo was killed. After the man killed him, he took his brother and followed the trail of the people who had skipped. "What is the reason you did this to my brother?" he said to them. "Did you people know anything at all? How to protect yourselves?" "That's all we know to do," they said. "We could not depend upon our own strength. Everyone in this camp would have been killed if it were not for you." This young man did not like the way his brother had been treated. (The people did not know he was mandauwizi [maandaawizi, endowed with extraordinary power]—he told no one.) Moral is that one had better die than all, and the windigo would eat the one that brought him [i.e., the boy who had burned the shoulder blade].

Context

Adam Fiddler, mentioned in the first case, was well known among the Ojibwe of Deer Lake and Sandy Lake for his strong spiritual powers, which he kept when he turned to Methodism in about 1901. James Stevens described him as "a Sucker clansman who could confront windigo, utilize the shaking tent, issue prophecies, and sing over his drum." In 1917 Fiddler built the first church at Deer Lake (Caribou Lake, as Stevens called it; Fiddler and Stevens 1985, 173, 177). Fiddler was still alive into the 1940s, but Adam Bigmouth made no mention of meeting him.

These two cases find a partial parallel in a Rupert House [Waskaganish] Cree story about a boy who "held the shoulder blade of an animal to the fire [a form of divination that children were forbidden to imitate]. The other child tried to stop him but he persisted anyway." An Atuk (Witiko) came after the children. They hid; otherwise "the Atuc would have killed and eaten them." Their father managed to kill the Atuk that night (Flannery et al. 1981, 66–67).

Scapulimancy, as defined by Frank Speck, is the widespread practice of "scorching an animal's shoulder blade for the purpose of obtaining an answer to a question and for divination of the future" (Speck 1977, 128–29). Speck (ch. 6) discussed at length its use by Naskapi hunters to help guide their pursuit of game by "reading" the cracks and spots that appeared on the scapula when heated. Adam was not the only one to note that mishandling of such bones could draw a windigo attack. Speck wrote that "for children to practice [scapulimancy] would attract a cannibal (*wi'ndigo*)" (1977, 149). Ruth Landes commented on the care taken with animal bones; they "were prevented from falling into the fire lest Windigo cause the scorchings to assume his appearance. This particular scapulimancy was read anxiously" (Landes 1968, 26). When James Bay Cree hunters practiced scapulimancy on caribou shoulder blades they exercised great care; women and children were kept out of sight (Preston 2002, 213). The stories do not explain why the accidental bone burnings would draw a windigo attack but indicate the high seriousness of the matter.

Sickness from Torturing a Windigo

A man [Flatstone] asked my father to help. His daughter was sick. She was spitting blood. A bone was set before him. I was there—Pay? [unidentified] was there too. My father told me to take out his rattle. I put it beside him. I tightened the leather before the fire. He talked for a few minutes, took the rattle and sang. When he was singing, he stopped suddenly. "I can't," he said. He began again—stopped. Said something—told the man she would not get better. "I guess it is your fault." The man did not answer.

[Then Owl asked him], "Did a windigo ever overtake you when you were travelling?" "Yes," said the man. "When he caught me (I was running away), I turned around—I got hold of him. I was stronger than he was. I yelled out for Mikinaak to hold him. When Mikinaak took hold, he did not move. I had nothing to kill him with. What should I use? First thing that came to mind was my knife. I stabbed him on his back—and kept on stabbing him. Now the blood came from his mouth. He did not last long then. I killed him at last. He was suffering a long time before I killed him. He was still moving but I knew he was going to die."

My father said, "Now you have told this, in two days your child will be better." (The kid got better. It was old Flatstone [Nabagaabik] that did it [stabbed the windigo].) "That's why your child is spitting blood. You did not tell the whole thing yet, but I think this will follow your family. Your child will be that way sometimes—now and then—because you did not tell all." It would have been OK if the man [Flatstone] had cut his head straight off—but it was the suffering that was wrong.

[Adam in another telling of this story stated that "old Flatstone's" father [Oshkiniiki] asked Owl to help his son ("my father called Flatstone 'my son'). Flatstone's son was spitting blood, and "blood does not come for nothing." Hallowell, in his brief published account of this episode, wrote of the son's ailment but also mentioned that the daughter was afflicted, seemingly at a different time (1963, 287–88).]

A Windigo's Head, Sickness, and an Orphan Boy's Cure

Long ago in the older days (I never saw this), a man was hunting, camping out. When he was following the trail, he saw someone had struck it—fresh tracks led towards his tent. He knew it was a windigo. He ran, trying to overtake him before he reached the camp. He came to a lake, saw him, then another lake—lost sight of him. At the end of the second lake, he reached the last portage before his camp. He filled his pipe—pointed it, and spoke to pawaganak, and told them to guard his family on the point where his camp was. Then he heard the noise already—the pawaganak were fighting. When he got there the windigo was killed already; they were cutting him up. Mikinaak got the liver; there was not much for anyone to get—there were so many pawaganak. So one of the pawaganak took the head and said, "This is for you." But the man said, "I don't want it"; he would not take it. The pawagan pressed him to take it. So he did—he cut holes in the ears and hung the head on a branch of a tree. After this, he went home—did not think about it.

Then all of a sudden, one of his kids got sick—this young boy is sore in the ear. He died. Another son had the same trouble and died. Four of his children died of the same disease—always the ear. He had one son left. This son got sick. So he asked one of the old men to treat his boy (pagitcigan [bagijigan, made offerings])—the last one. An orphan boy, not quite full grown, came in to where the old people were. This poor kid was an orphan, not quite full grown. He never had a proper place to sleep; he used to sleep in the doorway. Old people were [saying]— "no parents—what's this boy want here?" One old fellow spoke up then, as they were trying to cure the sick boy. He said, "Let's see what he will say. We don't know; perhaps he has had a blessing—an orphan like this."

So the orphan boy came in and was asked [to help]. The old man who wanted him gave his pagitcigan [offering] to the boy. He handed his pipe to him. The boy was not smoking yet, so he pointed the pipe—smoked for the first time—not long. After this he sat quietly for a while. Then he said, "What makes me sick [sit] quietly—is that I feel bad about this other boy—my playmate—I've missed him. That is why I came here. Now when I'm sitting here—just as if I were dreaming—I see something hanging on a tree." It comes to the man's mind now; the boy even named the tree and the side it was hanging on (N, S, E, W). The man was lying on his side as the old people were sitting there listening to the orphan boy. This man spoke up: "I can understand that. One time we had somebody at my camp" (he did not say who). "I had been away—when I came back, I found somebody on my trail and I followed him up. When I came to my camp—there where a point runs out, this monster was killed already— was cut up in pieces. I sat down and the head was brought before me. I threw it to one side—did not want it. I was told I had to keep it. I cut through the ears and hung it there—where you said." The orphan said, "Your boy will be better tomorrow. Tomorrow if I say the right thing [am correct] he will be better."

The next morning the boy was outside already. He got all right—no more sickness, and the rest of the children were never sick again. It was an orphan boy that found out [the problem]; not the old people—[he was] always invited to feasts after that.

("The challenge of youth. The point of this is that the man *should* have eaten the windigo's head—a real one, i.e., made out of a dream—and not hung it up. He disobeyed and did something else. Note that W.B. [William Berens] refers to this kind of a windigo as a '*real*' one as contrasted with a [human] person. Adam's father [Owl] was told to take the ear and a little finger of a windigo by pawaganak, but refused [see sequel to "Sighting a Fearsome Stranger," pt. 1]. But he did not get sick. Pawaganak tell a person what kind of medicine to use"—AIH.)

Windigos Killed by Two Women

[As a prologue to the present story, Hallowell asked Adam about women "using magic power to kill." Adam replied, "A woman *will only protect herself*—will not project magic. The girl in the story could have sent the migis and needles back but she didn't. She had the power all right." The story Adam invoked in his answer was that of the suitor's attempted killing (pt. 7).]

Two men, brothers, went off to set traps; both young married men—one child apiece. The women and children were alone in the camp while their husbands were off. When the brothers were two nights out, they made camp—birch bark—to hunt from there. It had been snowing that night. The younger brother said to his partner in the morning, "I have a queer idea" (thinking of something). He got pretty sure that something was near them. He spoke to his brother: "I'm thinking about our camp—something [about] going to save the women." So the older brother listened: "Well, if you think that way, we'll have to go back."

So they started home again. They came to their first camp and saw that someone had passed—a trail on fresh snow. Big foot marks on the snow—they tracked two persons using walking sticks. They followed the trail back to the [main] camp to see if their wives were OK, running for all they were worth. They came to another lake—could see nothing ahead. They came to the third lake—that is where the tent was, at the other end. They started to walk now. "Poor children," they said. "Guess our wives and children are killed already." When they came to the place where the tent was, they could see smoke coming out, but did not feel safe; they thought the women and children had been killed. Birch bark torn—everything. But a very strange thing: when they came close to the tent, they saw one wife rocking her cradleboard, the other just the same, wives and kids alive ("a very homely touch and an everyday sight in all Indian camps"—AIH). "I wonder how they can live?" they thought. Not far from the tent, they saw two windigos lying. Killed already. The women had been strong enough to kill these monsters—giants—windigos much larger than height of this building ("log house at Little Grand Rapids"—AIH). The elder brother pulled out his axe from his belt and tried to cut one of the windigos: "I would have done this to you if you had killed my kid"—he was mad.

How did these women do this? Even a lot of men could not do that. They could see the marks where the fight was on. This is the only case of women doing such a thing. They must have been strong. Who tended the children while their mothers were fighting? Must have been pawaganak. As soon as the women called out, they came.

They moved the camp then. They heard the pawaganak feasting on the windigos [that night]. The sound of the wind—they could hear laughing, egogwas [Roulette: name of a specific pawagan?] (that's the one that always laughs). Mikinaak—the liver for him.

Our father used to talk of tcig(k)anan [Roulette: Jigaanaan, unknown name]—the old woman; this [she] must have looked after the women when the fight was on. The women did not do this themselves; they must have had a dream when they were young. One [windigo] had a mark at the back of the neck; the other a mark on the forehead—as if a bullet had gone through them. Look how wonderful it was—no one knew what the women could do before this happened. Of course lots of times it was found out that a woman was *much* stronger through dreams than a man. The reason they were so strong was because no one knew what they had dreamed—*everything was secret until the time came when they needed their helper.*

Atsokanak [pawaganak] look upon a windigo as an animal to be killed to eat. After this thing is killed, those people leave the carcass of the windigo there. When it gets dark, one can hear all kinds of noise there. The sound of the wind; one even hears sounds like laughter there— egogwas (that's the one that always laughs). These pawaganak come—so many that when the windigo is shared out each one gets only a small piece. Mikinaak gets the liver. One gets the head. The man that kills him—sometimes his pawagan gives him a part of a nail—but [he] does not take it.

Context and Commentary

The preceding three stories all involve attacks by windigos "made out of a dream," as Hallowell described them. These powerful non-human beings were sent to destroy their victims although the senders were not identified. In all these episodes, the windigos were killed before they could murder and consume the humans they attacked. Hallowell published no articles focused solely on windigos. But sometime in 1938 or 1940 he made some detailed notes based in part on his conversations with Adam:

There are two basic kinds of windigowak that can be differentiated, although these are not distinguished in native terminology—and both are found equally terrifying. On the one hand (I) there is the windigo of what may be termed a superhuman order, and on the other (II), the windigo that is a human being turned cannibal. The extreme form of the superhuman windigo is typified by the statement that such a being can be made out of a dream, i.e., projected into existence by means of sorcery.

In the margin he listed three subsets of (I): A. The pawagan—the eternal windigo. B. The windigo "made in a dream" on some particular occasion and sent to kill some particular person or persons. C. The wandering type of windigo—the windigo "at large." On a following page he noted that the [windigo] pawagan "can make a windigo for you and you can send this cannibal to eat enemies. This is the type that would be conjured against."

In the stories prospective victims who confronted this type of windigo needed to summon their own pawaganak to defeat the attacker. Flatstone called upon Mikinaak, the boss turtle, who held onto the windigo for him. But then Flatstone violated a "rule of engagement" he surely had not thought about; he stabbed the windigo repeatedly, inflicting great suffering, which was to come back on his son and daughter, causing illness that required the ministration of Adam's father, Owl. (Adam assisted his father, giving this story a special first-hand quality.)

Flatstone's act of cruelty triggered a disease sanction, just as could happen when hunters caused unnecessary suffering to animals. Hallowell in fact discussed this case in the context of cruelty to animals, observing that "the breadth of the sanction against cruelty is as wide as it is deep in the Ojibwa ethos" (1963, 286)—and applied even to windigos. And on some level, windigos were like wild animals. As we have seen, Adam told Hallowell, "Atsokanak [pawaganak] look upon a windigo as an animal to be killed to eat." Some years ago Richard Preston drew suggestive parallels between windigos and animals: "Witiko is directly comparable to other non-human carnivores whose food is unwilling. Most, perhaps all, large carnivores are sometimes cannibalistic. Also comparable are owls (for which some Algonkian languages use a root meaning cannibal), dogs, and other creatures who occasionally fight, kill, and eat members of their own species" (Preston 1980, 129). Windigos also usually eat their prey raw like other carnivores; Brightman has discussed how, in this respect as in other ways, they were non-human, without culture (1993, 142–44). Yet as animate beings ("persons" in Hallowell's discourse), they too had rights of a sort.

The man who was given a windigo's head did not battle the windigo himself; his pawaganak did the fighting for him. Then one of them gave him the monster's head—which he was supposed to keep or even consume. Instead he cut holes in its ears and suspended it from a tree branch—a move reminiscent of the Algonquian practice of suspending a bear's skull in a tree (e.g., Berens 2009, 87; Speck 1977, 96, 107). His ignoring of the instructions he was given (and possibly the implied parallel with bear ceremonialism) must have offended the pawagan deeply, for four of the man's children died from ear ailments. It was finally an orphan boy (with the unheralded powers that orphans sometimes possessed) who saved the life of the remaining child by getting the man to confess what he had done with the windigo head.

The story of the women who killed the windigos is the most remarkable of the group. Adam himself told it in a tone of surprise; how could the women have accomplished this feat? They were so strong, he concluded, "because no one knew what they had dreamed—*everything was secret until the time came when they needed their helper.*"

For males, the dream quest was public in that everyone knew when a boy undertook it and had some inkling of its success, even though its content was not revealed. But Hallowell found that no one had any memory of girls being sent out to dream, though one man said it might have been done "long ago." When a girl was sent out alone, it was because of the onset of menstruation; her mother would build her a small tent a short distance from camp and supply her with a little food, water, and a fire (no fasting or ordeal of exposure). Hallowell asked if a girl would dream at that time. The answer was uncertain, but he was assured that "Pawaganak would not come to females in this condition." The corollary was, of course, that human males would also avoid all contact with such girls during their seclusion. Adam put it bluntly: "If any male is crazy enough to go and fuck her when she is there he will not live long."

Hallowell's follow-up question was whether girls might go off to dream at other times. In response, William Berens lightly made the suggestion "that if he were around and knew girls were out he might get after them." On recording this comment, Hallowell wrote, "Seriously, it may be that girls were not sent because of this possibility"—the risk of being bothered by males in the bush. Later, he concluded: "Although women also had "dream visitors" . . . any 'blessings' they received had only a personal significance." As in Adam's story "Windigos Killed by Two Women," the women's dreams conferred protection against a windigo attack, a blessing that was invoked when needed. In contrast, a male's relations with his pawaganak "determined a great deal of his destiny as an individual . . . and a few acquired exceptional skills that carried the greatest prestige in Ojibwa society. To a man, relations with other than human persons were an enduring source of his inner security" (Hallowell 1992, 88). Women did not need the help of pawaganak most of the time—until harassed or threatened by males, human or non-human. Yet men also felt uncertain and insecure about women's powers. As Adam said, after telling about the women windigo killers, "A young woman is the worst—she keeps what she has in secret—you don't know what she has."

PART 11

Human Beings Made into Windigos

Errant Windigo Kills Old Man

Two families, in separate tents, were getting short of food. It started to snow "that night"—("stated as before bed time"—AIH). One of the old men heard a voice outside the door. . . . "You are invited to a feast." This old man had two sons—the other old man, the same. The first old man took his "fire bag" and his pan, and went out. The tents were not far apart, but the young men in the other tent could not hear the voice of their father in the [purported] ceremonial feast.

"What's the old man doing?"—the second old man spoke up. "How can we put up a feast when we are all starving and it's snowing?" So one young man took a birch bark, twisted and lighted it, and went out to see where the old man was. He found tracks of his father, his medicine bag and pan on the trail, and tracks of another person—the person who had killed him—the windigo. He got mad. One fellow took his gun, the other his axe. The old man and his sons from the other tent went along. (What had happened was the old man had been choked right outside—he could not yell.)

They did not go far and saw a big fire; that's where the cannibal was. He split the old man, made a stage, and roasted him, turned him every once in a while. The fellows sneaked around. They heard him say, "I hope he will be cooked soon." He sat on a fallen tree. The men went up to the campfire. One of the fellows shot him in the back, and the one who carried the axe put the axe on him—split him in half. They put him in his own fire, added more wood. The whole day they burnt him—down to ashes—a long time to do it. The father was taken from the stage and buried. (This was not a windigo made out of a dream.)

Becoming Windigo from Eating Porcupine: Two Cases

1. Four families started to get short of food. The men went in different directions. One fellow brought in a porcupine. But another fellow, he never eats porcupine heart. One fellow was cooking the porcupine; the other spoke up: "Be very careful with that heart—don't put it in that pot." One of the other men spoke up then. "Throw it in; he'll never know anything about it." "Yes he will." "No, better not." This fellow jumped up, picked it up, and threw it in.

When this man got back at night from hunt, there was a little left in the pot. He looked at it but did not touch it—knows it already—he did not intend to take the food. Then he started to laugh—took the food and ate it. The one that threw the heart in lay close to him in [the] wigwam—not feeling too safe now—moonlight. The one that said no lay awake worrying, then thought he heard someone chewing, eating, as he lay under his blanket. He threw it off and looked up. [The porcupine-eater] ate the one next to him already—the one that threw in the heart. The one who did not want this done was alive and watching. The windigo knew this man had tried to protect him. "Now get ready as quick as you can," the windigo said. The man did so; he ran as hard as he could—told others what had happened. One old man knew what had happened already in the camp—this man got ready. At daybreak he could hear the windigo—he finished the other two men. The old man went to meet him and killed him. Everybody [was] scared. This old man who went to meet the windigo was a relation of the young man. Even the young man's parents were willing to have him killed—to save the camp. The children were terribly scared.

2. There was Kag [Gaag, porcupine]—just like a human being, and Marten—going to try one another. There was a band of Indians, a big camp—the young men used to have "nests" where they fasted. A couple of young fellows sleeping outside in a nest, called each other nita [my

brother-in-law]. One young man asked his kita [Porcupine], "Did you have any bad dreams about anything?" "There was one thing in my dream. If I ever eat kag by mistake I'll turn into a cannibal. But you nita, [don't eat] marten—even by mistake." "A marten would do that to me," the other one said.

The Indians divided—so the latter [Marten] went in one direction went with his father—quite a long way—used to sleep outside (way up high in his nest). He knew something was wrong with his kita. He came into his father's tent in the morning; his father gave him a rabbit, but the young fellow would not eat. On the third morning (he went to his nest every night) he could hear something in the distance—a cold and stormy day. That was his kita's voice turned into a windigo. He went to his tent early in the morning; dressed nicely. His father knew he was getting ready for something and warned him not to go in a certain direction. The boy said, "I'm not going there." So he took an axe, not gun, and killed a bear a little distance off—preparing now, did not eat anything yet—three days. But he had set his mind to see what his kita was doing. His father knew what the boy intended to do.

Next morning—the same, he did not eat. He went off in one direction and switched around to the direction from which the sound had come. When he struck a lake, he started to run—it was stormy that night. When he got to the other side, he saw tracks to the water hole [in the ice]. The foot marks were terrible—the human hair—you can see it down to the water hole, found some women in the water hole who had been killed. He sneaked up. When he saw the tents [they had] no coverings— all smashed up. There was only one from which smoke was rising. He sneaked up, looked through the door. The person inside had something on hot coals, turning it. (Version 2: "This was a woman's privates—a little hair on it—he was scraping it off.") He did not look up—he knew his brother-in-law was watching. "Well, nita," said Kag, "did you come to fight me?" Marten said, "Well, I'll try." Kag dropped those things. "Now we'll go out and pick a place. We'll go here." Then nita (Kag) [said] "You try first."—"No," said the other [Marten], "because I came over here." "No, you first."

They started to call now—got as big as trees, equal in height now.

Kag shouted again—way above the trees already; Marten grew to same height—Kag shouted a third time—away up now—Marten shouted and became as big. Kag shouts a fourth time—getting pretty close to clouds now—Marten the same—clouds begin to touch them. Marten shouted again, became bigger than Kag. Kag started to shout for help now—reaches beyond clouds. Marten comes to be taller—way above clouds. Now the fight starts—no sticks or anything. When Kag was shaking his tail (monster porcupine)—quills went in every direction just like snow, made the trees split. Marten shoved himself on his [Kag's] belly side—went over him—Kag getting weak now. Marten threw him on his back, chewed his throat, and killed him. After this he went down to camp now—the clothing of those persons Kag had eaten were put in a pile. The tent was only half covered—nothing but bones there—after smashing them to get the marrow out. Some of the people had run away for their lives; he found them in the bush. Had a little wound somewhere—leg or head. The cause of the trouble—the young man did not intend to eat kag. But someone had thrown a piece in his kettle and he had eaten it by mistake.

When Marten got home, his father knew he had been somewhere: "I told you not to go in that direction." He had not touched food for five days. One day he did not go out at all—heard something from the distance. When Mikinaak was getting the [windigo's] liver to eat, he heard someone laugh. Marten is one of the strongest atsokan [aadizookaanag, spiritual beings] if you dream about him. Hard to beat.

("William Berens heard Josie Josie tell this story—a different version—a trick was played on Kag; people did not believe he would turn windigo from eating porcupine meat. He told his kita to run for his life"—AIH.)

Infant Boy in Moss Bag Turns Windigo

A man had a large family—had two wives. One of his girls was nearly full grown. The sons were killing moose already—they were that old. Moving around, plenty of grub. One of his wives had a baby still tied up in a moss bag. The older daughter always got up first—cooked breakfast with help of one of her sisters, before the older people got up.

One of the wives was still sleeping although the sun was high. The old man gave his wife a push—"Sit up; you're the only one lying down yet." Her daughter said to her, "You better get up now—you are sleeping long." She tried to wake her but she did not move—yet the child was moving under the blanket. She wondered, what is wrong? She tried again—the woman was dead—stiff. But the kid was moving. She threw the blanket off—he was covered with blood on the mouth. He was eating his mother. He had finished one breast already, had eaten half of his mother—yet only a kid in a moss bag.

So this young woman sneaks out and starts to run for her life. Another camp was close. When she reached this camp, she found a man who knew already what had happened. You can hear this kid already shouting—the windigo had started to grow, he killed his father and other relatives already. The man in the second camp got ready, went to try and see what he could do. When he got to the camp, he saw smoke coming from tent. He opened the tent a little, looked in. The windigo had a big kettle on the fire—a pile of human meat there and he was cooking it. Bigger than a man now. He had been cooking pretty near everybody. His stepmother, his mother, his brothers and some small ones. Soon as the man looked in, the windigo knew it. He grabbed something—a birch bark dish, slapped it down by the fire and he stabbed the dish with an awl. Took migis—stabbed it all over, making it full of holes. The man only had an axe but he jumped right in, started to call for help [from pawaganak]. He got hold of him, threw him on ground (not depending on his own power), used the axe to kill him, split him in half, and found ice in him, along his backbone—that's what makes him a windigo.

The man collected wood, made a big fire, put him on the fire. All the body except the part where the ice was burnt up quickly. That part took a long time. (That's their belief—if you miss anything it will come alive and be stronger.) The girl who skipped was the only one left. After he burned the windigo down to ashes, lying there were the heads of the persons the windigo had killed last. All the meat he had cooked was all arranged nicely, all heads together. This man did not know what to do with the "remains." Finally he closed the door of the tent and went home.

What would make a child that way? The only explanation is that some-one did it. Another explanation—Someone had asked for the girl—the

one that ran away—but the father did not think she was old enough—
did not know enough—[say, to make] moccasins—so perhaps the man
got mad and took revenge that way. He was insulted. (Adam [said] if he
[the father] had let the girl go, nothing would have happened—AIH.)

Woman Turned into Windigo by a Jealous Suitor

A family was living by themselves, in fall in their trapping ground. One
day this man got back from his trap line—woman [would have] got
something to eat. (Years ago, men never took anything to eat while out
hunting—they waited until they got home.) He pulled off his moccasins
and threw them to his wife. She paid no attention—sat with her back
to him—faced the door. She looked strange—seemed to be big, would
make a funny noise once in a while. He never noticed she sat with an
axe near her. All of a sudden she made another noise—jumped up and
killed him with the axe. There was a young man a long distance away
who knew this was happening. He started off running to the place where
the couple had camped. Before he arrived the husband was killed. When
he got there she had eaten half of his back. The woman knew the young
man was coming. He opened the door and walked in. She made a noise
and grabbed the axe again. He grabbed her and threw her down near
[the] fire—killed her with the axe right near the fire. He piled up spruce
boughs, made a fire, and burnt the house and all—burnt to nothing. If
this young man had not found out, she would have killed all the people
she could have gotten hold of. This happened long ago.

When this woman was a young girl a man had asked for her. Her father
refused and she refused because she had her mind on [marrying] her
husband. The prospective suitor said she would not live long with her
man and would destroy him. This was the cause of it.

A Windigo Woman Destroyed

It did not matter what this woman was fed—she would vomit it up. You
could take boiling water and give it to her to drink—she would drink it
like cold water. [It was] getting cold [but] this woman had pulled almost
all her clothes off and she was sweating. A windigo starts to get big and
she was getting big. If no one had dreamed how to destroy her she would

have killed everyone. There were two old men who knew. Her husband said that anyone *able* to kill her [ought] to do so before she started eating anyone. Those old men tried to kill her. Had an awful time—she was pretty near a windigo all right. Cut her arms off and cut her up and still she was alive. One of those fellows then split her down the center. Her heart was still beating. The old man got hold of it and cut it off; then she died. Then they burnt her and her back. It took nearly two days to burn it. Inside of her back there was ice—behind each shoulder, these people have ice. If a windigo sees you, you drop right there, unable to walk any more.

A woman from Pauingassi was killed halfway between here [Little Grand Rapids] and Berens River on a lake. (Name? [Adam] does not know the name of the woman or husband. [It was] in Zhenawaakoshkang's time.) [Adam was probably referring to the 1876 case of the woman whose sons killed her because she feared she was becoming a windigo; a magistrate heard the case, but Chief Jacob Berens successfully argued that "the Indians had just come into Treaty and had no chance to learn anything different" (Hallowell 1992, 65).]

A Man Who Was Already a Windigo

Long ago the Company sent men out to camps to collect fur in bales. Two men (Indians) went out on such a trip. One a pure Indian (A); can't say for sure about the other (B) [John Thomas (Doggie): see commentary concluding pt. 11]. A was leading the dogs. After they had slept two nights out, they were boiling a kettle. B turned around to A and said, "What's wrong with you? You don't want to eat." They started off again. The next day they expected to reach the Indians' camp. Every time from then on, A would not eat—even at night.

At noon they were making a fire. A knew too that they were coming to a windigo. He said, "I know what you know. There is a person where we are going who is not doing the right thing." B [said]: "When we camp tonight it will be on a large lake. This windigo will arrive where we are going to camp. He's coming to meet us—knows we are coming." They came to the evening—late. Just at sundown they could see him coming. A said, "Watch—have the axe handy." B said, "If he is going to take hold of us do your best. Do all you can do; don't give in. If he is going to harm us, I'll get hold of him. When I throw him down, hit him." I guess they could manage because they knew ahead of time without anyone telling them.

One fellow tramped down snow and threw down spruce boughs. When the windigo got there, A said, "Stranger." The windigo never spoke. He was told to sit where [the man] had spread the boughs; "You can sleep there." A was not scared. The windigo had a pack on his back. They knew he had killed someone where he left. The windigo took the pack off and sat down. He lay down with his head between his legs and an axe in front of him. A and B watched closely. One fellow started thinking seriously: "This windigo is very big." He turned to his partner and spoke slowly: "Now, I'll get a hold of him. If I'm able to handle him, you jump in and grab his axe away from him. If the windigo handles me, you grab hold of him too."

The other fellow was watching his partner closely. As soon as his partner got enough courage, he grabbed the windigo. The other fellow then grabbed the axe and threw it away. He called on Mikinaak to help him. The windigo was not able to move—only moved a little because Mikinaak was helping. When [the man] saw this, he said to his partner, "Unloose those ropes on that toboggan and bring them here." He tied [the windigo's] arms, legs, and everything down. "Bring that toboggan here, and that tarp." They spread the tarp on the toboggan, spread the windigo there, and tied him down, as tight as they could tie him, then tied the rest of the stuff, bedding, and grub in there. One of the men then untied the windigo's pack. It had a kettle—pail half full of children's feet. That is what he had been eating. The other fellow was hitching the dogs up meanwhile. If they had not known ahead of time without anyone telling them, they could have done nothing.

They started off through the night, travelled all night. All of a sudden, the toboggan at times would come to a dead stop; sometimes the windigo would make a little noise when traveling—that is when the toboggan would stick. The driver would then jump on top of the toboggan. When daylight came they were closer to the Indians—walked all that day and through the night, then came to the camp. The fellows started telling people, explained the delay [in arriving], and the meeting with the windigo. Then the "boss" took the windigo into the house—toboggan and all—a very cold night. In the morning they tried to talk with him but he would not talk, could not be made to talk. There was wood stacked on end outside the building. They put him inside and poured coal oil all over his body and over the wood. Set a match to it. Wood started to burn, and the windigo too. Burnt up—a little was left, so they poured more oil on him. Nothing was left then.

The men then went off to where they were to collect fur. Matogans [madogaans, small lodges] were all broken down. This is what the windigo had done—no people left. He had eaten them all. It was then that he had started off. They brought the fur bales home.

Old John Doggie (Snake Island) was the one that held the windigo. This happened long before treaty [i.e., before 1875]. ~~Burnt up towards Sandy Lake—Deer Lake~~. Burnt at Norway House? (Turned back—to Norway House, then they went on.)

Context and Commentary

The stories in part 11 all tell of human beings who became windigos by various means, some unspecified. The story of the errant windigo who killed the old man is the only episode in which shortage of food was mentioned, but the hungry families did not turn to cannibalism. Rather, they told of how the old man was lured outside by a voice proposing a feast and then was killed and roasted. They tracked the windigo, killed him with both gun and axe, and burned him to ashes on his own fire. In Ojibwe terms this man may have been bewitched by a sorcerer who made him a windigo. Or he may have had an ominous dream. To dream of Kiwetin (North) could be a harbinger of turning windigo. Even more dangerous were dreams in which the dreamer was offered some delicious meat—human flesh, disguised. Fur trader George Nelson recorded one man's account of being so tempted; if he had not spotted the deception right away, he would have been fated to become a windigo (Brown and Brightman 1988, 90).

The stories about becoming windigo from eating porcupine echo a recurring theme. A young male on a dream fast may be enjoined by a pawagan never to eat a certain food; the story of the windigo man who was ordered never to eat whiskeyjack (gray jay) is one example (see "Windigo Man Consumes Family," pt. 12). Even accidental ingesting brought dire consequences. The man who ate the porcupine heart killed three victims before being destroyed by an old man, a relative who presumably had superior powers (pawaganak were not mentioned, however).

The second porcupine story tells of a contest of almost cosmic proportions. Two young men ("brothers-in-law," or cross cousins, to translate the Ojibwe term [Hallowell 2010, 73]), while fasting, received admonitions from their pawaganak never to eat their eponymous animals—Kag (Gaag, Porcupine) and Marten, or they would turn windigo. Kag somehow disobeyed, and his cousin realized the desperate situation that threatened the people around him. Both cousins grew to monstrous proportions and Marten finally killed Kag—by the classic method that fishers employ in killing porcupines. The metamorphoses that both cousins went through set this story apart from all the others.

The Ojibwe of Parry Island, Ontario, as in Adam's stories, made a linkage between porcupine and windigo. Porcupine, they told Diamond Jenness in 1929, is "one of windigo's creatures." One must never kill a porcupine idly. A boy who gets a blessing from a porcupine in a fast must not eat the meat, or he will become windigo and lose his blessing (Jenness 1935, 80).

A puzzle occurs in the second story. When "Marten" overcomes Kag (Porcupine), he kills him using the distinctive method that a fisher uses on a porcupine. Thomas Fiddler and James Stevens said, "It is only the fisher that can kill [a porcupine]" (1985, 3). Martens are much smaller and not known to attack porcupines. But in version 2 Adam told Hallowell that "wabidjesi [waabizheshi], marten is one of the strongest pawaganak." He made no mention of fishers (ojiig). Perhaps Marten, transformed, acquired some of the fisher's powers.

The story of the infant who became windigo entailed almost as radical a transformation, as the domestic circle was shattered by his fearsome growth and cannibalism. Adam cited a rejected suitor of the infant's mother as the probable agent behind the tragedy. The next story, about the woman who turned windigo and killed her husband, was more explicit on this point: "The prospective suitor said she would not live long with her man and would destroy him." "A Windigo Woman Destroyed," in contrast, does not provide an explanation of the woman's transformation but simply recounts her symptoms and the gruesome details of her killing.

The story of the man who was already a windigo closely parallels, up to a point, one that John Rae (Sturgeon clan) of the Deer Lake area told to his son, Edward, who shared it with James Stevens in the 1970s (Fiddler and Stevens 1985, 32–35). The two versions agree that John Doggie ("Doggy") and the other man knew the windigo was coming; they laid down spruce boughs, then seized him and bound him to the toboggan with ropes and a tarp. He had a pail with children's feet in it and made noises. They traveled all night, reached the main camp, presumably at a trading outpost, and put the windigo in a house or "a white man's lodge," as Stevens put it. Doggy was the only one who could hold onto him.

Then Rae's story diverges sharply. The people gave whisky to the windigo, then took him over Lake Winnipeg to Poplar River and gave him more whisky, whereupon he "woke up," cried, and said he killed his wife and kids. Then Doggy and the others "put him on the train" and he was taken to a mental hospital and was given "firewater and shots to control him"—anachronistic details that point to a story shift. Later his mind cleared but "he was still always crying," and "eventually, he just died." John Thomas (Doggie), born in 1838, died at Snake Island on Lake Winnipeg in May 1930 (*Manitoba Free Press* 1930, 12). Thomas is the surname of several old HBC officers. Whatever the original details, Doggie in later life may have decided not to reveal this old windigo killing, knowing the questions that could arise under Canadian law. But the published Stevens version took on a life of its own. Shawn Smallman in his recent book on windigo, lacking access to Adam's story, featured the John Doggy story as his prime instance of windigos being taken to mental asylums for treatment (2014, 164–66).

PART 12

The Curing of Windigos

Owl Cures a Windigo Woman

Otcibamasis treated one windigo case. The woman had ice on her back—my father took that ice. Another old man helped my father. My father hung a kettle over the fire—water boiling. He put the ice in it. It took a long time to melt, even in the water. He sang and held the ice between his hands; water dripped until it was all gone. The woman got better. (He did more than boiling water.) Women are afflicted much more often than men.

An Old Woman Cures Her Windigo Granddaughter

I saw a woman one time who was going to be a cannibal. In January (very cold), I heard there was a woman who had something wrong with her. She covered herself up—lay under blankets four days and four nights. Some of the old women—one of them knew what the trouble was. She said, "I think I can beat her." She had a small round dish. She had been filleting a dried duck (bones removed—skin and meat and fat—one fillet). This woman cut this duck in pieces and mixed kapigigin [gaabigigin, things that grow rigid/crunchy] (wild rice) with it in the dish. The windigo would eat nothing; she never spoke all this time.

This old woman said to the windigo (her own granddaughter), "If you can manage to eat this food I set before you, you will be different—everything will leave you. If you don't want to eat of this dish and turn into a windigo, I'll beat you anyway—you'll not live—that is sure." The woman did as she was told. She finished it. Then it was as if she were waking up. After that she was just like any other person—two days after. She had been sweating all the time—one blanket. She tried to forbid the others to make a fire; they did not like it—a man [was] watching in a cold tent—but the old woman would not leave her.

The young woman got married later—had two children. The old woman must have gotten this cure out of a dream—it was not medicine but acts like it. The South wind is the boss of the summer birds. That is why the association of ducks with the South wind can beat Kiwetin [North].

Windigo Man Consumes Family, Cured by Post Manager

One time long ago a man was hunting alone in the winter with his family. This old fellow did not like whiskeyjack (bird) around his tent, or even a feather. ("Dreamed he would turn windigo if he came near a whiskeyjack—under a dream injunction"—AIH.) He was off hunting every day. One day when he got back to camp, his food was cooked for him already. His kids had killed a whiskeyjack that day and eaten it. Somehow it got mixed with the hunter's food. When he sat down he ate regular food. When he finished, he saw rabbits all around the fire on [roasting] sticks—ate them all. The things he saw in this *vision* were his children. That same night he ate all his own children.

There were Indians in a neighboring camp, not far from a post. Another man with a family heard the kids screaming—knows that something is up. He got ready—tied his children to a sleigh—those who could not walk. He had two dogs. The hunter saw the "rabbits" again—ponask [roasting sticks, cf. apwanask, Cree term]—and was going straight for the camp (i.e., the other man's camp—the one that skipped). When the second man heard this other man coming, he killed a dog and left it behind; the other man came up and stopped and ate it. The second man was trying to reach the post. Almost when he reached the post, he heard the windigo coming again—eating the second dog. He managed to get to the post and saved his life—ran right in.

After he got in, he saw the other man [the windigo] on the lake—big storm, so cold—the man had nothing on, naked. The hired man and the boss of the post went to meet him. They picked him up—he did not try to put up a fight. They made a big fire. The boss went to the store, brought rum, and gave the windigo a drink—a lot. He started to sweat—a big man after he had eaten those people. The boss did not let him see the Indian he had followed. He gave him tobacco and matches. "Are you cold?"—no answer. He went to the store again—got a little keg—poured out another drink. Finally the man sat quiet, got smaller—like a real man. All of a sudden he burst out crying—knows then that he killed all his family. Each side of his backbone was just like ice on the outside.

Next day the boss gave him all the rum he could drink. When he came to his senses he was crying all the time. He asked for a knife—to stab himself. The manager would not do it; he hid axes. The white man did not want him killed; he kept him there all winter, never let him go anywhere lest he kill himself. He gave him employment at the post but kept weapons away. The man wanted a gun to hunt—the boss was scared to give him one. He was there one year—two years. Later he got an axe, a knife, and a gun—got all right again. Got married.

Context and Commentary

Adam Bigmouth's windigo stories provide some distinctive Ojibwe perspectives, which challenge interpretations offered by a number of writers on the subject. In 1933 John M. Cooper published a short article, "The Cree Witiko Psychosis," in *Primitive Man*. While doing fieldwork among the James Bay Cree, Cooper, a Catholic priest and trained anthropologist, heard stories of persons who, made desperate by famine, suffered mental breakdown and resorted to cannibalism. As a consequence, he wrote, they developed "an 'unnatural' craving for human flesh, or a psychosis that took the form of such a craving." They were said to develop hearts of ice, and if not cured, they were sometimes killed as posing grave danger to others. More rarely, "men or women who had not themselves previously passed through famine experience" might also be afflicted. Cooper concluded that this psychosis, "found among the eastern Cree and some kindred tribes," was derived from "prevalent environmental conditions," and was reinforced indirectly by Witiko folklore concepts of superhuman cannibal giants (Cooper 1933, 21, 24).

Hallowell, writing in 1934 soon after Cooper's article appeared, and before he had heard Adam Bigmouth's stories, was cautious about the use of such terminology. Without challenging Cooper directly, he cautioned that "the validity of all such hypotheses depends upon (1) the reliable diagnosis of individual cases in various cultures and (2) upon accurate data in respect to the incidence of different types of disorders in them. This is the crux of the problem" (1934, 2). In his later field notes and writings, he never framed the Berens River windigo episodes he heard about as psychosis.

Numerous other authors, however, extended Cooper's analysis to northern Algonquians more generally. Morton I. Teicher's monograph, "Windigo Psychosis: A Study of a Relationship between Belief and Behavior among the Indians of Northeastern Canada" (1960), was the most comprehensive, assembling thirty-one windigo stories from written sources, and the cases of seventy individuals "reported in the litera-ture as instances of windigo psychosis" (1960, 107). His tabulations and conclusions, however, subsumed a great variety of episodes under this category. Further, most descriptions of the cases were from outsiders and often anecdotal, leaving many questions unanswered. As Richard Preston pointed out twenty years later, "We have made the diagnosis without seeing the patient. . . . Some kind of compulsion and transformation is believed in by Northern Algonkians, but their words are too often taken as literal (rather than imagic or symbolic) representations of events, which we then use to construct our definition of a Witiko psychopathology" (1980, 112).

Later Robert Brightman warned that "windigo psychosis" had become over-simplified as "an Algonquian-specific psychiatric disorder whose sufferers experienced and acted upon obsessional cannibalistic urges" (Brightman 1988, 337). Brightman noted that outside observers, whether they supported the notion or critiqued it, as did John Honigmann and Lou Marano, paid too little heed to Algonquian perspectives. Honigmann, for example, complained about the lack of reliable accounts of cannibal impulses or behavior—the absence of "a trustworthy observer's eyewitness report of a person who . . . clearly admits to a compulsion to eat human flesh," and implied that a reliable observer would be someone who was, as Brightman put it, "sufficiently detached from Algonquian cultural premises to report cases in their objective factuality." Brightman pointed out, however, that outsiders' seeming objectivity could reflect ignorance. Most outsiders' texts "tell us little about what human windigos were experiencing. There remains a serious difficulty with the summary dismissal of all Algonquian testimony regarding the behavior of persons identified as windigo" (Brightman 1988, 346). As a qualifier, however, Brightman might have cited Regina Flannery, Mary Elizabeth Chambers, and Patricia Jehle, who in "Witiko Accounts from the James Bay Cree" (1981) published first-hand stories recorded in the 1930s.

The term *psychosis* first appeared in English in 1847. One modern definition is: "a serious mental disorder characterized by thinking and emotions that are so impaired that they indicate that the person experiencing them has lost contact with reality" (Healthline.com, accessed April 2016). Yet the Ojibwe windigo cases described by Adam (and others) exhibited a range of symptoms, mental and physical, and some persons described as windigo may even have been homeless strangers, ostracized for some reason (see Adam's "Sighting a Fearsome Stranger," pt. 1). In 2004 James Waldram in his *Revenge of the Windigo* (18) offered a strong critique of windigo psychosis as possibly "the most perfect example of the construction of an Aboriginal mental disorder by the scholarly professions. "Its persistence," he added, "dramatically underscores how constructions of the Aboriginal by these professions have . . . taken on a life of their own."

Adam's stories also raise questions about the relation between Ojibwe famine stress and the presence or rise of windigo cases. Teicher concluded that among his seventy cases, only eighteen were clearly precipitated by starvation (1960, 110). Charles Bishop, however, argued largely on the basis of Cree data that "the catalyst for the development of Windigo behavior was the decimation of game and the dependence on the trading post," and conjectured that by the early 1800s, the northern Algonquian belief in a windigo cannibal "became extended to include situations arising out of famine cannibalism concomitant with the dreadful fear of starvation. As famine became endemic . . . cannibalism became a constant social threat (Bishop 1973, 12, 16). Christopher Vecsey observed:

"Famine was not uncommon among the early Ojibwas, especially in the late winter, and the belief in the Windigo represented a tribal fear of winter starvation" (1983, 77).

Indeed winter hunger was often a serious concern to the Berens River Ojibwe, as Adam's starvation stories show. But those stories (pt. 9) did not relate hunger to windigo manifestations. Those of Adam's windigo stories that offered causal explanations linked windigoism to strong personal agency, not to lack of food. The other-than-human beings, the pawaganak, could visit and cause transformation through dreams, or enact penalties for mistreatment of scapular bones, for disobeying injunctions against specific foods, and the like. Human sorcerers such as rejected suitors could also use their powers to transform a victim into a windigo. Robert Brightman looked at numbers of human windigo cases in documentary and ethnographic sources to assess food availability (Brightman 1988, 347). His sources all described conventional food as being present during windigo episodes; people were not starving at the time, although in two cases famine had previously occurred.

The gender patterns of the eighteen windigos who appeared in Adam's stories are of interest. Fourteen were males, eight of whom were described as superhuman; there were no superhuman females. The superhuman windigos in Adam's stories never succeeded in killing and eating their victims; they were either driven away or killed. Among the humans were six males and four females. The six males had all murdered and eaten one or more victims; five of them were then killed, and one was cured—by a post manager. Of the four females, two were killed. One of them had killed one victim (her husband); the second woman, described as becoming a windigo, was killed without having murdered anyone. The other two females were incipient windigos who were cured. In sum, six human windigos were killed in Adam's stories: four males and two females. Adam thought that more women than men were afflicted by windigoism, even though male cases dominated in the stories he told. By comparison, Morton Teicher found that among the seventy cases of "psychosis" he gathered, forty were said to be male (1960, 108). Women windigos may indeed have been more common than men in Adam's experience. But they offered less drama for storytelling; they had fewer victims and less violent histories than the men. Possibly they also were more often cured at an early stage.

A common feature of windigo cases was "perception of internal freezing," as Brightman put it. Windigos were commonly said to have hearts of ice that had to be utterly consumed by fire, or else they might revive (Brightman 1993, 153–56). Adam made no reference to hearts, but four of his stories mentioned windigos having ice along their backs or backbones. In five episodes, windigo remains were intensively burned to destroy the ice. Three of Adam's stories described a different mode of windigo disposal, however—which was applied to the superhuman windigos. The pawaganak who were summoned to help in killing those windigos returned at night to feast on the remains, and Mikinaak, the main protagonist, got the liver. The windigos, instead of killing and eating their intended victims, were themselves killed and consumed by other pawaganak. William Berens told Hallowell that "*Windigo* is a *pawagan*— can be a helper. . . . It is this *pawagan* that helps a human being to make a 'dream' *windigo*" (to send against targeted victims; Berens 2009, 99). His identification provides an interesting turn: its implication is that the pawaganak were feasting on one of their own. Or did they really count the superhuman windigos as their peers? At the end of his story about windigos killed by two women, Adam said, "Atsokanak [pawaganak] look upon a windigo as an animal to be killed to eat." Brightman (1993, 146–47) did not make that precise equation, but his description of windigos as asocial and acultural, carnivorous, and perceiving humans as prey certainly suggests parallels with wild animals.

Adam presented all his windigo stories as part of human history, not set in mythic or legendary times. Six of them recounted his or his father's personal experiences or those of people he knew well. Two others referred to fur trade workers or to trading posts, placing them within the previous century and a half of active trading in the region. Some episodes occurred "long ago," with no clear historical markers. A few stories approached mythic dimensions, describing almost cosmic struggles between giant windigos and men who could call on powerful helpers. Hallowell in his field notes (while working with Adam in 1938 or 1940) wrote of such accounts, "There is probably no person now living who claims to have overcome a windigo by their magic power; these cases are all attributed to men of the past or to unnamed individuals." Such stories, as they were passed down through the generations, seemed to grow in drama and cosmic implications, acquiring a legendary quality.

PART 13

The Costs of Mockery and Cruelty

Consequences of Cruelty to Mosquitoes

There was one Indian living at about the time that mosquitoes began—
there were lots of them. This fellow could not sleep, there were so many
mosquitoes. So he said to his wife, "Make a rogan [birch bark basket]."
As soon as mosquitoes came along and lit on his hand, he put them into
the rogan. He kept them there the whole summer.

When winter came, on the very coldest day in January, he took this
rogan out and carried it outside. He was going hunting so he took it with
him; he struck right out on the lake and opened it up. As soon as the
mosquitoes came out and started to fly, they froze. "Last summer you
never left me alone—now I'll punish you for this," he said. So he started
to laugh at them now, flopping black on the snow. He left the rogan on
the ice and off he went.

When the summer came the mosquitoes came again. They did not
give him any chance to sleep; bad in daytime, too. He made a smudge
all round him, but they kept coming. Finally he took to the water to
escape—just his head sticking out. Still the mosquitoes were after him.
It did not make any difference. Finally he could stand it no longer, was
sure the mosquitoes would kill him. Then he heard a voice: "Will you do
this thing to us again that you did?" He did not see anyone, just heard
the voice. He said, "No, I'll promise never to do that again as long as I
live." "Don't you ever try to do that to us again. Next time, if you do it

we'll kill you." And the mosquitoes never bothered him anymore. He made a kind of pagitcigan [bagijigan, sacrifice].

A Man Insults Snow, Is Punished, and Barely Escapes Death

There was long ago a man—this was in the spring of the year. There were lots of places where sun struck the ground and it was getting bare already. He heard something crying—a person very sad for something. This man walked towards the sound to see. When he got there, he could see nothing but a snow drift that had been left. It was the snow that made this sound. The man stood there; he farted. "You are suffering with the heat because you are going now, but remember what you did to me last winter. You made me suffer lots of times. I could hardly stand the cold." The snow laughed at that. Then the man walked off.

He heard a voice now from behind him: "There is another winter coming—expect me again this coming winter." ("This was North Wind"— AIH.) This fellow was getting a little worried now—that summer he worried a lot. He knows another winter is coming; all summer he gathered grub—grease, oil, everything so he would have stock and not have to hunt during the cold days. He made a house, a fair sized house. He put in all the grub he collected during the summer and he built a kind of veranda of sticks, so that the snow could not come near to the door. Of course his children had lots to eat; he gathered quite a bit of wood too, everything was prepared.

When later it came to midwinter, he was very cold. January, when he made a fire, even he was that cold—could barely feel the heat inside the house. Even some of the wood, it would not burn good at all. He used the oil now to make a good flame—more heat. It was getting colder all the time—fire not burning good and his oil and wood getting lower all the time, but he still had lots of grub. Finally the oil would not burn; white frost was coming now. His children began to suffer. He was suffering now too.

Now someone came in and filled his pipe. Soon as this person started to smoke—the smoke that came out of his mouth—the logs began to crack with frost. The man knew his end was coming. This was the real man coming [the North Wind]. He had a young moose skin for a shipitagan [zhiibetaagon, pelt prepared as a bag], this visitor had. The man knew his end was coming.

The door opens again—another visitor walks in, a still bigger man. He had a swan skin for a medicine bag. The last visitor spoke to the first visitor; he said, "I think you are going to finish the man that lives in this house now." The last one that came in was the South Wind. He took his pipe now and started to smoke. It was not long before the cold began to disappear from the inside. The first visitor (North Wind) now pulls off his shipitagan and lays the moose skin before him. The frost comes back again—hear the cracking of the logs. South Wind now puts the swan skin before him. The frost disappears again. North Wind turns the moose skin on its belly side—the frost comes in. South Wind turns his skin again; the frost disappears, it gets warmer. The water runs out of Kiwetin [North] now. He turns the bag again—just a little cold. South Wind turns the swan skin; then the heat is felt again. Drops [come] out of North Wind's body—like sweat. He did the same thing—turns the skin— but is weaker. The other fellow turns the swan skin. When North Wind turns it, you can hardly feel the cold. There's no power to Kiwetin now. South Wind is getting the best of it—it's getting warmer. The last time North Wind turns [his moose skin], there's no cold at all. He is getting smaller all the time because he is melting. (You have seen the moose in the spring [how it] looks as if scorched. North Wind's bag looked just like that.) When North Wind found this out, he took his bag and flung it into the corner and ran out. Before he went, South Wind [said], "Don't you do that again to make a poor Indian suffer like that with the cold." That is the reason why the winters are getting a good bit shorter than long ago. Kiwetin is being beaten.

South Wind must have been one of the man's pawaganak. Still, he did not know how much strength the North Wind had. (Adam asked what whites thought about Kiwetin; William Berens mentioned "kabiboneke [gaa-bibooniked] = the winter maker—i.e., kiwetin = Jack Frost"—AIH.)

An Old Man and Woman Insult a Moose and the Animal Escapes

A man was living with his old father and mother. During the whole winter this man had been trying to kill a moose. But he did not succeed.

Finally the summer came. One day the father of this fellow saw a moose swimming across a lake. He called his wife and they jumped into a canoe and paddled after it. They caught up with the moose and the old man grabbed the animal by the horns. "I'm going to do something to this moose that he will remember," the man said to his wife. So he pulled off his breech-cloth, rubbed his hand on his penis and then put his hand to the nose of the moose. ("A gross insult"—AIH.) "Smell this," he said. "My son could not kill you the whole winter." Then he did the same thing again and said, "You'll have enough snuff on you now." Then his wife shoved her finger into her vagina and then stuck her finger up the nose of the moose. "My son has been walking enough this winter to kill you," she said. By this time they were approaching the shore and they let the moose go. The old man took up his gun. As soon as the moose got his footing near the shore he pulled the trigger. But the gun did not go off. Just as the moose was heading into the bush the gun went off. But the bullet did not hit the moose. The old man felt sorry now that he had lost the moose. (This was said to be a "kind of funny story"—AIH.) [The text, attributed to Adam, comes from Hallowell's "Myths and Tales" manuscript; it is not in his Little Grand Rapids files of 1938 and 1940.]

Abuses of Orphan Boy Lead to a Daughter's Sickness

There was a man who took another man's wife. This woman died. The adopted son was always put on the door side—a dog's place. Every meal time, they did not give him much to eat and said, "Don't look at anyone when they are eating." This boy always had his head down. They never even handed grub to him. Even sometimes they took a burning brand and scorched him with it; [he was] burnt so often he had scabs all over his face. Sometimes they threw coals at him, laughing at him. One old widow was looking after this boy, took pity on him and kept an eye on him. The old woman was not well off—could hardly support herself.

In the spring when the roads were getting bad, [they were] on the way to their camping ground. When they were portaging the canoes, when a man was running along, he tried to hit the boy by the bow end—it was a mozani [Moose clansman] who did this. Another one came along and pushed the boy with the point of the canoe. Every one of the men did something. The last one, he had a paddle; [he said] "You have been abusing this fellow long enough; why not kill him?" So he stabbed him in the ribs with the handle of the paddle. Another man hit him too. The last one smashed at him and killed him. And this father-in-law of mine, Zhenawaakoshkang, had a hand in this. My wife [Aanii] has been suffering because of her father's wicked deeds. The man who tried to help my wife found this out. She had to be carried when a girl—could not open her eyes for days. Zhenawaakoshkang confessed. After this she grew up nicely—pretty healthy now. ("Cruel treatment of an innocent child—orphan. Kiwasigan [giiwasigan]—orphan, no father or mother. W.B. said some people would act that way now if there was no law"—AIH.)

Context

Parallels to all three of these stories may be found in stories that William Berens told to Hallowell; see "Misdeeds and Consequences" (Berens 2009, 85–88). Along with his mosquito story above, Adam cited other examples of "cruelty to animals, like cutting off an animal's legs when it is alive and letting it go, just for fun, or plucking all the feathers from a live bird and letting it go, naked." Adam also told Hallowell about how, one time, he "found a snake and was playing with it took it by the head and tail—stretched it—worked it back and forth this way and that, finally pulled in two. His son was sick. A man dreamed that Adam had done something to a snake and mentioned it to him. He recalled then what he had done when a youth and confessed it. His son has been well since." In "Bad Doings" (pt. 5), Adam told about how his father cured a sick woman who had once tortured a frog; he got her to remember and confess the deed. The lessons were clear. Cree stories of the consequences of cruelty to animals provide parallels (see, for example, Bird 2005, 51; and Brightman 1993, 110–11).

Teasing and mockery could also bring severe repercussions, as when William Berens made fun of the hunchback son of a conjurer and had a frightening dream experience (2009, 86–87). The man who farted at Snow came close to death when Kiwetin visited in winter and was saved only by his connection with South as a pawagan. The moose who was so deeply insulted by the old man and woman foiled their efforts to shoot him. The consequences of a humorous gesture that caused offence to a powerful old man were highlighted in Adam's story "Those Two Wives of Tetebaiyabin" (pt. 4), when his sitting between his cross cousins led their husband to subject him to sickness and the menace of bear-walking.

The account of the abuse and murder of an orphan boy by Moose clansmen, including the man who later became Adam's father-in-law, is the only instance in the stories of such a group attack. The memory of it must have been disturbing, and it surfaced in Adam's telling of the sickness of his wife, Aanii, on account of her father's involvement in the deed. The story finds a parallel in William Berens's account of Betsey Grant, the wife of his uncle, William McKay. Her father had killed a man in an act that Hallowell heard was "unprovoked willful murder," and when he was dying, he bled from the nose and mouth. In her later years Betsey bled from the nose and "confessed" her father's sin (Berens 2009, 85–86). Numbers of other Ojibwe stories tell of the misdeeds of parents being visited upon their children: for example, Adam's stories of "Sickness from Torturing a Windigo" and "A Windigo's Head" (pt. 10). William Berens also told Hallowell of how his father, Jacob, one time, was suffering from an unexplained ailment. A conjurer used his shaking tent to summon Jacob's deceased father, who confessed to a misdeed that was causing his son's trouble (Hallowell 2010, 422–24).

PART 14

Magical Medicines and Powers

Hunting with Medicine: A Man Makes a Fatal Mistake

Some people used to be good hunters when they used medicine. A man once spoke to his wife and said, "I'll try to use what I have been told to do." Of course, long ago there were no steel traps.

This fellow went off a long distance. When evening came, he got back to camp and made a trap pretty close to his camp—as close as was necessary to hear a deadfall drop. (You can hear from here to Joe Alix's place.) When night came, he put medicine on his wife's hands—arms, face—even her knife and axe, and also right down to his door and his tent too. After he did all this, his wife was fixed. He started to sing now; then he heard the trap falling and dropped his drum. When he got near, he saw the trap had fallen. There was an animal in the trap; he brought it in and gave it to his wife to skin it. Another song—the trap went off again. He brought in another animal. The whole night he was busy singing, getting animals from the trap—and his wife skinning them. The trip he had made that day—all those animals that came to his trail—all followed his trail till they came to his trap. The whole night, then another night (the second)—four nights, he was supposed to beat the drum and not sleep. He did the same thing night after night.

A little before daylight, the third night, he dropped asleep—slept. Could not stand it any longer. When he woke up and went to his trap, a human being was there foaming—bloody. That same night, he died himself (caught in his own trap). This was due to the fact that he did not carry through for 4 nights. As long as he beat the drum and sang, he was OK.

He drew on birch bark (a picture of a man—something like Kiwitc [Giiwiich, Alex Keeper]), a picture of every animal as if they had a string tied on them leading to his tent. The trail was marked right into his tent. And every animal had a little tip of medicine on the heart. He would have had a wonderful hunt if he had kept up. The reason he put medicine on his wife was so that she would not get black; her hands would swell up, a cut would kill her. Protected by medicine, she could handle the animals. Can't call it good medicine though.

Root Medicine for Caribou

If animals get away without a shot, grind up [the root], place it in four tracks—wherever the animals would be paralyzed in their tracks. They could not raise their legs—only their heads; they would stay there and the hunter could come upon them. When you came upon them, you were supposed to leave a buck and a doe, but could shoot all the others. Anybody could eat meat of caribou killed in this way—it would not hurt them. One thing about it—the man who uses it must eat one part of the caribou himself. If anyone else does it he spoils it for himself—is not able to kill caribou. The person that eats it won't feel good. The tongue and heart are eaten, for example. The person who sold medicine [to the hunter] told him what to eat.

This medicine came from Deer Lake side. It was not dreamed of by a man for himself; it was bought—years ago. An old fellow at Sandy Lake—his father had it. This kind came from Midewiwin—where pictures of all the animals are drawn [on birch bark]. A Big Deer Lake Indian had all this medicine as part of the Waabano. He had all kinds of medicine for trapping—even when setting traps for otter. If the animal was caught, there was a rule to cut the "hand" that was caught in the trap underwater before removing. Open the trap underwater, and let the paw fall out under the water. Anyone who did this had no trouble in catching otter.

Medicine to Strengthen Dogs—and HBC Packers

[Medicine to cure trouble with legs and strengthen them] not much used now. But years ago it was used a lot for dogs—long ago. They never played out. If another dog train passed over the trail which had been traversed by a train with medicine, the second team would have trouble with legs. A man can get it [the trouble] from dogs [by crossing their trail].

In the old days of York boats, you could find men with medicine tied on their legs—they were the good packers. The other freighters, however, might get "sickness in the legs" [from them?] because you could not see the medicine under their pants. Sometimes they used medicine on their arms—the same kind to make a man strong—able to lift anything. Does not make any difference [in a fight] where he hit a man—chest, arm— he'd be sure to break a bone.

("Adam knows medicine to cure—[to make you as] good as you ever were then. If you have that medicine, no one can beat you no matter how small [you are]. Four things [in it]: ice, brown root, black one, another one looks as if it has hair on it. You had to be on the watch all the time years ago for this medicine—had to carry medicine to counteract [its use by others] or to cure yourself. Adam had medicine he carried in his mouth—so as not to be winded in running over portages. This is not bad medicine. You could work hard but the heart would not beat too fast. You could go to bed with clothes soaking wet—would not harm you. Adam had it—always carried medicine to cure pasikamauwin [bizika-maawin: medicine, usually bad, for someone to step on]. He never used arm medicine. Adam trained himself to run—without medicine. You can do some of these things if you start young enough"—AIH.)

Magical Capture of Otters

A Big Deer Lake Indian had all this medicine as part of the Waabano— all kinds of medicine for trapping, even when setting trap for otter. If an animal was caught, it was a rule to cut the "hand" caught in the trap *under* water before removing it. Open the trap under the water, let the paw fall out under water. Anyone who did this had no trouble in catching otter. If a man came to a place where an otter family was living, he would sit down, fill his pipe, and put medicine in his tobacco. It was not long before an otter would come up, and before you were through, all of them would come up ("one of things from Deer Lake Indian"—AIH).

One man was hunting otter like this. Early in the morning, he left in his canoe with his son (full grown) and came to a place where they saw fresh signs of otter. While paddling along, they came to a place where the rocks were near one another in the river—saw those otters close by. He turned to the boy: "We'll sneak up on them. Those otters are sleeping. I'll show you how sound asleep they are." They paddled up—very close. The old fellow got out of the canoe onshore. He spread a blanket inside his canoe. He goes and picks up an otter and puts him inside the canoe on the blanket—another—all the young ones and the old ones too. He tied them up tight in this blanket. Then they started to move and he killed the whole bunch. "You see now," he said to his son: "those otters don't sleep very sound." It was not everyone who could do this—only this man.

A Conjuror's Magic

Adam was never tied [up] before conjuring and did not know anyone on the river who was. But one man was tied, taken out on a lake, and thrown in. When the canoe got back to the shore, the man was there already. Adam's mother's brother: He was manao [mina'o, one who gives a drink of medicine, e.g., from the memegwesiwag, little people]. His wife had expressed skepticism: "You make those medicines yourself. You don't get it where you claim you do." He said to his wife, "Tie me up—my arms—anywhere you like." Near [Little] Grand Rapids on the Pigeon River, there's a little island below the big falls—an island between the two rapids. "Take me there to the falls and throw me in."

The women of course wanted to find out. So they tied him up, took him to the foot of the rapids—deep too. They threw him out of the canoe and went down. Those women, they followed the current down, watching. When they arrived at a high steep rock at the water's edge, the man spoke to them from the top of the rock already. "What are you looking for?" he said.

The Magical Manufacture of Canoes

In the spring of the year a man used to hunt beaver on glare ice. When warm weather came, he could not make his way home on the ice. He went into the bush and made some paddles. His wife said, "What are you going to do with paddles when you have no canoe?"

"You go over there and make a 'bedding' (just the shape of the bottom of a canoe—dug out of sand), and put a few stones there," he said. His wife thought he was going to build a canoe. But he had no birch bark. The woman finished her work as told and came back. "I'm through," she said.

When the night came you could still see the day sky in the west. They heard a noise—a partridge drumming all during the night. Just about broad daylight, they could not hear any more noise—the sun was up. The man got up and had something to eat, then said to his wife, "You better have a look where you did your work." There was a brand new canoe already made—made out of one piece of birch bark—the ribs and everything were just fine—no pitch anywhere. Now this fellow took the canoe and went home. He said to his wife, "We are all right—put it down in the water." So he paddled off to the main camp.

When he reached there, there were lots of people. People were puzzled because the man had never made a canoe before. Now he arrives with a new canoe. All in one piece and no pitch. People said he could not have made it himself—he must have had the help of his pawaganak. One Indian came along—gave him lots of stuff to purchase a canoe like that. So the man told his wife to do the same thing as before.

Before it was real dark, he heard the "drummer" (the partridge) again. He sent his wife to have a look to see if he had luck, i.e., before he said anything to the man who paid him. There was another fine looking canoe identical with the first one. "Go in that direction where you heard the drumming, and you will see something," his wife said. So he went and saw it himself. He was thankful to have such a wonderful looking canoe. He put it in the water. People now knew he did not make it with his own hands.

Another man came to him. The same thing happened. More and more people came. This man got rich. This was pipaski's work: the real name is matwe'onu—the sound made when a man is making a skiff or canoe— the sound comes from pounding. [Roulette: bapashki, ruffed grouse; matwe'on, making a sound; male grouse display for mates by "drumming" in spring.] ("Looks like a folk etymology—the sound analogy—then the story"—AIH.)

Afterword

Cousins and Connections, Power and Succession, Seeking Life

The stories and memories of Adam Bigmouth open a window into the lives and relationships of four generations of Ojibwe people on the upper Berens River. They offer glimpses of what Hallowell called the people's "culturally constituted world," which successive generations came to understand through "perceiving, remembering, imagining, judging, and reasoning" (1992, 80)—and through stories, whether they were myths and legends or the more personal, anecdotal tales that were Adam's specialty. The headings, contextual discussions, and annotations interspersed among the texts, and the glossary of Ojibwe names at the end of the introduction connect the stories to one another, revealing both concrete details of personal lives and larger themes and patterns to be understood in the context of both Ojibwe and outsider sources. Adam's stories also tell us, through names and allusions, about some of the most important familial and clan connections in which his life was embedded. A closer look at the dynamics of these connections illustrates how they and the values that underpinned them influenced and gave direction to the people's lives and communities in fundamental ways that outsiders could not easily fathom.

Cousins: No End to Relationship

Hallowell first came to Manitoba in 1930 with the aim of studying Cree-Ojibwe cross-cousin marriage, as scholars were curious about its presence in the region. His fieldwork soon demonstrated the pervasiveness of the practice. His summary article on the subject, written in 1937, remains a major contribution (Hallowell 2010, 6, ch. 5). Interestingly, he had one predecessor who had begun to get a grasp of Ojibwe cross-cousin relationships more than a century earlier—George Nelson, an HBC fur trader. In July 1822, when Nelson was traveling between Lake Winnipeg and Fort William on Lake Superior, he was startled to be accosted by an old Ojibwe woman, a stranger to him, who began to berate, scold, and tease him in a most familiar manner. When he got to Fort William, he finally realized that she was complexly related to his Ojibwe wife. She was "a cousin of a woman that thro' courtesy to her husband used to stile me 'Nee-nim'—brother-in-law; & as there is no end to relationship among the Indians, *she* also calls me thus!" (Peers and Brown 2000, 530).

Nelson had lived and traded among Ojibwe people for two decades and knew the language pretty well. He had an Ojibwe wife and family, like numerous other traders. But unlike his peers, he acquired a good understanding of the Ojibwe kinship system and the relationships that it generated, though he was still stuck with inadequate words to express them. "Brother-in-law" is an awkward English translation of "Nee-nim" (Ojibwe, "niinim"). The woman whom Nelson met was using the term that a female speaker would use to a kinsman who was not of her paternal line (or clan). In anthropologists' terms, Nelson was a cross cousin to her. That is, he was not related to her by descent from generations of brothers whose offspring were all parallel cousins (terminologically equivalent to siblings). Rather, he was connected by ties that crossed gender lines. The Ojibwe term in fact points to a much larger web of kin than does "brother-in-law."

More generally speaking, "in-law" is an irrelevant category in the Ojibwe context. As Hallowell wrote in 1937, "there are no specific terms for relatives by marriage" (2010, 73). The reason is that in Ojibwe kin terminology, everyone is defined as being related in one way or another, in or out of marriage. The parallel-cousin category encompassed all persons of the same generation who shared paternal ancestors and were thereby classificatory siblings restricted from intermarrying. Descen dants of a brother and sister, on the other hand, were spun off into different paternal lines (and clans) and could marry. The nature of their connection was acknowledged by the use of niinim and related terms specifying their place in the Ojibwe kin universe, and by their license to engage in joking, bawdy behavior and verbal abuse that was forbidden between cross-sex siblings and parallel cousins. Of course, not everyone appreciated the humor. Adam suffered sorcery from a Sturgeon parallel cousin—a jealous husband, Tetebaiyabin, when he found Adam sitting jokingly between his two wives—Adam's Moose cross cousins ("Those Two Wives of Tetebaiyabin," pt. 4). But cross cousins, married or not, were expected to carry on such performances, as William Berens himself freely recounted (Hallowell 1992, 55–56).

Generations

A second key concept that needs to be understood in Ojibwe terms is that of generations. Hallowell said of Ojibwe kinship that "the generation principle is paramount" and is accordingly reflected in kin terminology (2010, 73). English speakers commonly define generations in terms of measured time—the years between parents' and their children's births. The Ojibwe make no reference to chronology. Instead, they use a term that highlights the link between great-grandparents and great-grandchildren: "aanikoobijiganag, which evokes units of length that connect successive kin" across four generations (Brown 2010b). Ojibwe linguist Roger Roulette, and Cree historians speaking of the equivalent Cree term, aaniskotaapaanag, express the concept simply as "knots in a string." The underlying image is of lengths tied together, with the connotation of things being pulled along. As Cree teacher William Dumas said, it is like "when you tie one toboggan behind another," an apt way of describing links that reach from great-grandparent to great-grandchild (Brown 2010b, 296). Effectual family memories and stories commonly extend across four generations and not beyond. Few people get to meet their great-grandparents, but they may hear about them and are influenced (pulled along) by them, even if unwittingly, through parents and grandparents. More distant ancestors lie beyond the reach of living people's own recollections. William Berens's family memories reached back to Yellow Legs, his Moose great-grandfather, but no further. They were kept alive by vivid stories learned from his grandfather, Bear, and his father, Jacob, and were reinforced by his telling of them to Hallowell.

Adam Bigmouth's Sturgeon family line has been traced back through only three long generations, not four, but his stories and Hallowell's notes, supplemented by Gary Butikofer's research, convey the sense of knots in a string. Adam's father, Northern Barred Owl, was born in 1811 if census data hold up; he was in his forties when Adam was born. Adam's grandfather, Pisikasikaakwan, whom Adam never knew, was "very old, blind, and not able to get around well" when he died; he must have been born by about the 1780s. Owl's story about him ("Owl Rescues and Loses His Father," pt. 5), as passed to Adam, tells how Owl twice retrieved his father after camp members left him behind to die. It is one of the most poignant in the collection, and Owl's telling of it certainly conveyed a message to Adam about father-son relations and about his father's values. But we know nothing more about the old man except that he had two sons, Owl and Kaashaapowiiyaasit (Gaa-zhaaboowiyaazid)—who was doubtless the older one as he had grown children by the time he died, sometime before 1875 (Butikofer 2009, pt II.1, 56–57).

The sons' life paths diverged considerably. Both were probably born at Little Grand Rapids, but by the mid-1800s the older brother had settled at Poplar River, north of Berens River, on Lake Winnipeg. Adam referred to him only once in a remarkable story, "Owl Saves His Brother from a Windigo" (pt. 10). Somehow, from a great distance, Owl found out that his older brother was under a windigo attack at Poplar River. So "he got all his pawaganak together—just like an army," and after "a terrible fight," the monster was killed.

Adam told no stories, however, about another significant aspect of his uncle's life. Kaashaapowiiyaasit was one of the first Ojibwe to settle at Poplar River and founded his own Sturgeon line, a new series of knotted strings in a new place. He had three sons, two of whom produced descendants. The first, Neninkikwaneyaash (Neningigweneyaash, "affected by wind"), who became known as Alex Whiskis, had three sons, who carried on the Whiskis or Wiskis surname at Poplar and Berens rivers. Of greater note was the second son, Tetipaahkamikohk (George), who died in 1879–80. He had three wives at the same time and produced ten sons and two daughters. He took the surname Franklin, and as Butikofer wrote, he became the "ancestor of all the Franklins at Poplar River" (2009, pt. II.1, 57). Polygyny and reproductive success and survival assured his family a dominant role there for several generations.

In speaking of Poplar River and other settlements, an important qualifier is needed. In the periods discussed here, Poplar River, Little Grand Rapids, Lac Seul, and other places associated with these families were all relatively small summer fishing settlements where people gathered when they were not dispersed into their winter hunting camps on smaller lakes and rivers. The summer encampments were permanent in the sense that people returned to them regularly, but families described as living there would in fact be elsewhere for much of the year. The stories of how these individual settlements began provide concrete examples of the larger processes of Ojibwe expansions toward the Lake Winnipeg region from the mid-1700s.

While his brother's family grew, Owl maintained his summer base at Little Grand Rapids and his winter encampment at Eagle Lake. But his Sturgeon descendants did not proliferate like his brother's. His two sons by Pasho, his older wife, left no visible line; Maahtus died early, and records appear lacking for Kehkehk (Gegek). His and Injenii's younger son, Batis (Pachiish or John Baptiste) married a granddaughter of Zhenawaakoshkang and had seven children, of whom four survived to marry. But Adam, who was in his forties when he married Aanii, had only one surviving child, Peyak (John). Peyak and his only son drowned at Poplar Hill in 1968 (Butikofer 2009, pt. II.3, 308–9, 293, 297).

The fading of Owl's line contrasts with the demographic patterns found in the families of the other clan patriarchs with whom Owl and Adam interacted. Pazagwigabau, his son, Tetebaiyabin, and Zhenawaakoshkang, the Moose who first settled at Pauingassi, ten miles north of Little Grand Rapids, had multiple wives and many offspring. Hallowell's and Butikofer's researches supply their family histories and connections, reaching from the late 1700s to 1940, the year of Hallowell's last summer sojourn on the Berens River.

The story of Pazagwigabau and his descendants begins with a little-known great-grandfather, Nootinwep (Noodinweb, Wind Sitting), who turns up in Lac Seul HBC post records in the late 1700s and early 1800s. His two known sons, Pazagwigabau and a brother, were evidently born at Lac Seul, and Pazagwigabau's two wives, We'we and Mahkokwe, both came from there. Interestingly, the wives belonged to the Eagle and Bear clans respectively; those clans, well represented in the Lac Seul area, were not represented in the Berens River watershed itself. We'we had eight recorded children, of whom six married; Mahkokwe had five sons, all of whom married, assuring the strength of Pazagwigabau's family in the younger generations. The oldest children whose birthplaces are known were born at Lac Seul, and the later ones at Pikangikum (Butikofer 2009, pt. I.1, 9–14, 18). Pazagwigabau and his wives were the first Ojibwe people to settle at Lake Pikangikum—by about 1850, according to Butikofer (2009, pt. II.6, 471). We'we's married sons took the surnames of Strang and Turtle, and those names remain prominent at Pikangikum in the present. One daughter, Siipi (Ziipi), married Pindandakwan (James Shadow), a Pelican, and turns up in Adam's story of their son's death by sorcery ("This Old Fellow Was Pretty Bad," pt. 8).

The five sons of Pazagwigabau and Mahkokwe all took the surname Keeper. Most of them became connected with Little Grand Rapids, where Alex Keeper (Kiwitc, Kiiwiich, or Giiwiich; fig. 9), along with Alex's son John (Ketagas or Getagaash), became important sources of information for Hallowell in the 1930s. The eldest brother, William Keeper (d. 1894–95), was the second husband of Aanii, Adam's wife, as noted earlier. Another brother, Timothy (Pachahkaano) married Miskwimin, daughter of Zhenawaakoshkang and his fifth wife, Aanahk. Of the six marriages on record for their five children, five were with grandchildren of Zhenawaakoshkang (Butikofer 2009, pt. II.3, 325–26. Although a few marriages were with the smaller Duck or Pelican clans, Sturgeon and Moose cross cousins became intertwined time and again at Little Grand Rapids and Pauingassi, to an extent far beyond the examples mentioned here—a dense thicket of family trees.

The eldest surviving son of Pazagwigabau and We'we was Tetebaiyabin (Dedibaayaaban or Andrew Strang). His two wives were Kiitawan and Aasamwes, daughters of Otcik, a brother of Zhenawaakoshkang, and were probably born at Lac Seul. They had a total of seventeen children, of whom thirteen survived to marry, contributing mightily to the dominance of that family in the next generation. Tetebaiyabin was the first Ojibwe to establish the Poplar Hill summer fishing settlement. He died there in August 1925; his wives died in 1927 and 1929 respectively (Butikofer 2009, pt. I.1, 20–23; pt II.7, 522). As with Adam's older brother and his offspring, polygyny and reproductive success allowed certain men to found and maintain new communities that were based on their large extended families. The summer population of Pikangikum in 1932 was 122; that of Poplar Hill (Poplar Narrows in Hallowell's usage) was "a little over half as large" (Hallowell 1992, 48).

Families and Ceremonies, Sturgeon and Moose

Pazagwigabau and Tetebaiyabin during their lifetimes had the Sturgeon clan connections and power to achieve and maintain their hold on the Midewiwin along the upper Berens River, as related in the contextual discussions in part 5. In both their cases, however, Midewiwin leadership became strongly vested in one individual and was not passed to brothers or sons—except for Tetebaiyabin's successorship to his father. Other lesser Midewiwin leaders and assistants are mentioned in part 5 (for more details, see Hallowell 2010, ch. 21), but none took over the ceremony to the same extent. After Tetebaiyabin's death in 1925, no single strong practitioner came forward. Some of Adam's stories also point to another problem; Pazagwigabau and Tetebaiyabin sometimes used their powers in hurtful and damaging ways that led people, even their own relatives, to fear and avoid them (see examples in pts. 4, 5, and 6). They may have sown the seeds that sent the Midewiwin practice itself into decline along the Berens River.

Some other ceremonial trends also drew people away from the Midewiwin by the 1920s. Hallowell found in the 1930s that as the Midewiwin faded, the Waabano had "proliferated" and was being actively conducted by certain families at Little Grand Rapids and Pauingassi (Adam himself mentioned being a practitioner). Its leaders were held to have acquired special curative skills and knowledge from their pawaganak, and Hallowell recorded that "dancing in the Wabano pavilion is considered to be therapeutic" (1992, 84). Ceremonies at their best fostered the quest for pimadaziwin, "life in the fullest sense," as Hallowell put it.

Beginning in about 1912 another ceremonial innovation had also begun to draw attention at Little Grand Rapids and Pauingassi. A visitor introduced the Dream Dance from the south—involving the use of a large drum and songs and practices that went with it. Hallowell found that at Little Grand Rapids four men were active in these ceremonies, including members of the Sturgeon clan Keeper family. But the most striking and developed manifestation of the Dream Dance was at Pauin-gassi, under the aegis of Adam's brother-in-law Naamiwan (Fair Wind, John Owen) and his family (Matthews and Roulette 2003). His story leads us to the next major familial grouping whose members appear in Adam's stories.

Naamiwan was a younger son of Zhenawaakoshkang, the dominant figure of the Moose clan based at Pauingassi. Zhenawaakoshkang and Adam's father, Owl, were cross cousins and sometimes associates; see, for example, the story of their combining to drive away a windigo ("Owl and Zhenawaakoshkang Drive One Away," pt. 10). Zhenawaakoshkang equaled Pazagwigabau and Tetebaiyabin in his demographic impact on the small Ojibwe communities of the Berens River; he had six wives and twenty children. He was born at Lac Seul. The birthplace of his first son, Pishiw (Bizhiw or Lynx, Sandy Owen) is uncertain, but most of his later children were probably born at Pauingassi (subsumed under Little Grand Rapids in the records, as it was not recognized as a separate reserve).

Pishiw had almost as great a demographic impact as his father. One of his two wives (who were Pelican sisters) had ten children, of whom eight survived to marry. The other had eight children, six of whom married. Hallowell's article "The Incidence, Character, and Decline of Polygyny among the Lake Winnipeg Cree and Saulteaux" (1938) gave particular attention to five polygynous Berens River men who stood out when treaty records were first compiled. The names he listed included Zhenawaakoshkang and his son Pishiw, and Pazag-wigabau and his son Tetebaiyabin. Hallowell concluded that on the whole there was a "correlation between magico-religious functions, leadership, and polygyny" that "carried over into the treaty period"

(2010, 97, 100). The older descendants of Zhenawaakoshkang's son Pishiw put down roots at Stout Lake and other upriver communities, whereas later offspring such as Naamiwan and his family tended to stay at Pauingassi and Little Grand Rapids. Naamiwan's demographic footprint was smaller than that of his older half-brother Pishiw. Like others of his generation rising in the post-treaty period, Naamiwan had only one wife. He and Koowin (Pelican) had five surviving children (Butikofer 2009, pt. II.3, 193–94).

Hallowell never got to trace the roots of Naamiwan's big drum ceremony or the details of its transmission up the river along family lines. The Dream Dance had originated in Wisconsin and Minnesota, and a tenet of the ceremony was that the big drums that featured in it were supposed to travel so that the ceremony would be passed on. This happened with Naamiwan's drum. In about 1920 it passed from its Pauingassi home to Poplar Hill, and a new drum, its "younger brother," was built at Pauingassi to replace it. The Poplar Hill people purchased the original drum and ceremony so that they could "share the benefit of the dream blessings of Fair Wind [Naamiwan] and Angus [his son]." The purchaser was Omichooch (James Owen), a son of Pishiw. As Pishiw was the older half-brother of Naamiwan, so Omichooch, in his generation, was a parallel cousin (brother, in Ojibwe terms) to Naamiwan's son Angus (Aankas) who conducted the ceremony under his father's leadership at Pauingassi (Brown with Matthews 1994, 70). The drum moved but it very much stayed in the family. The ceremony thrived for a few decades and was warmly regarded for its emphasis on healing and consolation—evidently without the darker practices associated with the older Midewiwin leaders. But Omichooch died in 1937 at Poplar Hill, and Naamiwan in 1944. Angus died in 1957, leaving no sons, although his younger brothers assumed the care of the big drum and other items at Pauingassi. By the 1950s strong leadership succession was fading; external pressures of religious and other kinds increased, and the drums at Poplar Hill and Pauingassi fell into disuse for numbers of reasons, internal and external (see Brown with Matthews 1994 for details).

When Hallowell recorded Adam's stories in 1938 and 1940, he was hearing about a world that revolved around two major clans and certain families whose dominant males gave direction and form to ceremonial life, and to healing and its obverse, sorcery. Polygyny, and the siring of many children by a few fathers, assured that families were not equal; they varied in their power as in their numbers. Similar instances are known from elsewhere in the region. Edward and Mary Black Rogers, in their generational study of a northern Ojibwe extended family, the Cranes, remarked on "their origin from one extraordinarily large family most of whom lived to reproduce." They suggested that the Cranes "may represent a pattern of group evolution that has occurred repeatedly among Subarctic Algonquians" (Rogers and Rogers 1982, 172), setting up small-community demographic imbalances with wide social implications across generations. Hallowell in his article on polygyny (2010 [1938]) cited other examples from Manitoba and northwestern Ontario.

When such families interacted, a stage was readily set for competition and rivalry, often expressed through sorcery. When bad things happened, personal suspicions and animosities flourished. Berens River clans were meaningful in matters of determining whom one could marry, or not, and in the operation of hospitality and mutual aid. But strong families, even within the same clan, could be caught up in sharp antagonisms, as happened in the conflicts between Pazagwigabau and Owl. Back in 1815 an HBC trader left some comments suggesting that these patterns had a long history. George Holdsworth, writing at his Berens River post, observed that the people did not show strong territorial jealousies. However, "Feuds and animosities frequently exist between particular families, which not infrequently terminate in murder"—or at least accusations of murder, given the personalized explanations that were usually invoked when bad things happened (Holdsworth quoted in Brown with Matthews 1994, 71).

As Adam's stories indicate, outcomes of such contests were assessed in terms of relative spiritual power acquired from the other-than-human pawaganak, the dream visitors who endowed the ones whom they favored with the strength and aid to overcome threats and attacks, whether from other medicine men, or windigos, or illnesses sent against them by their enemies. The stage was a heavily gendered one. The protagonists were all males, sometimes old men, sometimes young boys proving themselves, enacting displays of power and aggression to secure their positions. Women had their own hidden powers, which offered some protection, but they were often on the receiving end of those displays. Yet women were the social glue that held marriages and families together, whether as wives or co-wives, grandmothers, mothers, or sisters. Through his stories Adam said a fair amount about women and girls and their situations—perhaps more than he realized, although he did not convey as much as we would wish, and when heard, their voices are at second or third hand.

Seeking Bimaadiziwin

From a broad perspective, Adam told Hallowell and now tells us a great deal about the dynamics of Ojibwe life as he experienced it. A theme that runs through many of the stories— sometimes implicit, sometimes explicit as in "Midewiwin Miracles" (pt. 5)—is the quest for bimaadiz-iwin (pimadaziwin, as Hallowell transcribed it)—the search for "life in the fullest sense," providing for health, security, and well-being in an uncertain world (2010, 285. 592). That world was full of animate beings whom Hallowell called "persons," both human and other-than-human. Nichols and Nyholm (1995) translate "person" as bemaadizid, which linguist Roger Roulette glosses simply as "one who is alive" (e-mail, March 8, 2016). Adam's world was full of animate entities interacting with Ojibwe people in multiple, complex ways. Many other entities were grammatically inanimate, though in certain special circumstances they might become animate. Navigating one's way toward bimaadiziwin involved learning and practical skills, caution, restraint, control, and a sense of direction and purpose that came from observation, experience, and listening. Adam learned from watching and listening to his father and from the stories his father told, just as Hallowell and William Berens, in turn, learned from listening to Adam.

Through watching, learning, and experience, Ojibwe people could follow several paths toward achieving bimaadiziwin. The Midewiwin at its curative best was one path, although it was sometimes undercut by some leaders' abuses of their powers. Hallowell's descriptions of the Waabano and big drum ceremonies at Little Grand Rapids, Pauingassi, and Poplar Hill suggested their contributions to healing and general well-being.

Adam himself said little about ceremonies, however. His interests lay mainly in ways of curing and healing, "making people better," sometimes through secular means (such as supplying food), but often through delving into life histories and past deeds and relationships to find the causes of people's symptoms. His father, Owl, had special gifts and skills in this domain. Sins of commission and omission that a patient had forgotten, or hidden, or never recognized as problematic came to light when Owl sat thinking in his sweat lodge and ferreted them out. Once they were revealed, public admission and confession afforded means of shedding the sickness and the penalties patients had suffered; trouble would not follow them anymore. If misdeeds were not uncovered and admitted early enough, however (as for example in "You Brought This Sickness on Yourself," pt. 5), they festered and could bring death. Charlie George Owen (Omishoosh) of Pauingassi, who knew Adam in the 1930s, spoke of these things in 1993, using words that Adam probably used as well. Wrongdoers sooner or later would be accountable for their deeds. The term that Owen used was "onjinewin"—the payment that had to be made sooner or later for a moral wrong (Matthews and Roulette 2003, 290).

The curing and confessional process had another critical function; it reminded everyone of core values that guided people's lives and of what could happen if they were violated. Incest, sexual transgressions, abuse of love medicine, egregious cruelty to animals—(and even to a windigo, as in "Sickness from Torturing a Windigo," pt. 10)—and the disregarding of injunctions laid down by one's pawaganak were among the misdeeds that came to light, and their admission served to warn the people of their possible consequences. Men with the greatest power and support from their pawaganak might sometimes escape any penalty, as did Sagaski, who married his sister (pt. 6). But misdeeds were believed to follow one, even to death, and could afflict a transgressor's family members later.

Sometimes doctors such as Owl could also help explain why other bad things happened. Some of Adam's stories told of jealous or rejected

suitors or other hostile personages who could impose a windigo afflic-
tion or other hardship, such as starvation. Owl and his medicine men
colleagues had techniques for recovering information about sources
of trouble and sometimes for finding remedies, as when Owl cured a
windigo patient (pt. 12). Use of the conjuring (shaking) tent, scrying
(pt. 5), dreams, and serious contemplation in the sweat lodge were all
means of finding answers to difficult issues. Troubles in the Ojibwe universe usually had personal names; they emanated from certain human
or other-than-human persons who could be identified, avoided, warned
against, or neutralized by some being with greater powers. A man's
pawaganak played critical roles in dealing with such beings, and his
cultivation of his relationship with them was a key means of pursuing
pimadaziwin—beginning in his youth with fasting and dreaming in
accord with firm rules and protocols about purity and good conduct.

Not everyone was a medicine man, however. Women were not
aggressors who launched attacks against others; they did not initiate
sorcery, project migis shells into bodies, starve people, or turn someone
into a windigo. But they sometimes had their own protective powers
and pawaganak, of which men were unaware; they might deflect an
attack by a powerful sorcerer or kill windigos to save their children
("Attempted Killing Because of Refusal of Marriage," pt. 7; "Windigos
Killed by Two Women," pt. 10). More generally, ordinary people who
lacked great powers, and even many men who could not predict the
possibly greater strength of their adversaries, followed quieter paths
to the good life. Hallowell pointed out that "both for the man who is
confident of his powers, as well as for the common man [and woman],
the best defense is to avoid offense if one seeks what the Saulteaux
call *pimadaziwin*—life in the fullest sense" (2010, 285). Older relatives
advised their sons or grandsons not to provoke or insult powerful old
men—even though the youths might prevail. The young man who was
teased by an old man's magic tricks felt obliged to press gifts upon him
to avoid any possibility of being harmed ("We Are Only Playing," pt. 8).
Circumspection, caution, and respect for bemaadizidag, all those "ones
who are alive" and who could not be completely known or judged by
their outward appearance, were needed qualities as people navigated

their way through life, and toward life in the fullest sense, along the Berens River.

Adam Bigmouth shared with Hallowell and William Berens many rich glimpses and insights into his world. Now readers may mine and contemplate his stories, for all the complex, interwoven strands and knotted strings that may be drawn out of them.

REFERENCES

Berens, William, as told to A. Irving Hallowell. 2009. *Memories, Myths, and Dreams of an Ojibwe Leader*. Ed. Jennifer S. H. Brown and Susan Elaine Gray. Montreal: McGill-Queen's University Press.

Bird, Louis. 2005. *Telling Our Stories: Omushkego Legends and Histories from Hudson Bay*. Ed. Jennifer S. H. Brown, Paul W. DePasquale, and Mark F. Ruml. Peterborough ON: Broadview Press.

———. 2007. *The Spirit Lives in the Mind: Omushkego Stories, Lives, and Dreams*. Ed. Susan Elaine Gray. Montreal: McGill-Queen's University Press.

Bishop, Charles A. 1973. "Ojibwa Cannibalism." Eleventh International Congress of Anthropological and Ethnological Sciences. Chicago.

———. 1978. "Cultural and Biological Adaptations to Deprivation: The Northern Ojibwa Case." In *Extinction and Survival in Human Populations*, ed. Charles D. Laughlin Jr. and Ivan S. Brady, 208–30. New York: Columbia University Press.

Black [Rogers], Mary. 1977. "Ojibwa Taxonomy and Percept Ambiguity." *Ethos* 5: 90–118.

Brightman, Robert A. 1988. "The Windigo in the Material World." *Ethnohistory* 35 (4): 336–79.

———. 1993. *Grateful Prey: Rock Cree Human-Animal Relationships*. Berkeley: University of California Press.

Brown, Jennifer S. H. 2006a. "Fields of Dreams: Revisiting A. I. Hallowell and the Berens River Ojibwe." In *New Perspectives on Native North America: Cultures, Histories, and Representations*, ed. Sergei A. Kan and Pauline Turner Strong, 17–41. Lincoln: University of Nebraska Press.

————. 2006b. "Older Persons in Cree and Ojibwe Stories: Gender, Power, and Survival." In *Actes du Trente-septième Congrès des Algonquinistes*, ed. H. C. Wolfart, 439–50. Winnipeg: University of Manitoba.

————. 2008. "Growing up Algonquian: A Missionary's Son in Cree-Ojibwe Country, 1869–1876." In *Papers of the Thirty-Ninth Algonquian Conference*, ed. Karl S. Hele and Regna Darnell, 72–93. London ON: University of Western Ontario.

————. 2010a. "Kinship Shock for Fur Traders and Missionaries: The Cross-Cousin Challenge." In *Papers of the Rupert's Land Colloquium, Winnipeg, May 2010*. Winnipeg: Centre for Rupert's Land Studies.

————. 2010b. "Afterword: Aaniskotaapaan—Generations and Successions." In *Gathering Places: Aboriginal and Fur Trade Histories*, ed. Carolyn Podruchny and Laura Peers, 295–311. Vancouver: University of British Columbia Press.

Brown, Jennifer S. H., and Robert Brightman. 1988. *The Orders of the Dreamed: George Nelson of Cree and Northern Ojibwa Religion and Myth, 1823*. Winnipeg: University of Manitoba Press.

Brown, Jennifer S. H., with Maureen Matthews. 1994. "Fair Wind: Medicine and Consolation on the Berens River." *Journal of the Canadian Historical Association*, n.s., 4: 55–74.

————. 1995. "Tackling the Women: A. I. Hallowell and Unfinished Conversations along the Berens River." Paper presented to the American Society for Ethnohistory.

Butikofer, Gary. 2009. The Butikofer Papers on Berens River Ojibwe History. Transcripts made at the Centre for Rupert's Land Studies, University of Winnipeg; copies in author's possession.

    Part I.1, 2. Family Histories

    Part II. 1. Berens River [BR] Family Histories

    Part II.2. Lac Seul Family Histories

    Part II.3. Little Grand Rapids [LGR] Family Histories

    Part II. 4. Bloodvein Family Histories

    Part II. 5. Pauingassi Family Histories

    Part II. 6. Pikangikum Family Histories

    Part II. 7. Poplar Hill Family Histories

    Part II. 8. Stout Lake Family Histories

    Part III. 1. Upper Berens River Family and Community Histories

    Part III. 2–7. Berens River History, Interview notes

    Part IV. 1. Material Culture

    Part IV. 2. Artifacts: Descriptions and Sources.

    Part V.1. Translations of Indian names.

    Educational Notes

Chapman, W. M. 1912–15. Fur trade journal kept at Little Grand Rapids. Winnipeg: Archives of Manitoba, MG 1, C5.

Cooper, John M. 1933. "The Cree Witiko Psychosis." *Primitive Man* 6: 20–24.

Dewdney, Selwyn. 1975. *The Sacred Scrolls of the Southern Ojibway.* Toronto: University of Toronto Press.

Dunning, R. W. 1959. *Social and Economic Change among the Northern Ojibwa.* Toronto: University of Toronto Press.

Fiddler, Thomas, and James R. Stevens. 1985. *Killing the Shamen.* Moonbeam, ON: Penumbra Press.

Flannery, Regina, Mary Elizabeth Chambers, and Patricia A. Jehle. 1981. "Witiko Accounts from the James Bay Cree." *Arctic Anthropology* 18 (1): 57–77.

Hallowell, A. Irving. A. Irving Hallowell Papers. Manuscripts, field notes and research files. Manuscript Collection 26. American Philosophical Society, Philadelphia.

    N.d. "Aggression." Typescript.

    N.d. "Myths and Tales." Manuscript.

    N.d. Research file on conjuring.

    N.d. "Sexual Behavior." Typescript and unnumbered pages.

    1932. Field Notes. Brief diary, June–July.

    1938. Adam Big Mouth and Windigo—Field Notes. Series V, Research Files.

    1940. Little Grand Rapids—Field Notes. Varia Adam Big Mouth.

———. 1934. "Culture and Mental Disorder." *Journal of Abnormal and Social Psychology* 29: 1–9.

———. 1942. *The Role of Conjuring in Saulteaux Society.* Philadelphia: University of Pennsylvania Press.

———. 1951. "Cultural Factors in the Structuralization of Perception." In *Social Psychology at the Crossroads,* ed. John H. Rohrer and Muzafer Sherif, 164–95. New York: Harper and Brothers.

———. 1963. "Ojibwa World View and Disease." In *Man's Image in Medicine and Anthropology,* ed. Iago Galdston, 258–315. New York Academy of Medicine. New York: International Universities Press.

———. 1992. *The Ojibwa of Berens River, Manitoba: Ethnography into History.* Ed. Jennifer S. H. Brown. Fort Worth: Harcourt Brace College Publishers.

———. 2010. *Contributions to Ojibwe Studies: Essays, 1934–1972.* Ed. Jennifer S. H. Brown and Susan Elaine Gray. Lincoln: University of Nebraska Press.

Hudson's Bay Company (HBC) Archives. 2017. Biographical Sheets. HBCA, Winnipeg, Manitoba. https://www.gov.mb.ca/chc/archives/hbca/biographical/index.html.

Jenness, Diamond. 1935. *The Ojibwa of Parry Island: Social and Religious Life.* Bulletin no. 78, anthropology series no. 17. Ottawa: Department of Mines, National Museum of Canada.

Landes, Ruth. 1968. *Ojibwa Religion and the Midewiwin*. Madison: University of Wisconsin Press.

Leach, Frederick, OMI. 1973. *Fifty-five Years with Indians and Settlers on Lake Winnipeg*. Winnipeg: no printer named.

Library and Archives Canada (LAC), RG 10. Department of Indian Affairs and Northern Development fonds, "Manitoba Regional Office" series, "General operational records" sub-series, "Registry records of Manitoba Regional Office," 1984–85/402 GAD, volume 13761, file "[Admission of Pupils-Brandon Industrial School]," 1895–1933, Application for admission, October 1908; Quarterly Return, 30 September 1913. Courtesy of Anne Lindsay.

Lindsay, Anne. 2012. "Tapastanum: 'A Noted Conjurer for Many Years, Who Long Resisted the Teachings of Christianity.'" In *Papers of the Fortieth Algonquian Conference*, ed. Karl S. Hele and J. Randolph Valentine, 223–40. Albany: SUNY Press.

Lytwyn, Victor P. 1986. *The Fur Trade of the Little North: Indians, Pedlars, and Englishmen East of Lake Winnipeg, 1760–1821*. Winnipeg: Rupert's Land Research Centre, University of Winnipeg.

———. 2002. *Muskekowuck Athinuwick: Original People of the Great Swampy Land*. Winnipeg: University of Manitoba Press.

Manitoba Free Press. 1930. "Red River Pioneer: John Thomas (Doggie)," obituary, p. 12. With photograph. 25 June.

Matthews, Maureen, and Roger Roulette. 2003. "Fair Wind's Dream: *Naamiwan Obawaajigewin*." In *Reading beyond Words: Contexts for Native History*, eds. Jennifer S.H. Brown and Elizabeth Vibert, 263–92. Peterborough ON: Broadview Press.

Nash, Alice, and Rejean Obomsawin. 2003. "Théophile Panadis (1889–1966), un guide abénaquis." *Recherches amérindiennes au Québec* 33 (2): 75–91.

Nichols, John D., and Earl Nyholm. 1995. *A Concise Dictionary of Minnesota Ojibwe*. Minneapolis: University of Minnesota Press.

Peers, Laura, and Jennifer S. H. Brown. 2000. "'There Is No End to Relationship among the Indians': Ojibwa Families and Kinship in Historical Perspective." *History of the Family: An International Quarterly* 4 (4): 529–55.

Podruchny, Carolyn. 2006. *Making the Voyageur World: Travelers and Traders in the North American Fur Trade*. Toronto: University of Toronto Press.

Preston, Richard J. 1980. "The Witiko: Algonkian Knowledge and Whiteman Knowledge." In *Manlike Monsters on Trial: Early Records and Modern Evidence*, ed. Marjorie M. Halpin and Michael M. Ames, 111–31. Vancouver: University of British Columbia Press.

———. 2002. *Cree Narrative: Expressing the Personal Meanings of Events*. Montreal: McGill-Queen's University Press.

Red River Ancestry.ca. 2017. http://www.redriverancestry.ca/.

Rogers, Edward S., and Mary Black Rogers. 1982. "Who Were the Cranes: Groups and Group Identity Names in Northern Ontario." In *Approaches to Algonquian Archaeology: Proceedings of the Thirteenth Annual Conference*, ed. Margaret G. Hanna and Brian Kooyman, 147–88. Calgary: Archaeological Association of the University of Calgary.

Schuetze, Luther L. 2001. *Mission to Little Grand Rapids: Life with the Anishinabe 1927 to 1938*. Vancouver: Creative Connections Publishing.

Smallman, Shawn. 2014. *Dangerous Spirits: The Windigo in Myth and History*. Victoria BC: Heritage House Publishing.

Speck, Frank G. 1977 [1935]. *Nascapi: The Savage Hunters of the Labrador Peninsula*. Norman: University of Oklahoma Press.

Steinbring, , Jack H. 1981. "Saulteaux of Lake Winnipeg." *Handbook of North American Indians*, vol. 6, *Subarctic*, 244–55. Washington DC: Smithsonian Institution.

Teicher, Morton I. 1960. "Windigo Psychosis: A Study of a Relationship between Belief and Behavior among the Indians of Northeastern Canada." In *Proceedings of the 1960 Annual Spring Meeting of the American Ethnological Society*. Seattle: University of Washington.

Vecsey, Christopher. 1983. *Traditional Ojibwa Religion and Its Historical Changes*. Philadelphia: American Philosophical Society.

Waldram, James B. 2004. *Revenge of the Windigo: The Construction of the Mind and Mental Health of North American Aboriginal Peoples*. Toronto: University of Toronto Press.

Young, Elizabeth Bingham, and E. Ryerson Young. 2014. *Mission Life in Cree-Ojibwe Country: Memories of a Mother and Son*. Ed. Jennifer S. H. Brown. Edmonton: Athabasca University Press.

INDEX

Ojibwe people were known by different names, including nicknames and anglicized names. Individuals are indexed under the name most commonly used in the book. Alternative names are indicated in parentheses.
Italicized figure numbers refer to illustrations following page 88.

Adam Bigmouth's stories (*continued*) 170–71; on medical practices, 29–31, 89–91; on Midewiwin miracles, 171; on mistreatment of the dead, 41; on mockery and cruelty, 149–54; on old man's winter threat, 93–94; on power of women, 124, 129; publication of, xxiv–xxv; recording of, xxiii; about sexual relations, 73–74; of starvation, 101–13; of Tetebaiyabin's jealousy, 36–37, 38; transcription of, xxiii–xxiv; of warfare, xvi–xvii; about windigo, 9–10, 117–19, 147–48

Adin Kakegumic (Gaakekamig), 33

Ahak (Thomas Ross), xxii, 29, 80

Alix (Alec) (Lebanese trader), 13

Amo (old wicked man), 105–7

Andwewe (Adam's daughter-in-law), 30–31

Angus (Aankas), 169

animate beings, 171

Asagesi (Ashaageshi), 13; Waabano pavilion of, *fig. 15*

Ayassa (Small One). *See* Owl (Adam's father)

bad medicine, 32, 38, 89–91

Batis (Baachiish or John Baptiste): children of, 165; at conjuring ceremony, 2; death record of, xx–xxi; and fasting in winter, 25, 27; hunting by, 59; marriage of, 165; photograph of, *fig. 5*; possible baptism of, xxi

Bazigwiigaabaw. *See* Pazagwigabau

Bazil (Pindandakwan's son), 91–92, 93

bear: as disguise of medicine man, 36, 38, 89, 90

Berens, Gordon, *fig. 3*

Berens, Jacob (father of William), 2

Berens, William: account of Betsey Grant, 154; at conjuring ceremony, 2; experience with love medicine, 35; family memories, 163–64; on insecurity of women, 83; introduction of, 3; marriage of, 18; memoir of life of, xvii–xviii; occupations of, xvii; photographs of, *fig. 2*, *fig. 3*, *fig. 4*; and repercussions of mockery, 153; translation of Adam's stories by, xiv; travels of, xiii–xiv, xvii; on windigo, 124; on winter maker, 151

Berens River, xxxvi, 8, 13

Berens River Indians, 119

Berens River post, 5

Bezhig. *See* Pesk

Bigmouth, Adam. *See* Adam Bigmouth

Bigmouth, Maggie, xxii–xxiii

Biindaandakwan. *See* Pindandakwan

Biindakik. *See* Pindakik

bimaadiziwin. *See* pimadaziwin

birch sap collecting, 9

Birchstick. *See* Wiigwaasaatig

Bird, Louis, 52, 99

Bishop, Charles, 8, 145

Bittern, Antoine, *fig. 3*, *fig. 4*

Bizhiw (Pishiw, "Lynx"), 30, 36, 101, 104, 168–69

Bluffhead (Pikwakwastigan or Bikwaakishtigwaan), 55, 90

Booshii. *See* Potci

Boucher, Alex (Poshi), 59

Brightman, Robert, 128, 144–45, 146, 147

Bushie, Alex (Noochipine), 22, 24

Bushie, Joseph (Choome), 24

Butikofer, Gary, xix, xxv, xxix, 19, 20, 33, 63–64

cannibalism, 112–13, 115, 143. *See also* windigo

canoes: magical manufacture of, 159–60

Cenawagwaskang. *See* Zhenawaakoshkang

ceremonies: Dream Dance, 168, 169; drums at Poplar Hill and Pauingassi, 169; families and, 169–70; Midewiwin practice, 167; Waabano, 167–68

Chambers, Mary Elizabeth, 145

Chiichiik (Jiichiik), 64

conjuring, xiv, xv, xxi, 1–3, 25, 27, 32, 48

conjuring lodge (shaking tent), *fig. 13, fig. 14*

Cooper, John M., 143

Cree people: cannibalism by, 143; and windigo psychosis, 143–44; and women in hunting dreams, 85

cruelty: abuse of orphan boy, 152–53; to animals, 153–54; insult of moose, 151–52; insult of snow, 150–51; to mosquitoes, 149–50

dead people: consequences of mistreatment of, 41

Dedibaayaaban. *See* Tetebaiyabin

diseases, 11–15

dreams: Christian themes in, 23; experiences of, while fasting, 24–25, 26–27; of males and females, 128–29; power of, 28

drinking, 12–13

Duck, George (Shiishiipens or Zhiishiibens), 24, 26, 31

Duck, John (Makochens), 2, 3, 26, 35, *fig. 6*

Duck, Maamaan, 28

Duck, William. *See* Potci

Dumas, William, 163

Dunning, R. W., 82

Eagle Lake (Moar Lake), 6

Everett, Joe, 16, 18, *fig. 3*

Everett, Nancy, 18

fasting, 24–25, 26–27, 83, 84

feasts, 94

Fiddler, Adam, 120, 121

Fiddler, Thomas, 139

Fiero, Charles, xxv, xxix

Flannery, Regina, 145

Flatstone (Nabagaabik), 9, 10, 52, 55, 59, 93, 122–23, 127

Gaa-zhaaboowiyaazid (Kaashaapowiiyaasit), 116, 164

G.B. (Grey Balls), 105, 106–7

Gegek. *See* Kehkehk

gender relations, 81–83

Getagaash (Ketagas). *See* Keeper, John

Gezhiiyaash (John Owen), 30

Gibeault, William, 20

Gichi-ogimaa (Ktciogama), xxi, 35, 36

Giiwechinwaas (Kiwetcinwas), 24, 26

Giiwichens. *See* Keeper, John, Sr.

Giiwiich. *See* Keeper, Alex

Ginoozhewinini. *See* Green, Joseph

girls: dream quest, 128–29; isolation during menstruation, 128

Gisayenaan ("Our Elder Brother"), xiii, xxiii

Goosehead, Samuel. *See* Pineshiinsh

Goosehead, William, 2

Grant, Cuthbert, 18

Gray, Susan Elaine, xvii

Green, Joseph (Ginoozhewinini), 19, 20, 32, *fig. 8*

Gwiikwishii (Maggie Ross), xxii, 3

Hallowell, A. Irving: commonly used Ojibwe words in works of, xxvi–xxvii; on conjuring, 1–3; and conversations with Adam Bigmouth, xiii–xiv, xxiii–xxiv; and expedition to Manitoba, 161–62; family history research by, 165; fieldwork of, xvi, 3, 6; and first trip to Berens River, 1; "Glossary of Ojibwe Words and Names," xxv; on incest, 67, 71–72, 73; on interaction of opposite-sex siblings, 66; on kinship relations, 33, 162; and memoir of William Berens's life, xvi; observations of women's lives by, 82; on Ojibwe ceremonies, 167–68; photograph of, *fig. 4*; on polygyny of Berens River men, 168; *The Role of Conjuring in Saulteaux Society* by, xiv, 11, 52; on soul abduction, 57; and stories about windigo, 11, 119, 126–27, 147–48; and study of Cree-Ojibwe cross-cousin marriage, 161–62; transcription of Ojibwe personal names by, xxix; on violations of clan exogamy, 63; on windigo psychosis, 144
Holdsworth, George, 170
Hole-in-the-Sky (Ojibwe doctor), 32
Honigmann, John, 144
hospitality, 31–33
Hudson's Bay Company (HBC): and competition with North West Company, 8; sickness of employees of, 19–20; steamboats of, 16, 18; trade posts of, 6
hunger. *See* starvation
hunting: for caribou, 8; with medicine, 155–56; sex as metaphor for, 85; in winter, 101–2

Ihkeweshenshish (Ikwewiizhenzish), 26
illness: from causing animal suffering, 51; caused by cruelty toward windigo, 123–24, 127; caused by homosexual relations, 46–48, 49; caused by masturbation, 49; caused by oral sex, 50; caused by wrongdoing, 64; sins and, 46–50
incest: between brother and sister, 62, 63; between father and daughter, 69–70; with father's sister, 65–66, 67–68; intergenerational relations and, 73–74; and magical conception, 68–69; man's sickness due to, 64; marriage within the same totem, 61–62; between old man and daughter-in-law, 72–73; sickness of children as result of, 61; between young woman and grandfather, 71–72
Injenii (Fanny Bigmouth), xx, xxi, 12, 59, 165
intergenerational competition: old man's magic tricks, 97–98; orphan boy *vs.* old conjurer, 95–96, 99; young man's trick, 96–97

James Bay Cree. *See* Cree people
Jehle, Patricia, 145
Jibo, Willie, 19, 20, 45–46

Kaashaapowiiyaasit. *See* Gaa-zhaaboowiyaazid
Keeper, Alex (Giiwiich or Kiwitc), 166, *fig. 9*
Keeper, Bella. *See* Noonaawas
Keeper, John (Getagaash, Ketagas), 2, 166
Keeper, John, Sr. (Giiwichens), 3, *fig. 4, fig. 10*
Keeper, Timothy (Pachahkaano), 166

Noonaawas (Bella Keeper), *fig. 10*
Nootinwep (Noodinweb, Wind Sitting),
55, 165
North West Company, 8
North Wind spirit, 68, 150–51
Norway House man, 116

Ochiibaamaansiins. *See* Owl (Adam's
father)
Ojibwe people: concept of generation,
163; concept of soul, 93; contacts
with masters of game animals, 27;
disease theory of, 66–67; drinking by, 12–13; kinship system of,
xviii–xix, 33–34, 162–63; marriage
traditions of, 63; murders by, 81–82,
88; and occupation of men, 8; and
"percept ambiguity," 11; personal
names of, xix, xxv–xxvi, xxix–
xxxiii; polygyny of, 170; potato crop
of, 34; and purity of people and
animals, 26; and quest for pimadaziwin, 171–72; rivalry between
families of, 170; sexual behavior of,
27–28, 46–50, 65–68, 80; spirits of
the dead of, 60; territory of, xviii,
165; trade and, 14; and universe of
sound, 119; view of sins, 46–50;
wild rice harvesting of, 13–14
Okadjisi (Okachesi), 33–34
Okawapwan (Ogawapwan), 80
older men: competition with young
men, 95–97; magic tricks of, 97–98,
99; social isolation of, 100
Omichoosh (James Owen), 35, 36, 169
Omiimii, 43
Oniichipo. *See* Winiichipo
orphan: powers of, 95–96, 99
oshkaabewis (helper or apprentice),
46, 53

Otcibamasis. *See* Owl (Adam's father)
Otcik (Ojik), 82, 166
Otcimazo (Ojiimaazo), 101, 102, 103, 109
Otci-tcak (Ojijaak, Crane Strang), 55
Owagigat (Owaagigaad), 6
Owen, Charlie George, xxiii, 172
Owen, James. *See* Omichoosh
Owen, John. *See* Naamiwan
Owen, Thomas. *See* Tomi
Owl (Adam's father): and ability to
control weather, 52; and ability to
find lost objects, 51–52; children of,
xx, 165; contests with Pazagwigabau, 56–58; curing skills of, xiii,
xiv, 29–30, 32, 39, 42–54, 141, 172;
death of, xix-xx, 58–60; duel by
sorcery, 57–58; and employment by
Hudson's Bay Company, 5–6; and
fight with windigo, 10, 11, 116–17;
harm caused to, 56–57; multiple
names of, xix; personality of, 57;
and refusal to eat windigo parts,
124; and relations with Zhenawaakoshkang, 116, 168; and rescues and
loss of father, 39–40; rivals of, 55;
saving his brother from windigo,
115–16; and visit to Midewiwin
lodge, 52–53; year of birth of, 164

Pachiish. *See* Batis (Baachiish or John
Baptiste)
Pagak, 10, 102, 108, 109, 120
Panadis, Theophile (Theo), 3, *fig. 3*
Pasho (Owl's older wife), xx, 7, 82, 115, 165
pawaganak (dream visitors): disposal
of windigo by, 147; and impact on
humans, 146; as protectors from windigos, 114–15, 123, 124, 126, 128, 173
Pazagwigabau (Bazigwiigaabaw): children of, xxii, 7, 37; and connection to

Sturgeon clan, 167; and contests with Owl, xvii, xxii, 56–60; death of, 60; duel by sorcery by, 57–58; family of, 165–66; Midewiwin practices of, 52, 90; personality of, 57; powers of, 55–56; use of bad medicine by, 90, 91

Pelican clan, xviii

Pesk (Bezhig), 12, 76

Peyak (John Bigmouth), xxiii, 22, 25, 32–33, 165

Pikangikum settlement, 166, 167

pimadaziwin ("life in the fullest sense"): meaning of, 32, 171; quest for, 54, 110, 168, 171–74

Pindakik (Biindakik), 68

Pindandakwan (Biindaandakwan or James Shadow), 55, 91–92, 93

Pineshiinsh (Bineshiinzh or Samuel Goosehead), 13

Pishiw. See Bizhiw

Pisikasikaakwan (Adam's grandfather), 39–40, 41, 164

Piwanuk (Biiwaanag, Flint), 69

Poplar Hill summer fishing settlement, 167

Poplar River settlement, 164–65

porcupine: connection to windigo, 131–33, 138–39

Poshi. See Boucher, Alex

Potci (Booshii or William Duck), 25–26, 27, 28

Preston, Richard, 127, 144

Rae, John, 140

red ochre. See love medicine

Rogers, Edward, 170

Rogers, Mary Black, 170

The Role of Conjuring in Saulteaux Society (Hallowell), xiv, 11, 52

Ross, Maggie. See Gwiikwishii

Ross, Thomas (Ahak), 29

Roulette, Roger, xxv, xxvi, xxix, 83, 163, 171

Sagaski (Zagashkii), xxii, 36–37, 62, 63–64, 67, 172

Sagatciwe (Zaagajiwe), 52, 53, 54–55

Sagatciweas (Peter Stoney), 54

scapulimancy, 119, 121–22

Schuetze, Luther, 28

scrying, 52, 173

sexual relations, 86–87

sickness. See illness

Siipi (Ziibi), 7, 93, 166

Smallman, Shawn, 140

snow: cost of insult of, 150–51

South Wind spirit, 150–51

Speck, Frank, 121

Spencer, Dorothy, 82

starvation: bear-walking incident, 104–5; cannibalism and, 112–13; defeat of, 107–8; and killing of an adopted boy, 110–11; magic and, 104, 105–7, 108–9, 110; offense of, 109, 110; rescue from, 111–12; stories of secular, 110–12; and story of monster man and giant dog, 107–8; of a thief, 108–9; windigos in stories of, 110, 112–13, 145–46; in winter time, 101–3, 104

Stevens, James, 121, 139

Stout, Alexander, 5–6

Sturgeon clan, xviii, 166

Sucker clan, 33–34

sucking tubes, 44, 49

sweat lodge (bath), 50, 84, 172, 173, *fig. 11, fig. 12*

Tapastanum (Tepastenam), 103, 116

Tcakabec (mythic being), 67

Teicher, Morton I., 144, 146

www.ingramcontent.com/pod-product-compliance
Lightning Source LLC
Chambersburg PA
CBHW051726260326
41914CB00031B/1752/J